THE YOUNG CHE

The father of Che Guevara, Ernesto Guevara Lynch was born in Argentina in 1900 of Irish and Basque origin.

Lucía Álvarez de Toledo grew up and was educated in Argentina. Having worked as a journalist and broadcaster in her native Argentina, she settled in London in 1968 and established herself as a professional interpreter and translator. Her background, knowledge of Latin America and long-standing interest in the life and works of Ernesto Che Guevara have enabled her to bring a unique understanding to the first English language translation – and the editing – of this book.

ERNESTO GUEVARA LYNCH

The Young Che

Memories of Che Guevara

EDITED AND TRANSLATED BY
Lucía Álvarez de Toledo

VINTAGE BOOKS
London

Published by Vintage 2007

2 4 6 8 10 9 7 5 3 1

First published in Spanish under the titles *Mi hijo el Che* and *Aquí va
un soldado de América* in 1981 and 1987

First published in Great Britain in 2007 by Vintage
Random House, 20 Vauxhall Bridge Road
London SW1V 2SA

www.vintage-books.co.uk

Addresses for companies within The Random House Group Limited
can be found at: www.randomhouse.co.uk/offices.htm

Map copyright © Reginald Piggott

The Random House Group Limited Reg. No. 954009

A CIP catalogue record for this book is available from the British Library

ISBN 978184590736

Penguin Random House is committed to a sustainable future for
our business, our readers and our planet. This book is made from
Forest Stewardship Council® certified paper.

Printed and bound in Great Britain by Clays Ltd, Elcograf S.p.A.
Typeset by SX Composing DTP, Rayleigh, Essex

Contents

Acknowledgements

I wish to thank Aleida March de la Torre for permission to publish Che Guevara's letters, my editor Mandy Greenfield for her invaluable editorial advice and insight, and my literary agent Margaret Hanbury for her commitment and guidance.

I am also grateful to Charles Carlino, Alexandra Potts and Matthew Reisz for their continuous assistance and support throughout the project.

Lucía Álvarez de Toledo

Introduction

Ernesto Che Guevara has been dead forty years and yet there is a continuing fascination with the young and charismatic guerrilla who went to his death in a remote and desolate corner of the world with the cheerful elan he had displayed throughout his life. But how did a sickly boy from a comfortable background become one of the great revolutionary heroes of the twentieth century?

The Young Che offers us an intimate portrait of Guevara from his birth in 1928 up to the turning point of his life in 1956, when he joins Castro to train for the invasion of Cuba. It can be read as a record of a remarkable and lovable personality, as the journey (both real and psychological) of a revolutionary in the making and as a colourful tour of Latin America in the 1950s. All these things and more, it is now available in English for the first time.

The Young Che has been created from two separate books written by Che's father Ernesto Guevara Lynch: *Mi hijo el Che (My Son Che)* and *Aquí va un soldado de América (Here Goes a Soldier of the Americas)*. As such, it offers an intimate picture of Che *en famille* by one of the people who knew him best. Until these books were published in Spanish in 1981 and 1987 (the latter posthumously), very little was known about Che's early years. All subsequent biographies have drawn on them extensively for their chapters on his childhood and youth. This edition gives English readers access to the primary sources, with the essential background information set out in a Chronology, and with Biographical Notes giving brief descriptions of all the people mentioned.

We get to see the young Che through the loving eyes of his father, who often looked after him as a child during his frequent bouts of asthma and who, having been one of Che's political role models, became one of his most ardent followers. Yet much of the book consists of Che's own words, since Guevara senior quotes extensively from his diaries and from his letters to his parents, his close family and his best friend and fellow student, Tita Infante. There is simply no other detailed first-hand narrative of the trips Che embarked upon, of his reactions to what he saw, of the scrapes he got into in Bolivia, Peru, Ecuador, Panama, Costa Rica, Nicaragua, Guatemala and Mexico. His irony and self-mockery show him capable of great humour even in the face of adversity. All his dominant qualities – the qualities that spurred him into political activism and helped him inspire such devotion – stand out vividly here: his idealism, sharp observation and spontaneous empathy; his love of archaeology, his curiosity and constant desire for adventure.

The first half of *The Young Che*, originally published as *My Son Che*, offers a unique account of his Argentine childhood in a nonconformist bourgeois family, which was always committed to radical causes. Despite their class, the Guevaras were clean-scrubbed, unaffected people, never influenced by material fashions. Their homes in Alta Gracia, Córdoba and Buenos Aires were always open, friendly places, where no one ever knew exactly how many people were coming to dinner – relatives, the children's fellow students, visiting academics, professional colleagues or exiled Spanish Republican politicians and intellectuals. The younger generation grew up self-sufficient and free, but with a strong moral sense. Because of his upbringing as well as his chronic asthma, Ernesto's education was unlike that of his peers and he matured quickly, becoming an iconoclast as well as a young man in a hurry. We discover the single-minded fury with which he played rugby; the impact of the books he read voraciously when his illness kept him at home; and the political events that rocked the world of his teens – the Spanish Civil War and the effects of Nazism in Argentina.

This section of the book also contains Che's diary of his journey around northern Argentina in 1950, which Guevara Lynch discovered by accident in 1975 when the storage room in the basement of his flat in downtown Buenos Aires was flooded. Che covered around 4,700 kilometres on his bicycle, often going without food or sleep – an endurance test that would be good training for his future career as a guerrilla. This first trip was followed by another, in 1952, when Che was a medical student and decided to cross Latin America on a motorbike with his close friend Alberto Granado, who was a few years older and already a doctor. Both men kept diaries of the journey, which have been published in English as Guevara's *The Motorcycle Diaries* and as Granado's *Travelling with Che Guevara* (Pimlico, 2003). These formed the basis for Walter Salles' film, *The Motorcycle Diaries*, which was released in 2003.

Before embarking on this adventure, Che promised his mother that he would return to sit his remaining exams and graduate as a doctor. He kept his promise and flew back to Argentina to finish his studies, only to leave again with another close friend, Carlos (Calica) Ferrer, shortly afterwards. He was only to set foot in Argentina again very briefly in 1961 – as Comandante Che Guevara, the famous guerrilla leader – while visiting neighbouring Uruguay at the head of a Cuban delegation to the Economic Summit of the Organisation of American States.

Even during his first trip across the continent with Granado in 1952, Che became acutely aware of the misery in which the poor lived. Both men did voluntary work in leper colonies in Peru. When he returned home Guevara said that he was no longer the man who had left Argentina a year earlier. But he still saw the continent's shortcomings through the eyes of a physician.

It was his next trip across Latin America, which forms the second half of *The Young Che*, that truly radicalised him and turned him into Che Guevara, a man who believed that armed struggle was the only answer. Bolivia, his first port of call, opened his eyes to the exploitation of the continent – and it was there that he realised that it was pointless to be a doctor. One had to attack the underlying causes of the people's suffering, rather than just eradicate illnesses that were the result of malnutrition, scarcity of water, poor hygiene and lack of medicines.

Guevara travelled on from Bolivia to Ecuador with Calica Ferrer and other fellow Argentines whom they met en route. Together they would see how the country's production was controlled and exported by companies owned by Americans, while the locals were low-paid employees with no say.

From Ecuador they travelled through Panama and on to Costa Rica, where Che met two other young men who were spending time on the road: Romulo Betancourt and Juan Bosch. All three were looking for answers to the political and social problems of Latin America, and they argued and discussed what they had seen and experienced as they went from one country to the next. Betancourt was later to become the President of Venezuela and Bosch that of the Dominican Republic.

Che then went on through Nicaragua to Guatemala, the

original 'Banana Republic', where he had his first direct experience of US intervention in Latin America. The CIA, backing the interests of the United Fruit Company, helped topple the legitimately elected Socialist government of Jacobo Arbenz. Guevara even took part in the defence of Guatemala City. It was then that he first came to the attention of the CIA, who opened a file on him. His letters to his family let us witness this turning point in his life and observe his progress towards revolutionary activism.

After the debacle in Guatemala, Che arrived in Mexico City following a brief stay at the Argentine Embassy in Guatemala City, where he had been forced to ask for asylum. By now he was psychologically prepared for the event that would change his life and would soon have an impact on the political landscape of the whole continent: his meeting with Fidel Castro and his fellow revolutionaries.

It was in Mexico that Che became a fully fledged revolutionary. He studied Marx and Engels, began training with Castro for the invasion of Cuba, was taken into custody and then forced to go underground when released. He had married his constant companion, Peruvian economist Hilda Gadea, and now became a father, famously saying that he was prepared to lay down his life if need be, since his little daughter, who looked just like Mao Tse Tung, would be the continuation of his lineage.

The Young Che opens dramatically with his family's visit to Cuba after the triumph of the revolution. No other book gives such a strong sense of the path he had taken to help achieve this extraordinary victory.

The books on which *The Young Che* is based were written during a particularly grim period for Argentina and most of Latin America. This helps explain the rather pessimistic

Preface

The difficulty with writing a biography is that so many factors have to be taken into account if a true picture of a life is to be revealed. But to write the biography of one's own son is even more difficult. It is not a matter of talent, or a feat of literature, of expression or imagination.

To tackle the life of Che[1] Guevara is an arduous task because it was a very rich life, both within the family circle and beyond it. Once he had finished his secondary school, Che went on to university where he studied economics, politics and social sciences. He did scientific research, was interested in archaeology and worked as a male nurse for the Argentine merchant navy. He graduated in medicine and specialised in wartime medicine. He was a site manager/foreman. He was an international revolutionary and he fought as a guerrilla in different parts of the world. He cooperated with the organisation of the new Cuban government, he was Governor of the National Bank and the Minister for Industries of Cuba. He wrote literature and essays, and participated in economic debates of the highest level . . .

[1] Che: this is an expression generally used in Latin America to refer to people from Argentina, as it is an interjection with which they often pepper their conversation. It was Guevara's Cuban comrades in Mexico, while training for the invasion of the island, who nicknamed him 'El Che'. Nobody knows the origin of the word: it could be Mapuche or Guaraní (two indigenous Indian tribes of the continent) or it could have come from Andalucía with the conquistadores. In any case, Guevara promptly adopted it and went so far as signing bank notes in Cuba simply 'Che' when he was Governor of the National Bank.

Preface

The difficulty with writing a biography is that so many factors have to be taken into account if a true picture of a life is to be revealed. But to write the biography of one's own son is even more difficult. It is not a matter of talent, or a feat of literature, of expression or imagination.

To tackle the life of Che[1] Guevara is an arduous task because it was a very rich life, both within the family circle and beyond it. Once he had finished his secondary school, Che went on to university where he studied economics, politics and social sciences. He did scientific research, was interested in archaeology and worked as a male nurse for the Argentine merchant navy. He graduated in medicine and specialised in wartime medicine. He was a site manager/foreman. He was an international revolutionary and he fought as a guerrilla in different parts of the world. He cooperated with the organisation of the new Cuban government, he was Governor of the National Bank and the Minister for Industries of Cuba. He wrote literature and essays, and participated in economic debates of the highest level . . .

[1] Che: this is an expression generally used in Latin America to refer to people from Argentina, as it is an interjection with which they often pepper their conversation. It was Guevara's Cuban comrades in Mexico, while training for the invasion of the island, who nicknamed him 'El Che'. Nobody knows the origin of the word: it could be Mapuche or Guaraní (two indigenous Indian tribes of the continent) or it could have come from Andalucía with the conquistadores. In any case, Guevara promptly adopted it and went so far as signing bank notes in Cuban simply 'Che' when he was Governor of the National Bank.

He also worked as a hired hand in industry, in construction, in mines and in the countryside. He travelled across Latin America on foot, motorcycle, lorry, train and plane. He found time, however, to practise all types of sports and even reached the top category as a chess player.

He studied in depth the causes of underdevelopment in Latin America, which he had seen at first hand. Because of the influence he had over his fellow workers, it can be said that he was a true educator.

In brief, during the thirty-nine years of his life he did so much that in order to publish his complete biography one would require many years of research.

These difficulties would hinder anyone who tackled the subject, but for someone with blood ties as well as emotional ones, such difficulties are multiplied tenfold.

To write about him in order to judge him is not something I should really do.

However, I would like the reader to have an idea of who Ernesto Guevara de la Serna was as a person – in his childhood, his teens and his youth – within our extended family. I would also like to bring him to life within his milieu, surrounded by his parents, his brothers and sisters and his friends.

I would like to tell you about all that I have seen, lived, felt and suffered by his side. This is the task I have set myself.

If I can transmit the emotion that overwhelmed me when I had to reread his letters and retrieve his words and familiar expressions, then I believe I will have accomplished what I set out to do.

I want to speak about what I have seen and heard, and about those events in which I have also taken part – that is, about all that I know so well.

I also want to tell you about his life within the family.

Only I and my immediate family can speak about this knowledgeably.

I believe that to be able to study a man from all sides it is necessary to know in depth the social and family atmosphere in which he moved and what he lived through. That is why in this book I not only describe the events that took place in Alta Gracia, in Buenos Aires and in the nearby areas – all the places he visited during his childhood – but also in Argentina in general and in particular in the province of Misiones.

Ernesto lived in Misiones for a very short time and left the area at a young age, so he barely remembered it. But Misiones had a great influence on the family between 1927 and 1947. We had property there and were in close contact with that region and all that took place there.

A man does not exist in a void. He is related to all that surrounds him, and his destiny is inevitably linked to that of his ancestors. This is why I mention, albeit briefly, events that took place during the lifetime of Ernesto's ancestors (his grandparents and great-grandparents), in the certainty that this will contribute to understanding that great fighter called Ernesto Guevara de la Serna, whom the world knows as Che.

Ernesto Guevara Lynch
1972–3

Central and South America

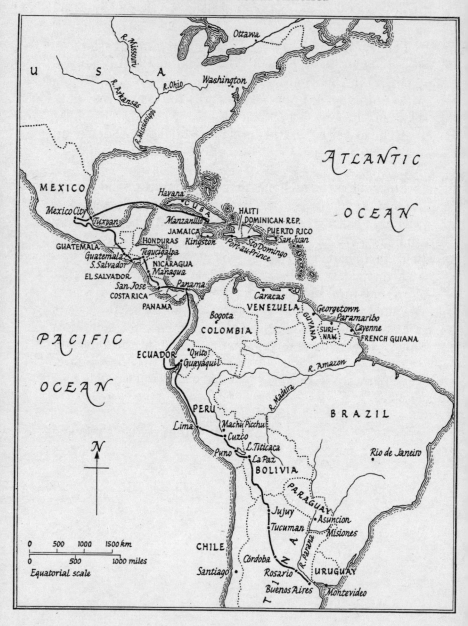

List of Illustrations

Part One: Che in Cuba, 1956–9

It was early December of 1956 and the world's major newspapers were publishing accounts of Fidel Castro's* failed attempt to invade the island of Cuba. The ex-Sergeant Batista*, then self-elevated to the rank of Major General, spread the news, by means of the international agencies, that Castro and his men had been killed during an attempt to invade the island. This took place on 2 December of that year.

Fidel Castro had launched the threat to invade Cuba over a year earlier by saying: 'We shall be free or we shall be martyrs.'

Our family in Buenos Aires was not aware of this threat, but began to understand what was going on when we read in large headlines the first news of it that the leading newspapers of the world were publishing. They were devoting space to the disaster that had taken place when Fidel and his men disembarked near the city of Manzanillo, in the province of Oriente. It was a bombshell.

We knew that Ernesto was involved in a conspiracy and that he had been taken into custody in Mexico with Fidel Castro and his men.

The Guevara family discovers the real destiny of Ernesto Guevara de la Serna

On 6 July 1956 I received a letter from Ernesto, in reply to one of mine that I had sent to the jail of the Gobernación of

Mexico City, on Miguel Schultz Street, in which I told him that we had just learned from the newspapers that he was in jail and asked him to tell me what the situation was, plainly and without beating about the bush.

His reply to my letter cleared any doubts that anyone might have had about Ernesto and his position within Fidel Castro's army.

The news, particularly when it came from the United States, gave details of the extermination of the whole contingent.

When the news reached Buenos Aires, our friends started telephoning incessantly. They wanted to know what was happening. I was told over the telephone the dreadful news that my son Ernesto had been mortally wounded during one of the skirmishes. The reports said that both Fidel Castro and his brother Raúl* had been killed, as well as several of their comrades. I remember the names of Juan Almeida* and Ramiro Valdés*. The news said that the motorboat *Granma*, in which the eighty-two had sailed from a small port in Mexico called Tuxpan, had been captured with all members of the invasion force on board and that the majority of the crew had died. The remaining few had been dispersed, according to the newspapers, and would soon have to give themselves up.

The whole world believed the news because of the disparity between the regular army of General Batista – formed by selected troops of the rural guard, the marines and the armed police force – and the tiny guerrilla group of just eighty-two men under Fidel Castro. It was impossible to believe that the latter might topple the military government of Batista, far less defeat its army and air force, trained by the United States of America and equipped with the most modern weapons.

When we received the news we were depressed. I went to

the offices of the newspaper *La Prensa* of Buenos Aires asking for confirmation. They said, as consolation, that they were unable to tell me if it was true until official confirmation came and, as such confirmation had not arrived, there was still hope.

I went home in despair. My wife, Celia, was sitting at a table with a pack of cards playing a game of patience. My children had learned from other sources what the wires were announcing, which was by now in any case in the public domain. When they saw me arrive, they did not utter a single word. They did not say anything to their mother. It was up to me to deliver the awful blow. I sat opposite her and waited for what seemed to me a century until she had finished her card game. She then lifted her head and, perhaps because she had a premonition, asked, 'What is it?'

'Look,' I replied, 'there are some reports that I don't think are true.'

She was livid. 'Ernesto?' she asked.

'Yes. But I can assure you that I do not believe it.'

She jumped to her feet, went to the telephone and called the news agency Associated Press and, with a dry but firm voice, said, 'I am the mother of Dr Ernesto Guevara de la Serna, whose death you have just announced and will be published in the newspapers. I want you to tell me the truth. Is it true?'

She later told me that they had tried to console her, telling her what I had already been told: that most of these reports ended up not being confirmed.

We were used to putting up with all sorts of worries when it came to Ernesto. I imagine the majority of our family and friends believed the terrible news, and I imagine that the government of Batista himself also believed it. But I was not totally discouraged. There was something that told me it could not be true, even if the evidence was to the contrary. I had an intuition – something like a remote hope in this avalanche of unconfirmed news – and that is why my words could be of some comfort to my family.

At that time I was in contact with civil servants who worked for the government of General Aramburu*. I went to the President's private secretary and asked to see the President to request him to intervene with the Cuban government, so that in the hypothetical event that Ernesto had been taken prisoner, he would not suffer the fate that Batista was in the habit of meting out to his prisoners: torture and assassination.

General Aramburu intervened and the Argentine Foreign Ministry moved with speed. We were continually in touch with the ministry, but neither denial nor confirmation was forthcoming. We were unable to find out anything.

My home, normally so noisy and lively, had become a sombre place. Nobody spoke, everyone foresaw the catastrophe, and around us there was an air of desolation. As for me, I must confess that I found it impossible to concentrate on anything that was not related to Ernesto. I abandoned my job, I didn't even turn up at the office. I went from one place to another seeking information. The newspapers dropped the story. But some newspapers and magazines arrived by air from Cuba. I remember an issue of the magazine *Bohemia* that I forced myself to read. It contained the same news that the first agency wires had issued, but in great detail: Ernesto, who was reclining against a tree talking to his mate Dr Pérez, had been mortally wounded. It had happened at Alegría del Pío. Fidel Castro's men had been surprised by the army, and the rural guards had fallen upon them before they had been able to see them, and the guards had machine-gunned them from a few metres away. The air force had rained napalm bombs on the woodlands and sugar-cane fields. The army had surrounded the area, and it was assumed that nobody could have escaped the ambush alive. For the government of Batista, this was the beginning and the end of the much-heralded invasion by Fidel Castro Ruz.

And then a letter from Ernesto, written in Mexico, arrived. For the family this was simply dreadful. It was his farewell letter to his parents. In it he made some philosophical observations. His message was that for him death was not important; what was important was the struggle for one's ideals. He also said that he was leaving Mexico to enter Cuba as a revolutionary. My wife read the letter in front of everyone without a tear. I clenched my teeth and did not understand why Ernesto had to get involved with a revolution that had nothing to do with his homeland.

How wrong I was. My son Ernesto had to teach me – I who had guided him through his first steps in life – the duty of men who fight for humanity. It was not clear to me at the time; I could not separate the heroic event in which one gives one's life for an ideal from a warlike adventure with no precise direction. I would compare Batista with any of the military men who had at one time or another been dictators in my country. I had fought against them, but what eluded me at the time was something that Ernesto had already fully understood: for the oppressed people of the world, the enemy was one and the same, and that enemy was not in Argentina, or Cuba, or Peru, or any other part of Latin America; the enemy was further away – it was from where the capitalist elite originates, and from where it sends its forces against those oppressed people via the heads of governments who serve their interests.

Early one morning the phone rang. I was being summoned by the Ministry of Foreign Affairs to meet the secretary of the Foreign Minister. He saw me in his office; his demeanour was quiet. What must I have looked like! I do not know, but I can imagine. He looked at me with pity and said the following: 'I have just received a telegram from the Argentine Embassy in Havana, which reads: "Dr Ernesto Guevara de la Serna, according to enquiries made by this embassy, is not among the dead, nor among the wounded, nor among the prisoners of Batista's army."'

Had I been thrown into the air by an earthquake I would not have left the premises with greater speed. I ran all the way home with the news, and that same afternoon everything changed for us. An air of optimism enveloped us all and my home was once again noisy and filled with youthful exuberance.

Some days went by. We lived in a state of anxiety awaiting confirmation or denial, but neither arrived through the official channels. So we believed the news that had arrived at the Ministry of Foreign Affairs from our embassy in Cuba.

1956 was coming to an end. On 31 December we were getting ready, as usual, to celebrate the arrival of the new year, although this time uncertainty hung over us. It was then that the unforeseen happened. It must have been around ten o'clock that night when an envelope was slid under the front door by an anonymous benefactor acting as postman. Nobody in the family will ever forget it. It was a small airmail envelope addressed to Celia de la Serna postmarked from Manzanillo in Cuba. Inside there was a little piece of paper. It was a page torn from a small notebook and was in handwriting that we all knew well. It read:

Dear Viejos:[1]
I am fine, I only used up 2 and have 5 still left.[2] I am still doing the same job, news will reach you sporadically and will continue to do so, but trust that God is an Argentine. A big hug to you all.
Teté[3]

We felt such a great sense of relief. After a whole month of agony, we became euphoric. The news did the rounds of the entire family and all our friends, and that New Year's Eve turned into a real rowdy celebration. The blow we had been dealt by the earlier false report of Ernesto's death had been such that this brief message lifted our spirits dramatically: he would continue the fight, despite the overwhelming odds and with little regard for his own safety. That night we felt some optimism as well as pride in our beloved Ernesto.

The champagne flowed and the toasts started. A few minutes before the church bells began to ring and the noise in the streets announced the arrival of the new year, another letter appeared mysteriously under the door. This time it was a larger, square envelope, also an airmail envelope like the previous one, but my wife's name and the address were written in a female hand. We opened it quickly. It was a printed card. The first page was covered with a red rose. It read more or less as follows: *Happy New Year. Teté is perfectly well.* It was signed by someone whose name I have forgotten, but it was a woman's name. This surpassed our expectations. The bells pealed and all those who had come

---

[1] *Viejo, vieja, viejos*: literally, old man, old woman, old men and women; but in many countries in Latin America these terms are used affectionately to address people of any age, particularly one's parents.
[2] 'I only used up 2 and have 5 still left': in Spanish, cats have seven lives, as opposed to nine in English.
[3] Teté: a nickname given to Ernesto by his parents a few days after his birth.

to our home were jubilant. Ernesto had been spared, at least for now.

After this, we continued to wait anxiously. I invited my daughter-in-law Hilda Gadea*, who was in Peru with her parents, and our granddaughter Hildita* to visit us. They came to Buenos Aires to stay with us. Hilda brought fresh news, but it dated from before Ernesto's departure for Cuba. She was very reserved and one could tell she was trying to observe the strict silence imposed by Ernesto. However, with Hilda and Hildita in our midst, we gradually began to understand why Ernesto had joined the Cuban Revolution.

Hilda also brought a letter to her from Ernesto. It read as follows:

28 January 1957

My dear Vieja,

Here I am, in the Cuban jungle, alive and thirsting for blood, writing these fiery lines inspired by Martí* as if I were a real soldier (I am dirty and in rags, at least). I write on a field mess-plate with my weapon by my side and a new addition between my lips: a Havana cigar. We had a hard time. As you probably know, after seven days of being packed like sardines in the already famous *Granma*, thanks to the pilots we disembarked in an infected mangrove swamp and our misadventures continued until we were surprised in the now-famous 'Alegría' ambush and disbanded like pigeons. I was wounded in the neck and I stayed alive due only to my catlike luck, since a machine-gun bullet hit the ammunition box I was carrying close to my chest and it bounced on to my neck. I walked the hills for a few days, believing myself to be badly wounded, because the impact of the bullet had left me with a serious pain in the chest. Of the boys you have met, only Jimmy Hertzel was killed, executed for surrendering. A group of those whom you and I had met together, including Almeida and Ramirito, spent seven days of terrible hunger and thirst until we broke the encirclement and, with the help of the *campesinos*,[4] we regrouped with Fidel. (One of the ones who is believed to be dead, although it has not been confirmed, is poor Ñico*.) After serious problems we reorganised ourselves, we found weapons and we attacked a barracks, killing five soldiers. The army, who thought we were disbanded, got a huge surprise and put the whole country on alert, and for forty-five further days they set on us the elite troops; we dispersed them again and this time they had three dead and two wounded. The dead were left in the scrub. Not much later we captured three guards and took their weapons. If you add to this that we did not suffer any losses and the woodland is ours, you can imagine how demoralised the army are, seeing us slip through their fingers when they thought we were within their grasp. Of course, the struggle has not yet been won and we still have many a battle to fight, but it is tipping in our favour, and will do so more and more.

Now, talking about you two, I want to know if you are still at the same address, and how everybody is, in particular 'the deepest petal of my love'. Please give her the biggest kiss and hug that she can bear. For the others, a hug and regards. As we had to leave in a hurry, I left my things in Pocho's house, and the photos of you and the baby are there. When you write to me, please send them. You can write to me at my uncle's house

---

[4] *Campesino*: peasant. In Spanish, *campesino* does not have the negative connotation peasant has in English. A *campesino* is a political word for a member of the rural working class.

care of Patojo*. The letters will take a while, but they will arrive, I think.

A big hug from Chancho.[5]

For Mrs Hilda Gadea, Paso de los Andes, 1028, Puebla Libre, Lima, Peru.

We found it difficult to relate to this new Ernesto, a combatant in the jungle, not the one we knew. I would never have believed that he could have been that bloodthirsty. But an episode sprang to mind that I will tell you about, as it might help you to understand my son's character.

We lived in Buenos Aires in a street called Aráoz, number 2180, on the corner of Mansilla Street. Our house was the oldest of the neighbourhood – it was in fact so old that the people who had lived longest in the area believed it to be the first house of the then-remote borough of Palermo. Given its age, the ceilings were very high, as was usual in the previous century. We occupied the first floor of the house, which had a huge terrace corresponding to the ceilings of the lower floors; the terrace was surrounded by a wall that separated it from the street. Embedded in this small wall there was a ventilation duct, which was higher than the wall by some 2.5 metres. This old pipe placed there (no one knows how long ago) had a groove on the end a few centimetres wide, in which a poor bird had caught one of its wings. Ernesto and I were watching the desperate little thing frantically flapping its wings, foreseeing its end. Its wing was really caught in that groove and it would have been impossible for the bird to break loose, no matter how hard it tried. One could see how tired it was and could guess that it had spent several minutes in this situation, as the flapping of its wings was

---

[5] Chancho: a nickname given to Ernesto by his friends in Argentina. It means pig, and reflected his careless attire and his disinclination to wash often.

becoming less frequent. The fragility of the pipe prevented us from placing a ladder against it and there was nothing we could do. This took place in 1949. Ernesto was by then a grown man. He looked at the bird and decided to set it free. I, on the other hand, realising what he was about to do, decided to prevent him. The freedom of the bird could represent the loss of Ernesto. We were some seven metres from the ground. All my arguments were useless: the pipe was too high and too frail; it would not support his weight if he climbed through there; it was better to wait for help. Knowing the danger he was in, I sat astride the small wall and tried to hold the pipe as far as possible, while Ernesto without further delay climbed the wall as best he could. A few seconds later the bird flew away free.

I now had before me the letter Ernesto had written from the Cuban jungle, and I understood how a man could become hardened by his decision to fight for a just cause. My sensitive, emotional son was overcoming his sensitivity to comply with an irrevocable sense of duty.

Now we began to understand the magnitude of the exploit of that small band of men who disembarked on 2 December 1956 on the beach of Las Coloradas, on the island of Cuba, in order to put an end to the military dictatorship and change the political and social structure of that country for good.

Our family calmed down and began to interpret the news from Ernesto – news that was expressed in a somewhat cryptic manner in his letters. And we understood his earlier imprisonment in Mexico, his hunger strike and his clandestine existence later on.

Each one of us read something different into the decision he had taken to fight with the revolutionary army. All of us, however, were wishing with all our hearts that things went well for him and that he would come out of it alive. None of us had any faith in the triumph of that tiny guerrilla force that had to face an army trained by the United States of America, technically supported by that country and armed with the most modern welfare equipment of the time. We thought it was an impossible task, because we did not know the strength of resolve of men who do not fear death because they have decided to fight for freedom for the oppressed; but neither did we know the strategic and tactical value of guerrilla warfare when confronted by conventional armies. We did not know all this because, although the political persuasion of my family did not differ much from that of Ernesto, none of us (myself included) had understood, as he had, the depth of need of the 'underdeveloped' countries – a lovely word that serves as a useful pretext for imperialists to trample underfoot the oppressed of the world – to set themselves free from the colonial yoke, which has kept the humble mired in misery through the ages.

The family is distressed by the plight of Ernesto as a guerrilla in Cuba

Newspapers from all over the world spread the news that Batista divulged for circulation. Naturally, these stories were meant to demoralise the men and women of the 26 July Movement[6] – for that was the name of the revolutionary movement founded by Fidel Castro – and to persuade the peasantry of Oriente province, as well as all the revolutionaries of the island of Cuba, that the war was totally lost.

And this was the news that the Argentine newspapers published as well. However, reading between the lines, one could learn things that Batista's army did not intend. Nor

[6] 26 July Movement: the revolutionary movement named after the date of the failed attack on the Moncada Barracks led by Fidel Castro in 1953 in Santiago de Cuba, as a result of which he was exiled.

could they silence the battle of La Plata[7] or that of El Uvero.[8] Although we did not know the importance to Batista of these areas, the fact that the papers published news which referred to skirmishes that had taken place in those areas, saying that the invading forces had been routed, was encouraging, because they implied that the rebels were attacking and that Batista's forces were on the defensive.

I started to make my own enquiries. I contacted General Bayo*, who was the instructor of the budding Cuban liberation army in Mexico. This general, who had fought for the Republican side in Spain and against the Franco* uprising, was instrumental in the invasion of Cuba. For it was he who prepared the young invaders militarily, and who should have been on board the *Granma* with them; he was unable to go because of the restricted space on the vessel. He replied to my letters with great warmth and always tried to raise my spirits.

As I explain further on, I was in constant contact with the 26 July Movement in Buenos Aires, since they operated out of my office. However, I could not find out much from them because they knew very little themselves. With a group of friends, we had installed a special aerial connected to a very powerful radio and we listened to the news that was continually being transmitted on shortwave from Cuba. But through these channels we did not obtain news of Ernesto.

After the letter that had reached us on 31 December, we only learned about him from the letter he had written to Hilda Gadea, which I have already commented on, and from another one, the exact date of which I cannot establish, but which must have been from February or March 1957.

[7] La Plata: on 17 January 1957 Castro's guerrillas, now known as the Rebel Army, attacked a small army garrison at the mouth of the La Plata River in the Sierra Maestra. It was their first victory.
[8] El Uvero: on 28 May 1957 the Rebel Army captured a well-fortified garrison at El Uvero in the Sierra Maestra.

As can be appreciated, it had been written so that it was impossible to identify the sender. He used the name Teté again, which only my family knew of, as it was a nickname we had given him as a baby; and he gave the name and address of a young lady whose fiancé he claimed to be, in order to be able to receive our news.

The letter read as follows:

Dear Viejos,

After such a long time, I can take advantage of a favourable event to give you my news.

I am really sorry that I am not able to receive even a miserable little note from you telling me how things are. At the beginning I had thought that the business would fail and that the resolution would be quick, but then the boss stabilised matters and started to straighten them out, and now it seems that he will give me a holiday in a few months' time when the business comes to fruition and he can pay for the load.

I am beginning to really know the business and I think I could have a career with the help of the boss, who is a very good chap. Of my personal situation I cannot tell you anything of interest because you have not met my new friends. What I can tell you is that I still love going on excursions and, whenever I can, I go on one with a group of friends.

I am waiting for the business to be complete to invite you to visit this marvellous island. Also, I would like you to know that I am engaged to Miss Norma Llopis Sánchez, at whose address at Mazó Twenty Six Manzanillo, Oriente, you can write to me until I have my own home. A big hug for all of you.

Teté

In this letter, written in Ernesto's style so that only we understood it, he gave us some news of what he was doing and what his immediate objectives were, but he could not give more details without endangering the person who took it to the post office, as well as risking its non-delivery.

The information provided by our country's newspapers was the same as that transmitted by the international agencies. The majority of these agencies were at the service of American imperialism. They told us what the Batista government wanted us to think: the fatalities of the revolutionary army were so numerous that in very little time there would be no rebel soldiers left. On the other hand, when it referred to the Cuban army, it hardly admitted that there were any casualties, and only every now and then one fatality.

We were encouraged by such clearly false information. It showed how desperate the Batista government was to spread lies. The morale of the government's army had to be raised, and the people had to be prevented from taking sides with the rebels. All this was evidence that Castro's guerrilla army was taking hold.

Our family was by now immune to the pessimistic news that appeared in the papers. Ernesto's name appeared many times in the news, and many times he was reported dead. Fortunately, we did not trust the news and we had learned to control our anguish.

Not all the newspapers gave completely false information. Dolores Moyano, the daughter of a friend of ours, lived in New York and would often send us press cuttings from the *Diario de las Américas*, published in Miami. In a section called '*El Reloj*', almost every day there was news from the Rebel Army. This is how we managed to find out how the revolutionary struggle was progressing in Cuba.

The representative of the 26 July Movement in Buenos

Aires was Dr Jorge Beruff*, whom I saw every day. It was he who put me in touch with the representatives of their committee in the United States. From New York I received communications and communiqués from the Rebel Army.

One day I met the North American journalist Jules Dubois*, who claimed to be against Batista. He travelled regularly to Buenos Aires and stayed at the Plaza Hotel, where he rented an apartment. He would invite me round for a glass of Scotch and to chat about the Cuban Revolution. I did not know his background; I only knew, because he had told me himself, that he was one of the editors of the newspaper *Diario de las Américas*. He would ask me lots of questions about Ernesto, about his childhood and what political ideas he had when he lived in Buenos Aires.

He also asked my opinion of Fidel Castro and if I knew whether he was a Communist. I would tell him all that I thought prudent about Ernesto and of his way of thinking, but when the conversation touched on Fidel, I would invariably tell Dubois that I knew very little about him. Between one conversation and the next I managed to extract from Dubois what he thought about Ernesto and Fidel. That is how I found out that he believed that Fidel was only a liberal, and that Ernesto and Raúl were pro-Communist.

I did not suspect that this journalist could be from the CIA. I believed Dubois when he stated the source of his news: Radio Rebelde, which transmitted from the Sierra Maestra. It was credible because Miami, the home base of his newspaper, was very close to Cuba.

Whenever he arrived in Buenos Aires he brought news of Ernesto, and that news was never denied me, so I waited anxiously for Dubois' calls. He would tell me that Ernesto had taken part in this or that skirmish, that he commanded a suicide battalion, that on one occasion he had been wounded in the foot, but that the wound had not been serious; as well as many other details.

But one day I began to suspect something, because of the questions Dubois asked me. This suspicion increased when he asked me in writing for a summary of all I knew about Fidel Castro. He made this request by means of a letter that I still have. Some time later the veil fell from my eyes when I learned, from a very reliable source, that Dubois was in fact no less than a colonel with the CIA.

Whatever he was, he did not cause me any harm, nor did he get from me anything that might be to the detriment of the Cuban Revolution; on the contrary, Dubois gave me a lot of news that was true.

For our family, the sources of information were growing. Although Ernesto's letters were becoming less frequent, we had more information. Of course we had to filter it carefully, since many of the sources were suspect and their purpose was to deceive and to confuse.

Amongst the war communiqués, the commentaries from the *Diario de las Américas*, international wires, the news provided by Jules Dubois and information provided by some of the few Cuban refugees who sought asylum in Buenos Aires, we had enough to form our own network of knowledge. But we lacked the main thing: direct news from Ernesto. This was sparse and infrequent and it made us all very anxious.

The whole world had now begun to take an interest in that small guerrilla army, which although the Cuban government tried to belittle its actions in the Sierra Maestra – was showing that it constituted a serious threat to the Batista dictatorship.

Renowned journalists, the representatives of some large newspapers, discovered that the revolutionary war undertaken by the 26 July Movement under the command of

Fidel Castro Ruz was not simply one more coup d'état or another uprising in the Caribbean, but a real national liberation war. Consequently, interviewing its leader at the site of the operations would represent a journalistic coup. The first one to do so was the veteran reporter from *The New York Times*, Herbert Matthews*, who went into the Sierra Maestra to interview Fidel Castro. He also took many photographs, one of which was published all over the world. In these photos Fidel appeared with his brother Raúl, Juan Almeida, Calixto García*, Crescencio Pérez*, a *campesino* who was a great help to them, Universo Sánchez* and with the Argentine doctor of the expedition, Ernesto Guevara.

You can imagine with what interest we read Matthews' story and with what emotion we examined the photograph from *The New York Times*. Yes, that guerrilla who appeared with a rifle in his hands and sporting a new beard was Ernesto. There was no doubt. The article comforted us a lot because it gave us the impression that by its very publication Fidel Castro and his people were being recognised as an incipient army. The article put paid to the versions spread by Batista, according to which they were a band of common criminals, men operating outside the law who had already been encircled by the troops in a small redoubt of the Sierra Maestra, where they would soon be exterminated.

The New York Times was, beyond doubt, one of the most authoritative newspapers in the world and, consequently, one of those with a discerning and influential readership. After Herbert Matthews' articles (which had a great impact on all circles close to the Cuban revolutionaries), the stature of Fidel Castro grew and the 26 July Movement was elevated to the category of 'army at war'.

For us it was a great relief. Now we knew that Ernesto was fighting for a cause that was recognised as just, and was in the company of a group of men who knew what they were fighting for.

It is one thing to tell stories from the past, as I am doing now, and another to have lived through those moments in a state of permanent anguish, trying to fathom out that revolution through the haze of confusion that enveloped it. It was no longer just Ernesto's life and health that interested us. Our family was now totally engulfed in the unfolding drama of that small band of men who had turned into the 'Rebel Army'. Any piece of news about them was a piece of news that touched us all. Fidel Castro, Raúl Castro, Juan Almeida, Ramiro Valdés, Calixto García, Gustavo Ameijeiras*, Crescencio Pérez, Camilo Cienfuegos*, Universo Sánchez – all these names now belonged to our family. These men were Ernesto's comrades and consequently had become his brothers.

We lived in a constant state of anxiety and were always in search of any news about Cuba. Of course much of it was anti-Communist propaganda and a lot was merely sensationalist. But at times we did receive valuable information. I received a North American magazine, dated May 1958, which contained a story by a journalist called Bob Taber. The title of the article was 'Will Che be able to change the fate of America?' – Taber had interviewed both Fidel and Che. We knew that the Cubans called Ernesto by the nickname Che, but we did not know that his nickname was known abroad.

The story was well written, and in it Taber told all that he saw on his way to Fidel's headquarters. Thus we were able to get an idea of the atmosphere of the Sierra Maestra during the revolutionary war, and his articles made us live through a little of that war, which we were so passionate about.

It is evident that Che made a great impression on Taber, who made predictions showing his admiration for Che. I must admit that Taber's writings impressed all the family. Ernesto now was not just one more guerrilla; he was being described as a future leader of men.

'The Invasion'

After the serious defeats suffered in Oriente province by Batista's army, Castro decided to open new fronts. The project consisted of taking the revolutionary war to the populated areas nearer the capital, Havana.

With the intention of opening new fronts to the west, two columns were to leave under the orders of Che: Column 8, which he commanded himself, and Column 2, under Comandante Camilo Cienfuegos. This operation was known as 'The Invasion'.

On 27 September 1958, from a small village called El Jíbaro, situated in the foothills of the Sierra Maestra, Comandante Ernesto Che Guevara left for the Sierra del Escambray, in the province of Las Villas, at the head of an armed group of 146 men. In the hills of El Escambray different groups of men operated sporadically without a unified command and attacked the government forces.

On a parallel course to that of Che's forces, but a little earlier, Comandante Camilo Cienfuegos moved in the direction of the Sierra del Bamburanao, also in the province of Las Villas. Both forces were to stay in touch with each other and join up near the city of Santa Clara, the capital of Las Villas province. Then Cienfuegos was to continue towards the province of Pinar del Río, where the Órganos range would offer good refuge for his forces, and he was to open a new revolutionary front in order to be able to attack the rearguard of Batista's army.

The beast would thus be encircled in his lair. The international news agencies were continually transmitting news of clashes between Batista's army and these columns, but were always giving the impression that the columns were only a band of outlaws on the run. Che covered a distance of approximately 600 kilometres on foot along the south of the island; the march was extremely painful. They had to overcome all sorts of difficulties, hiding in the small woods of the region, walking through the swamps (often with water up to their necks), engaging in combat against troops that greatly outnumbered them, enduring bombardment from aircraft, and holding up pharmacies in small villages in order to treat the serious foot infections of their men, caused by the mud of the foul marshes. Thus, after forty-two days, they reached the first hills of Escambray. Column 8 had had only three casualties, but the whole column had become a group of hungry, sick and exhausted men.

In 1959, the Brazilian magazine *O Cruzeiro* published an article by Che about this famous march. Let me add here a few paragraphs from that article to give the reader a more accurate idea of how the crucial march of Column 8 took place.

Che tells us:

Once the regiments that attacked the Sierra Maestra were annihilated and the front had recovered, and we had increased the number of our troops as well as boosted their morale, we decided to begin the march to the central province of Las Villas. The military order I was issued stipulated that my main strategic task was to systematically cut communications between the two ends of the island . . .

With these instructions, they set out in lorries on 30 August 1958.

In a letter to Fidel, Che says the following:

I'll give you a short account: we left by night on the 31st with four horses because it was impossible to leave by lorry, due to the fact that all the petrol from Magadan had been taken and we feared an ambush in Jibacoa. We went through this point, which had been abandoned by the guards, without incident, but were unable to go on for more than a couple of leagues, sleeping in a small clearing in the woodland on the far side of the highway. On 1 September we crossed the highway and took vehicles, which broke down with frightening frequency, reaching a smallholding called Cayo Redondo, where we spent the day as a hurricane was approaching. The guards arrived, about forty of them, but they withdrew without fighting. We carried on with lorries, assisted by four tractors, but it was impossible to go on like this and we had to give up until the next day, 2 September, when we continued on foot, arriving on the banks of the Cauto, which we could not cross at night due to an extraordinary flood.

Che goes on in the magazine *O Cruzeiro*:

On 1 September a fierce cyclone [. . .] rendered all means of communication useless, with the exception of the Central Highway, the only paved one of this region of Cuba, forcing us to give up travelling in vehicles. From that moment on, we had to use horses or go on foot. We had a lot of artillery with us, a bazooka with forty rounds of ammunition, and all that is needed for a long journey and for establishing a camp quickly.

The days that followed turned out to be difficult although we were in the friendly territory of Oriente: we crossed flooded rivers, channels and brooks that had turned into rivers, struggling continuously to prevent the artillery and the shells from getting wet, looking for fresh horses and leaving the tired ones behind, avoiding the populated areas as we left the eastern province.

We walked on difficult flooded ground, enduring the attack of plagues of mosquitoes that made the hours of rest unbearable, eating little and badly, drinking water from muddy rivers or simply from swamps. Our days began to grow longer and to become truly horrible. Already a week after we left the camp and crossed the River Jobabo, which is the boundary between the provinces of Camagüey and Oriente, our forces had grown weak. This river, like all the previous ones, as well as those we would cross later, was flooded. The lack of footwear was also felt by our troops; many of our men went barefoot and on foot through the quagmires of the south of Camagüey.

Their misery was compounded by having to travel around the mosquito-infested Laguna Grande. But Che then tells us worse news. They fell into an ambush at La Federal and lost two comrades. This encounter had given away their presence in Camagüey, and from then on they would have to endure the punishing attacks of Batista's army and air force.

He continues the story in *O Cruzeiro*:

These are days of exhausting marches across desolate areas, where there is only water and mud; we are hungry, we are thirsty and we can barely advance because our legs weigh like lead and the weight of the weapons is colossal.

The guides that Comandante Cienfuegos must have sent

had not arrived, so they had to carry on regardless. Che's story goes on like this:

> . . . we threw ourselves without further ado into the adventure. Our vanguard clashed with an enemy post at the place called Cuatro Compañeros and the exhausting battle commenced. At dawn we managed to gather, with great effort, a large part of our troops in the area, but the army was advancing by the sides and we were forced to fight hard to make it possible for some of our stragglers to pass through some rail tracks towards the woodland. The air force spotted us then, and started bombing us with B-26s, C-47s, the large C-3s and the light aircraft used for reconnaissance, over an area no greater than two hundred metres wide. After all this, we retired leaving one dead, killed by a bomb, and several wounded, among them Captain Silva, who took part in the rest of the Invasion with a broken shoulder.

From that moment on, the air force continued to follow systematically in the steps of that small army and bombed them every time it spotted them.

We were never without encouragement from the *campesinos* in spite of the difficulties. We always found someone to act as our guide, or who gave us what food we needed to be able to carry on. It was not, of course, the unanimous support of all the people that we had in Oriente, but there was always someone who helped us.

They found out, by means of a portable radio, that General Tabernilla boasted that he had destroyed Che's guerrilla force and gave the names of the fallen – names that he had obtained from a rucksack that someone had lost at the battle of Cuatro Compañeros. The false news on the radio about the death of the combatants filled them with glee, but things were not going well for the guerrillas. Che goes on with his story:

The news of our false death brought about a joyous reaction in the men; however, pessimism was winning them over little by little: hunger and thirst, fatigue, the feeling of powerlessness when confronted with enemy troops that were gradually encircling us, and above all the terrible disease of their feet, known by the *campesinos* as *mazamorra* – which turned every step that our men took into intolerable pain – had turned us into an army of shadows. It was difficult to advance, very difficult indeed. Day by day the physical condition of our troops grew worse and the food – some one day, none the next, some maybe the following – did not contribute to alleviating the level of misery that we were enduring. Our hardest days were those spent in the vicinity of the Central de Baraguá, in foul swamps, without a drop of drinking water, constantly harassed by the air force, without a single horse that might have taken the weakest through the inhospitable marshes, with our shoes totally destroyed by the muddy water of the sea, with vegetation that hurt our bare feet; our situation was truly disastrous when we left behind, with much effort, the encirclement of Baraguá and reached the famous Trocha de Júcaro a Morón, a site of historic fame, having been the scene of bloody battles between patriots and Spaniards during the War of Independence. We did not even have time to recover a little before a new downpour, the severity of the climate, as well as attacks from the enemy or news of their presence in the area forced us to march on. The men were growing more and more tired and discouraged. However, when the situation was at its worst – when only by means of insults, pleadings and every type of curse could I get the exhausted men to walk – a single remote vision on the horizon lit up their faces and infused the guerrilla force with a renewed spirit. This vision was but a blue spot towards the west, the blue spot of the mountains of Las Villas, which our men were seeing for the first time.

From that moment on, the deprivation became far more bearable and everything seemed easier. We dodged the last encirclement, we swam across the River Júcaro, which separates the province of Camagüey from that of Las Villas, and it seemed as if a new light guided us.

Two days later we were in the heart of the Trinidad-Sancti Spiritus mountain range, safe and ready to start a further stage of the war. [. . .] We had reached the mountainous region of Las Villas on 16 October. We had little time and an enormous task. Camilo was doing his part in the north, sowing fear among the men of the dictatorship.

This audacious and brilliant tactical operation paved the way for the eventual triumph of the Rebel Army.

The fall of Batista

For those who were part of the larger Cuban scene, at the time it was difficult to comprehend what was going on, to weigh what was happening there; consequently it was far more difficult for us, who had only our immediate knowledge of events from the news issued by the international agencies, which were constantly changing their version of events prior to the fall of the dictator Batista, as if it were a fantastic kaleidoscope.

But in the end the news we had hoped for arrived: Batista had fled. Early on the morning of 1 January 1959, having celebrated the arrival of the new year with a party at the government palace, he fled the country together with his closest collaborators, abandoning to their fate many of those who had been with him during his ill-fated tenure. Now all the rebels had to do was to clear up the scattered remnants of Batista's defeated army.

Comandante Camilo Cienfuegos, with one final push, had in his turn defeated the army that tried to ambush him. On 1 January, Comandantes Camilo Cienfuegos and Ernesto Che Guevara, in a single joint operation, completed their pincer movement on Havana and entered it not much later with their small rebel force, which carried along with it, because of their enthusiasm and courage, a large section of the population of the island. Their arrival in Havana was truly triumphant.

Newspapers worldwide carried the news of this incredible feat in large headlines.

The sirens of all the newspapers in Buenos Aires sounded at length. The people poured out into the streets. The fall of Batista was a rude blow for the United States, whose government was not appreciated by our people, who on the whole viewed with suspicion any interference by them in Latin America. In any case in our country, although we enjoyed relative freedom, the people had sampled the bitter taste of a military dictatorship, which had labelled itself 'Revolución Libertadora'[9] and had for many years misruled Argentina.

At home we had barely put down our glasses from toasting the fall of Batista when a terrible piece of news arrived. Ernesto had fallen, fatally wounded when taking the

[9] Revolución Libertadora: the name that the Argentine military junta gave itself in 1955 when it ousted President Juan Perón.

Cuban capital. Wires originating in Cuba said so. We would not believe the international telegraph services. According to reports, he had been wounded and killed so many times, but he had always survived these alleged deaths. But when each of these blows was announced we crumbled. I immediately got in touch with Jorge Beruff, who in turn got in touch with the central office in New York, and within two hours we received a correction of what the newspapers had published.

We celebrated the new year that night with the joy of knowing that Ernesto was alive and in charge of the barracks at La Cabaña fortress in Havana.

Euphoria had taken over our lives. The triumph of the revolutionary troops seemed unbelievable. Over the two years that the war had lasted, anxiety had eroded our spirits drop by drop. Although we all tried to disguise our concern, each one of us knew that our thoughts were always centred on Ernesto's life.

Now everything had changed. On 2 January 1959 the newspapers brought all sorts of good news. We became less tense; we could at last relax. That race between life and death that the Cuban rebels had endured since 1 January 1956 had now come to an end. Although their path was covered in blood and strewn with corpses, the murderous dictator Fulgencio Batista was no longer in power. Twenty thousand lives were lost over the years he was in power. Now the situation was different: a revolutionary government had just taken power, sustained by the Rebel Army with Fidel Castro at the helm.

The revolutionaries entered a new phase of very challenging struggle. Government stability had to be maintained at all costs and they would have to rebuild the whole of Cuba.

In Buenos Aires nobody talked about anything else. I felt

as if suspended on air. Our relatives and friends kept asking
questions and we replied as best we could. But the truth was
that for our family the main concern was Ernesto's life. And
Ernesto was alive and the war was over.

Hundreds of letters and telegrams of congratulations
arrived at home. Many years have gone by and today, when
I reread those telegrams and cards, crude reality shows me
that many of those who congratulated us then are now on
the opposing side. For the world around us, the fall of Batista
should signify the return to a 'democratic type' of government, where the people would elect their representatives
and leaders.

Experience has shown us that it is precisely in this type of
government that the greatest contradictions are hatched.
The conditions in which Cuba found itself then were so
disastrous that, in order to be able to put that nation back on
course, what was done was essential.

The die was cast. The Cuban Revolution had to become a
Socialist Revolution, and with it would start the liberation
of Latin America from the imperialist yoke.

I myself had not totally grasped the sense of this
revolution. And from Buenos Aires I could not see it all that
clearly.

On our way

On 6 January I was surprised, but elated, to hear that an
aircraft sent by Comandante Camilo Cienfuegos was to
transport my family to Havana, together with some Cuban
exiles.

We began to prepare for the trip with great haste. One
month earlier we could not have dreamed it, and now we
had to prepare quickly, because the plane had just left Cuba
for Buenos Aires.

Our family would be represented by my wife Celia and

myself, our daughter Celia and our son Juan Martín. My other two children could not travel because of their professional commitments.

By the time we arrived at Ezeiza, the main airport for Buenos Aires, the aircraft from Cuban Airlines was already there. I introduced myself to the captain and, while I was chatting with him, I could see the Cuban exiles arriving with bulging suitcases. I remember that one of them, Luis Conte Agüero (who later behaved atrociously towards the government of the revolution), expected to be allowed to carry with him more than a hundred books. I expressed my fears about the excess baggage, but the captain assured me that the total weight of the plane would not exceed the limit.

And so it was. A few minutes later we bade farewell to friends and family. We reached cruising altitude above our city and very soon were flying towards the province of Mendoza. The crossing of the Andes was carried out impeccably. I knew the mountains well because I had crossed them riding a mule, when I was in my twenties. Now, within a few minutes, we had flown over what had previously taken me several days to cross. Under the wings of the aircraft, places that I recognised immediately began to appear. We left behind Tupungato and Aconcagua with their snowy peaks, and a few minutes later we landed at Santiago's airport in Chile, where many journalists and curious people awaited the flight.

We had lunch at the airport and took off straight after that. I had never been on such a long flight. While I thought about Ernesto, about how lucky he had been, how happy he must be in Havana, and about all that we would witness there, I was fascinated by the landscapes unfolding below us, all of which were new to me.

It was already night when we flew over Peru and at dawn

we realised the plane was landing, because of the way it shook. We were at the airport for Guayaquil, Ecuador. We left the aircraft; it was unbearably hot. We spent four hours there and I later learned that this was because they were trying to fix the landing gear. The passengers were not aware of this. At six in the morning we took off again and not long afterwards we flew over the Panama Canal at more than 6,700 metres.

For one moment we could see both the Pacific and the Atlantic Oceans. Below, a broken line indicated the canal, and some little black dots the vessels at sea. Alongside, some little red dots, the roofs of some modest houses, could be seen. Soon afterwards we could see only water and clouds.

Around midday we landed at Rancho Boyeros, the main airport for Havana. As soon as the steps were placed against the aircraft I leaped out and, with one knee to the ground, kissed Cuban soil.

We were immediately surrounded by several bearded soldiers in rather dirty uniforms, armed with rifles and machine guns. The regulation greetings took place and we made our way in a hurry to the airport building, where Ernesto was waiting for us. As I understand it, they had wanted to surprise him and he had only found out that we were arriving a few minutes earlier.

My wife ran into his arms and could not contain her tears. Many photographers and television cameras recorded the scene. Then I hugged and kissed my son. It had been six years since I had last seen him.

I did not know Havana – I had never been there. The car drove through crowds who showed their joy and celebrated the triumph of the revolution. Amongst the crowd were poorly clad soldiers, almost all of them bearded and deeply tanned by the tropical sun. Most of them moved with ease and carried their weapons casually, sometimes carrying them over their heads. Many of them wore necklaces with the Virgin Mary or crucifixes, or the seeds of trees, and some even sported dogs' teeth. Their lack of discipline attracted our attention, but there was something that was noticeable above all else, and that was the enormous joy and euphoria all the people were expressing. They shouted, they sang and some danced. A few minutes later we arrived at the Hilton Hotel, today known as the Havana Libre, and were lodged on the sixteenth floor.

That midday we had lunch with Ernesto in the living room of the apartment we had been assigned. There was a large table in the middle. As soon as we entered the room a group of soldiers and officers came forward and, with a great display of camaraderie, embraced Ernesto and greeted us. There was a festive atmosphere. In the confusion of those arriving and leaving, we began to make contact with that group of combatants who had fought the revolutionary war side by side with Ernesto. Cubans, on the whole, speak not only with their lips, but also with their hands. We were astonished by the euphoria with which they communicated with each other in a language spoken so fast that many syllables went unpronounced. Between gestures, back-slapping and loud laughter, they expressed their happiness.

As well as these men in uniform, a group of civilians had also greeted us. Among them I recognised some of those who regularly visited the Committee of the 26 July Movement in Buenos Aires.

We sat at table. We had brought some bottles of red wine with us, remembering how much Ernesto liked it, and his eyes lit up when he saw them and the labels of the wine that we usually drank at home. Seeing them probably brought back the memory of other happy times, when the whole family lived together in Buenos Aires.

We would have liked to capture the joy felt at that moment, but it fleeted by as if it were lightning. It would be impossible to put into words the emotions felt by us then.

A group of soldiers and officers sat at our table and I specially remember Camilo Cienfuegos. He and Ernesto treated each other with great familiarity and camaraderie. We already knew that they were the greatest of friends.

We could not help noticing the sunburned bearded faces of those combatants, whose faded uniforms still showed traces of their battles.

Today, so many years after that luncheon, it is difficult for me to reproduce that moment. We missed the opportunity of recording the voices telling the story of what they had lived through. There we were, celebrating the triumph of the revolution with Cubans who were also celebrating the arrival of Che's family in Havana!

Toasts were proposed amid exclamations and laughter. Now we were with the winners, the incredible winners, and Ernesto was one of them. In his physical appearance, his expression, his joy, he was the same young man who had left Buenos Aires one cold afternoon in July more than six years earlier.

From the living room, through the large windows on the sixteenth floor of the Hilton Hotel, we could see in the distance the neighbourhood of El Vedado and, further away, the imposing stone wall of El Morro fortress protruding into the bay, and beyond the calm green sea and the intense blue sky.

The healthy joy of the place engulfed us all. We could not even begin to think that the cruel war had not yet come to an end. Just as previously, during the sad times of the war, victory seemed incredible, now it seemed to us that this triumphant revolution could not be vanquished.

But in front of us, beyond that calm sea – only 150

kilometres away – was the spearhead of the USA, aiming straight at the heart of Cuba.

Many foreigners had arrived at the hotel. The ground floor seemed to be awash with people coming and going: journalists with their camera equipment, cameramen, local people, foreigners in elegant attire, military men from other countries, hotel waiters in impeccable uniforms and soldiers and officers from the revolutionary army wearing fatigues – the cheeriest of the lot.

I remember going down in the spacious lift from the top floor, when on a lower floor an American couple boarded the lift. He wore a white tuxedo and she was in evening dress. When we reached the ground floor the doors opened automatically, and before our eyes there was a bearded soldier lying on the floor across the door with his rifle between his legs. The soldier was resting and, as it was probably the first time he had seen a lift and a hotel of this category, it may have seemed to him that it was more comfortable to wait for the lift in that position. The American man did not know what was going on and neither did his wife. They took a step back with a gesture of horror, and only when they saw the Cubans laughing at this spectacle did they leave the lift cautiously.

Outside the hotel, the streets were packed.

Havana was in a turbulent state. On the one hand, the revolutionary army was arriving from various parts of the island: they were ragged and dirty, poorly shod, wearing different types of clothes and behaving in an unruly manner. The majority had never seen a city like Havana, and many had not even seen a small city. Among them there were illiterate men whom one could barely understand, many of them *campesinos* who had risked their lives, day in and day out, and now walked among people who cheered them, applauded them and kissed them. And they looked in amazement at the buildings and at all the luxury they had never dreamed of seeing.

On the other hand, an invasion of Americans and Europeans filled the large hotels. They wanted to see this new social phenomenon, and that was how the encounter between 'refined' and stylish people and the plain and simple men who were Fidel Castro's soldiers took place. The soldiers walked the streets without paying attention to any conventional rules, like animals that had been let loose. In any case, the city was theirs because they had fought in the revolution. They felt safe, even if they looked with distrust at the well-dressed people who crossed their path.

A conversation with Ernesto

Those were unforgettable days for us. We saw Ernesto whenever we could, or rather, when his commitments allowed him the time to chat with us. But he always managed to find a moment for his family.

One afternoon Ernesto came to visit us at our hotel. I took the opportunity to ask him to see me in private. I wanted to talk to him alone and did not want any interruptions. I had tried to do so on previous occasions, but he was always too busy.

We went into the room and he sat quietly. He had changed a lot. When he left home he seemed not to have any facial hair and now he had grown a full beard. He was very thin and very suntanned. He spoke slowly, but the eyes were the same old eyes, both scrutinising and mocking. In the old days he used to speak fast, ideas piling up before he could express them, and he used to chat nervously, sometimes leaving out half his words. Now he was more poised, thinking quietly before replying, something he had never done before. I asked him what he was going to do with his medical degree.

He looked at me sideways, thought for a moment and then, with a smile, he replied: 'Medicine? Look, viejo, as you and I are both called Ernesto Guevara, you can place a plaque with your name in the premises of your construction company, with the word Doctor in front of the name, and you can start to kill people at your discretion.'

And he laughed at his joke.

I persisted with my question, so he turned serious and replied: 'I can tell you that I abandoned medicine a long time ago. Now I am a combatant who is working to support a revolutionary government. What will become of me? I myself do not know in which land I will leave my bones.'

I could not totally understand what Ernesto was saying. He had just entered Havana in triumph with the revolutionary army. I expected him to tell me that he would stay there for a while to do this or that, but Ernesto was telling me that he did not know what was to become of him.

I shall never forget his words because they contained the enigma that I have so often tried to decipher, in relation to his disappearance from Cuba and his resurfacing in far-away lands as a guerrilla leader.

We then spoke about family matters. I said: 'Che, my boy, you have had it your way. You left to go on the road and have been on the move for six years; now it is my turn. Why don't you go back to Argentina, take over from me looking after the family and give me an old rifle to go to the mountains?'

He laughed. In the hours we spent chatting together we went through many old family stories and caught up with the current news.

I was seeing a different man. It was difficult to see in him the Ernesto from home, the everyday Ernesto. A huge responsibility seemed to weigh him down. He wasn't having us on, he was never capable of that. It took me a long time to understand and come to grips with this transformation.

I think that, upon his arrival in Havana, Ernesto already knew his destiny. He was conscious of the power of his personality and was turning into a man whose faith in the triumph of his ideals was almost mystical.

But his attitude towards us had not changed. He was affectionate with his family at all times.

Havana as it was then

Havana at the time had approximately one million inhabitants. The Old City had been built on a bay, with typical colonial streets, narrow and winding. The buildings were just like they had been 300 years earlier. The people who lived in those houses lived without any comfort; their lodgings were like tenements. Many of these old houses were half in ruins, dirty and insalubrious.

On the other hand, modern architecture of American style, well built by good architects, could be seen in the neighbourhoods where the rich lived, such as Miramar, Marianao, El Vedado. There were well-designed buildings surrounded by wonderful tropical vegetation, in luxurious neighbourhoods where one could see that money had been lavished on the buildings. One must not forget that Havana had so far been the playground of American millionaires.

Other neighbourhoods, somewhat modified and with a particular style, still exhibited their typically Spanish influence from the colonial period. These were one- or two-storey houses with elegant columns supporting corridors along the façades, all of them painted in lively colours, separated from each other by gardens.

And lastly, very close to the centre of Havana, facing the sea, there was a group of huge buildings towering over the rest of the city.

Havana is separated from the sea by a wide avenue called

El Malecón, a waterfront area where the population goes for a walk on hot days.

A few kilometres from the capital there were resorts along the beaches. When we arrived it was the beginning of winter in Cuba and the beaches were empty, but we were able to see the beautiful villas that rose up along the coast, and which in summer would be filled with tourists from all over the world.

The richer clubs, which were famous in Cuba, rose up along the sea front facing the capital, and when we arrived we saw many yachts at anchor in the bay. We experienced some of Havana's high life, such as the extremely luxurious Tropicana, with its world-famous dancers and musical tableaux; and went to parties in nightclubs, where the privileged still squandered their money. I saw all this ten years later, totally changed, since the privileged classes who kept those clubs going had disappeared.

The revolution confiscated all the clubs, beach resorts, hotels, palaces and residences, which became assets of the State. The population, who were once forbidden to approach them, can now enjoy them. Those magnificent buildings, those stupendous resorts and those esplanades and yacht clubs are today for the use of the people.

One afternoon we visited a small and beautiful fishing village called Cojímar, situated a few kilometres from the capital city. This village, with its humble little wooden houses and rustic inhabitants, has a particular charm. The great American novelist Ernest Hemingway* was inspired by it when he wrote his superb work *The Old Man and the Sea*. It seemed as if all the peace and quiet that the rest of Cuba lacked had been concentrated in this little village.

Ernesto agrees to be interviewed

The newspapers, the majority of which had been in favour of

Batista, were crammed with news. Naturally they had now changed their political stance and were trying to fraternise with the revolutionaries.

The pages of these newspapers were filled with countless personalities of the revolution who were being interviewed. That is how I found out about many heroic exploits of the men whom I knew from the war reports that had arrived in Buenos Aires through the Committee of the 26 July Movement in New York.

A newspaper from Havana published an interview with the then Comandante Ernesto Che Guevara. The journalist asked him, among other things, the following: 'What was the most moving moment of your life as a guerrilla, Comandante?'

Ernesto replied without hesitation: 'When I heard the voice of my father over the phone, ringing from Buenos Aires. I had been away from my country for six years.'

I was deeply moved when I read that newspaper. I was able to understand Ernesto's decision to stay to the end, to fight in a struggle for the freedom of one of the most oppressed peoples of the Americas. These people were not his own, but they were comrades.

So although Ernesto had spent many years away from his family, and often we had had no word at all, his words now – precise and almost dry – conveyed the enormous affection he felt for all of us while he was away giving himself completely to the cause in which he believed.

Comandante Cienfuegos

One morning I received an invitation to lunch from Comandante Camilo Cienfuegos. We met at the bar of the Hilton Hotel.

He was an extremely charming, thin, short man, who moved nervously. He had a large beard that reached down to his chest, and his long black hair touched his shoulders. There was a strange vivacity in his expression and he seemed to be able to understand everything. Before a question was asked he had an answer for it, and he always included a funny phrase or a sharp adjective.

A photograph shows us sitting at a table accompanied by two Cubans, who I believe later died in combat. Also with us was Armando March, an Argentine trade unionist who had been a childhood friend of Ernesto, as well as Lieutenant San Martín, an Argentine who had joined the revolutionary army.

During lunch I was able to chat at length with Camilo. After lunch he came up to my rooms and we went on chatting. As usual, Camilo laughed and joked.

'Do you know,' he asked me, 'that I am the only man ever to take Che prisoner?'

And he looked round at all those present to see the surprised faces. So he told us the following:

'Che and I had gone to carry out an operation. He went in one direction and I in another. Suddenly, I reached an empty area and noticed that there were some armed men who were dropping to the ground and starting to shoot. We had exchanged a few shots when I saw a rifle being raised with a white handkerchief tied to it. I ran towards them and, to my extreme amazement, saw that the rifle was Che's. He had realised before I had that we were shooting at each other by mistake and had the idea of producing the white hand-kerchief in order to avoid casualties.'

And Camilo laughed and said that, whenever he wanted to tease Ernesto, he would remind him that he had once been his prisoner.

Changing the subject, he asked: 'Guevara, do you know who Mujal* was?'

As I replied that I barely knew of him, Camilo went on:

'He had sold himself to the Americans and to Batista's government when he was the top trade-union leader in Cuba. If you knew how I would have liked to get him! And guess what happened precisely to me, who could not even bear to hear his name: I had to protect him from a lynch mob.'

And Camilo told us how Mujal, after the fall of Batista, had asked for asylum in the Argentine Embassy. So when he had carried out all the negotiations to leave Cuba, it was Cienfuegos who was given the task of protecting him, and when Camilo was escorting Mujal to the airport at Rancho Boyeros so that he could leave for Buenos Aires, at that precise moment a group of men who wanted to kill Mujal appeared on the landing strip and attacked him.

'I had to defend that traitor using violence myself!' Camilo said.

Through another channel I learned at a later date that Mujal left on that flight. An hour later the plane was forced to return because of engine trouble. Mujal knew he was lost and collapsed into his seat, because he realised nobody was going to protect him this time round; but as the plane was registered in Chile, the Chilean Consul intervened at the airport by putting Mujal under the protection of his government, thus saving him from revolutionary justice.

I also learned that when Mujal arrived in Buenos Aires, people from the US Embassy were waiting for him and escorted him to the Continental Hotel, where he went in and out again after signing the register. A few hours later Mujal was installed in a New York hotel.

I asked Cienfuegos about his own life. I wanted to know how he had joined the guerrilla force.

'Very simple,' he replied, 'I worked underground. At a given moment I had to leave for the US and then went on to Mexico, where I got in touch with Fidel Castro's people.'

It was a pleasure to talk to him. I knew from the other guerrilla leaders that he was one of the most courageous and capable men in the revolutionary army.

A shooting competition

When Ernesto was a child he liked to watch me shoot with a revolver or a pistol. He was a few years old when I taught him to use firearms in Alta Gracia. When he was older we used to compete against each other.

When we were at El Pedrero, shortly before going up to visit the Sierra del Escambray, Ernesto asked me: 'How do you feel about a little shooting, viejo?'

I had been taunting him since my arrival about having a shoot-out competition. I replied that I would love to do it then. I had been a good shot in my day, but Ernesto had the reputation of being a crack shot.

We were on a slope on the edge of the village, and behind us there was a woodland and some slopes. We chose a tree for our target.

Ernesto drew his pistol and I drew mine. He took aim and fired, but before I could shoot at the target in turn, a huge noise was heard all over the area. Hundreds of shots were heard everywhere.

What had happened? The soldiers had realised that we were going to try our weapons and, as soon as their *comandante* fired, they fired too. It was their opportunity to infringe the established order: nobody must use his firearm unless under attack or in self-defence. They saw their *comandante* infringing the order and, as if they were all in agreement, started shooting. It was like being in combat. The tree we had chosen as a target was riddled with bullets. It was useless for me to shoot now. No comparison was possible.

These people were so used to daily warfare that they took

no precautions. They were all armed for war and, when they heard a shot, after two weeks of peace, they were unable to contain themselves and all of them fired.

Learning to fly

Ernesto had gone on a course to learn how to fly. He was training to take off and land in a small area inside the grounds of the barracks at La Cabaña. The barracks had been built next to the sea; the great walls that surrounded it fell steeply into the water. Had the take-off or landing failed for one fraction of a second, an accident was unavoidable. I saw Ernesto carry out this operation several times next to his instructor and, had this happened long before, when we all lived in Buenos Aires, I would have been horrified. By now I was so used to his behaviour that my original anxiety had turned to indifference. Ernesto had escaped so very many dangers that the situation I was witnessing was just one more danger and nothing else.

Ernesto tells us how he was injured at the battle of Alegría del Pío

One afternoon I was chatting with Captain Alberto Castellanos* at La Cabaña barracks. He was one of the men who had gone with Ernesto from El Jíbaro (a small village of the Sierra Maestra) up to El Escambray.

While Alberto Castellanos tried to explain to me some of the details of the battle for Alegría del Pío, at which he had not fought, Ernesto overheard our conversation and approached our table, and told us with precise details what Captain Castellanos had attempted to describe.

On a piece of paper he drew a sketch explaining how the attack at Alegría del Pío, where he had been wounded, had taken place. On this little piece of paper, which I still have, he drew the cane fields, the lines between the rows of sugar cane and the woodland. He gave us some details, which he later included in his book *Reminiscences of the Cuban Revolutionary War*.[10]

They had arrived there after disembarking from the *Granma* on a beach called Las Coloradas, and crossed mangrove swamps and open woodland. A local man had guided them and, after he left Fidel and his small group of men, had retraced his steps and informed Batista's army.

The men, still novices in this type of operation, were exhausted and almost without weapons, because they had lost most of them in the swamps they had crossed after disembarking. At that moment many of them were lying on the ground and were not wearing their boots, as they were tending to the wounds on their feet that had been opened up by the sea water.

Although some of Fidel's men stood guard around the camp, both the rural guards and Batista's army managed to approach unnoticed within a few metres of the unwitting revolutionary troops.

Next to the woodland there was a cane field with open spaces between the rows of cane. In this field Ernesto hid with some comrades. He had a backpack with medicines and a heavy ammunition box. When Batista's men fired the first shot, a sentry who was standing on a tree trunk fell off and was killed. Immediately afterwards heavy rifle and artillery fire rained down on Fidel's men.

Ernesto was carrying the ammunition box hanging around his neck, and when he heard the shots he tried to cross the lines that divided the rows of sugar cane. When he jumped into the air, a machine-gun round hit the box, destroying it and ricocheting onto his neck. He fell flat on

[10] *Reminiscences of the Cuban Revolutionary War*: by Ernesto Guevara de la Serna, published in Cuba in 1963 in Spanish, and later on in various other languages.

the ground and the bullets continued to pass over his head.

Ernesto told me that Juan Almeida reached him and tried to pick him up, grabbing him by his armpits. He shouted at him: 'Leave me, I have been killed.' But Almeida dragged him and, assisted by Ramiro Valdés, took him to the other end of the sugar-cane field. The place was an inferno at the time – they were being shot at from the air and from the ground, and napalm bombs had started to burn the sugar cane. Ernesto was being carried aloft by Almeida and Valdés. I remember exactly what he said:

'I kept asking them to look at my wound, but they kept running, dragging me with them. As they did not do as I asked them, I opened my shirt and looked for the bullet hole and – you know, my old man, when I realised that I did not have any hole in the chest and only a superficial wound on the neck that oozed blood – I grew wings on my feet and began to run alongside them. The impact of the bullet on the box had been so strong that I could not breathe, but with the help of my friends I managed to escape the fire and take to the woodland with them.'

When chatting with us, Ernesto told us the details of the odyssey of the small contingent, which managed to regroup from the original force of eighty-two men who had invaded the island.

I will tell you some of those details, because Ernesto left them out of his book.

His group was hiding along the coast and there was no drinking water there. In the hollow of some stones a minimal amount of dew water had collected. He used the inhaling device he always carried with him, because of his asthma, to suck up these drops of water and then pour them into a small broken half-cup that they had with them. They rationed this minimal amount of water, and that enabled them to march on to where they hoped to meet up with some comrades.

For several days they walked along the coast, hiding under the rocks during the day and walking at night. The small troop marched desperately hungry and thirsty. They ate raw crabs, which mitigated their hunger somewhat, but gave them a greater need for drinking water. Ernesto saw a hut near the beach and decided to run the risk of approaching it. A man was standing in front of his home and turned out to be an Adventist, who greeted them kindly and gave the group his protection. According to Ernesto, their benefactor later told him that he had seen them before they saw him and had said to his wife, 'There are some brethren out there who need me.'

It was through the Adventist that the group headed by Almeida, which included Valdés, Chao, Benítez and Ernesto, was able to rejoin Fidel Castro.

When I arrived in Cuba in 1959 I tried to visit all those places, but it was impossible. In 1969 I went back and then I was able to visit them. I saw Alegría del Pío. Everything was different there – even the cane fields no longer existed, and in their place there was arable land and some brushwood. It took a lot of effort to recognise the places. None of the people who had witnessed the events were with me, and the then-inhabitants had moved on and the one or two I did meet did not talk much. Many crosses marked the disaster. At the foot of them there were inscriptions commemorating the defeat at Alegría del Pío.

I brought back the casing of an exploded bullet, thinking that it might be one from the steel box Ernesto had been carrying all those years ago.

At La Cabaña fortress – Che's headquarters

Once when we were at La Cabaña barracks, where Ernesto was the officer in command in 1959, he told me many stories about the war. So I asked him: 'Tell me, Ernesto, which was the most dangerous moment you found yourself in during the invasion?'

He looked at me smiling and said: 'I saw death very near me in Oriente, on a slope of the Sierra Maestra. I was leading a guerrilla force that was harassing Sánchez Mosquera. You know that he was one of the most ferocious men at the service of Batista. I was complying with the orders to attack and withdraw, but when I tried to do this, I suffered a huge asthma attack that knocked me down. Seeing that I was unable to run, I ordered my men to disperse and leave me. I had to repeat the order because nobody wanted to obey it, but in the end they did. One of them, a young man, hid near where I was and, without my knowing, waited in order to help me. The hours went by and the boy appeared. I told him off, but I could no longer send him back to the camp because I knew that Sánchez Mosquera's troops were combing the area from all sides in the hope of finding me. I never knew how they found out, but in the enemy ranks it was known that I had not returned to the camp.

'Without making the slightest noise, my comrade and I listened to how Batista's soldiers went through the woodland inch by inch, and the hours went by in this way and then a couple of days, too. I had such a violent asthma attack that I thought it would kill me. I had run out of the medicine I used to put into my inhaler and was practically at the mercy of my asthma attacks.

'Well,' Ernesto said to me then, 'at that moment I thought I would never return to camp – not because of enemy bullets, but because the asthma would finish me off. Fortunately, some hours later it gave way and, helped by my comrade, with great caution, we were able to withdraw and break away from the encirclement and reach the camp where I was expected.'

Departure

When I arrived in Havana I showed Ernesto the wristwatch I was wearing.

'Do you remember it?' I asked.

'Yes,' he replied, 'it is Granny's watch, and you are going to give it to me.'

He had adored his grandmother. She used to wear an old gold watch, which had one of those covers that you opened to see the time, although hers had a little glass window that enabled you to see the time without opening the cover. It was the sort of watch ladies wore some seventy years ago. It had her initials inside the cover. She always wore it hanging from a little chain. The watch was really beautiful. When my mother died, my family decided that I should have it and I converted it into a wristwatch.

'When I leave,' I said, 'I will give it to you.'

The time to leave had come. My commitments in Buenos Aires required my presence. I decided to return home on the spur of the moment. I telephoned Ernesto and told him that I was leaving that evening. He came to the airport to see me off with Raúl Castro. We spent our time there discussing trivial matters, as you do when you have to bid farewell to a person you love and do not know whether you will see them again.

The revolution had triumphed, but the struggle was certainly not over. Although the regular army was no longer fighting, I knew that the island had not been entirely pacified. I also thought these Cuban leaders were very careless. They mingled with the people and took few or no precautions.

Ernesto detested having bodyguards and, whenever he could, gave them the slip. The escorts themselves told me so. But it was very difficult to convince him. When he wanted to be on his own, he managed to leave them behind. But if one took into account that the revolution was going to affect both Cuban and foreign interests, one had to realise that those interests would find a way to perpetuate themselves, and the easiest way of doing so was by eliminating the leaders of the revolution.

We had spent a month in Cuba. We had seen so many different things! We had visited the most beautiful places and seen the happy outbursts of a people who felt free. During those few days amongst them we had also become infected with the euphoria of the Cuban people. We too, in the beginning, had thought the road that lay ahead for the revolutionaries was an easy one. But if you really thought about it, you reached the conclusion that the armed struggle would now turn into a struggle against all odds for that small republic, which, until the day before, had been dominated politically and financially by the nearby North American colossus.

At the airport of Rancho Boyeros large numbers of people were seeing other people off. It was an international crowd. Someone among them saw Ernesto and, realising who he was, approached him quickly and asked: 'Comandante Guevara?'

Ernesto nodded with his head and the man said in a perfect Buenos Aires accent: 'Comandante, will you allow a fellow Argentine to shake your hand?'

Ernesto smiled and, without uttering a word, held out his hand.

Our fellow national found a notebook in one of his pockets and proffered it to Ernesto, saying: 'Please, will you give me an autograph?'

Ernesto, while turning his back to the man, replied: 'I am not a film actor.'

I was now in front of Ernesto and I had to say goodbye.

'Here is your grandmother's watch,' I said, handing it over.

He took the watch from me and then took his off his wrist and handed it to me, saying: 'Keep this as a memento, this watch was given to me by Fidel when he made me Comandante, after a battle.'

I put it on my wrist. It has never left me.

A few minutes later the plane was taxiing down the runway of Ranchos Boyeros and, after a few seconds, all that was left of Havana were a few little lights twinkling below.

I was sad when I left. I had arrived happy and joyful, but now I understood that the separation from Ernesto would be long. I had my business in Buenos Aires and he had his commitments in Cuba.

A few seconds later we had left the island behind, enveloped in total darkness.

In Buenos Aires

Once back in our own country – the impressions that had shaken me so much were beginning to blur – I tried to put my thoughts in order. I had witnessed such incredible things that I thought I had dreamed them.

All that we had lived through in Cuba now came rushing back to my mind. In a disorderly manner and in slow motion, I could see blinding lights, mouths laughing and kissing, eyes that cried, shouts of joy, bodies shaking to the sound of an African beat, marching out of step, worn and dirty uniforms, clothes of every possible colour, faces tanned by the tropical sun, black faces, pale faces, sallow faces that still showed hatred, breasts beating with courage, clenched teeth, fingers still ready to press the trigger, hordes frantically embracing, looks of fear, beards and more beards, rifles and more rifles, boards and flags carried aloft, *mochas*[11] thrown into the air by sinewy arms amid the tobacco smoke and the smell of rum, and crowds drunk with enthusiasm, revelling in their incredible victory.

I sail on in my imagination and I see the public trials of the dictatorship's criminals, among the deafening screams of thousands of spectators; and I see multitudes with torches lit to pay homage to José Martí, their apostle; and I see President Urrutia* in his palace and the solemn, self-important magistrates next to the rustic militias who clutch with their rough hands the weapons that have given them their victory; and I see Fidel and Raúl, and Camilo and so many other *comandantes*, each a hero in his own right, at the head of a ragged army while, behind the walls, death lies in wait and a whole generation crushed by a dictatorship puts its best hopes in this revolution, which is sweeping away the old and all its misery.

And all of this went by so fast, and reached so deep inside me, that I was unable to step any distance from that jumble in order to analyse what I saw and felt.

Cuba had been left behind, far away, in a whirlwind, and in the vortex of this whirlwind was my son Ernesto with his comrades in-arms.

I could understand that the danger of the revolutionary war was over, but a different kind of danger was hanging over Cuba and its inhabitants: the reaction of the United States of America, owner of many interests on the island.

---

[11] *Mochas*: large, flat knives with a straight blade sharpened only on one side, used for cutting sugar cane.

Part Two: Ernesto's ancestry and early years, 1850s–1933

It seemed impossible to me that the asthmatic and underdeveloped child in far-away Alta Gracia, who tried by sheer will power to comply with his daily school tasks, was the same man who now defied the obstacles before him with unique strength and who was in the headlines of all the main newspapers in the world.

I decided to analyse his life. I recalled Ernesto's infancy, his childhood, his adolescence, his primary and secondary schooling, his adventures in the hills of Alta Gracia, his favourite sports, his bicycle and motorcycle trips all over Argentina and Latin America. I went through his work and his friendships, and I studied all the letters he sent to the family in which his socio-economic-political development is reflected.

The following pages are the result of this painstaking work.

My ancestors

During the dictatorship of General Juan Manuel de Rosas* (1829–52) many Argentines went into exile in order to escape the political climate of the times.

My grandparents were political exiles. My mother, who adored my son Ernesto and delighted in his conversations with her, used to tell him about her life in California, where she was born and lived until the age of twelve. She would tell him about her father Francisco Lynch, who had to leave his country estate in Baradero in the province of Buenos Aires for Uruguay, with several of his relatives. He had refused to join Rosas' army and that was tantamount to a self-imposed death sentence. He left from Montevideo in Uruguay, sailing through the Straits of Magellan and reaching Chile, and from there he went on to Peru, where he became ill with cholera.

From Peru he went on to Ecuador, where he caught smallpox. From there he went on experiencing a thousand ups and downs until he reached California, where he settled in the then-new city of San Francisco. He married a nineteen-year-old girl, Eloisa Ortiz, who was a widow with a child, and from this marriage my mother and her brothers were born.

My paternal grandfather, Juan Antonio Guevara, who was born in the city of Mendoza, Argentina, had to leave the country because of his political ideas. He crossed the Andes and established himself in Chile for some time, and then joined some of his brothers and fellow Argentines on an expedition to the 'Pleasures of California',[1] a place to which many people from the Argentine provinces of Mendoza and San Juan went. They were all political exiles. This must have had an influence on Ernesto as a child, as he heard talk of my grandparents, who in their youth had had to leave their homes and earn their living in a foreign country.

[1] Pleasures of California: the discovery of large gold fields in California, a region that had been Mexican before its annexation by the USA, after a cruel and unjust war, attracted thousands of men who arrived from all over the world in search of a fortune, which they imagined could be amassed from one day to the next. History coined the phrase the Gold Rush to describe the human invasion to the 'Pleasures of California', where few actually managed to make money.

Francisco Lynch, my maternal grandfather, was exiled for more than thirty years and amassed a fortune working in San Francisco. He returned to Argentina once the government of General Rosas had fallen.

Juan Antonio Guevara, my other grandfather, was a direct descendant of the founders of the city of Mendoza; his was the ninth generation of Guevaras born in Argentina. His prior ancestors were Chilean.

He was twenty-five years old when the obsession with Californian gold reached Chile. He left with some of his brothers and several fellow nationals for the north and, after much deprivation, they reached southern Mexico; as they had very little money, they bought some wild horses to travel on to California on horseback. They displayed magnificent horsemanship and tamed the horses.

The 'Pleasures of California' turned into a total failure. After the disillusionment with gold, my grandfather established himself in the region and married Concepción Castro Peralta, a descendant of illustrious Spanish-Mexican ancestors. Once the political climate in Argentina had changed, he returned to his homeland with his wife and his children born in California – among them my father Roberto Guevara.

My father did his secondary studies in the province of San Juan, which is near Mendoza. He studied civil engineering in Buenos Aires and graduated as a geographical engineer in Córdoba. He carried out many surveys throughout the country and set the boundaries between the province of Santiago del Estero and the region of Chaco in 1898, an assignment that took two years to complete. A military party from the Sixth Cavalry Regiment escorted him, in order to protect him from attacks by the local Indians. The survey was a difficult one to carry out because they started from the meteorite at

Campo del Cielo[2] in the region of Chaco and had to reach the Orán hill in the province of Salta by means of a line set astronomically. During that time, working and living in the jungle entailed great hardship. The Indians, who were savage and indomitable, attacked them continually. There were no rivers or streams in the area, so water had to be taken from excavated wells more than eighty metres deep. I still have my father's survey papers. In one of his notebooks, it says:

Forty-eight degrees in the shade. We have totally run out of water. The water convoy should have arrived two days ago. The animals are beginning to go mad. The hired hands make no effort and just lie under the trees. The troops are showing signs of rebelling. If the Indians have attacked the water convoy, we've had it.

And the following line reads: 'I hear shots, either it is the Indians or a salute to the arrival of the water convoy.'

And the water convoy arrived, having brought the water over a distance of twenty leagues. My father's notebook says: 'Not everything is thorns in life, there must be roses as well sometimes.'

All this that I am writing now is part of the story I told many times at home during meals in front of all my children, and I remember that Ernesto did not miss a single detail of my tale. I had great admiration for my father and I

---

[2] Campo del Cielo: in the eighteenth century a meteorite fell in the area of Chaco in Argentina called Campo del Cielo. According to a legend of the aboriginal population, it lit up the sky during the night and for several days afterwards. Its location is known thanks to the Spanish sailor Rubín de Zelis, who marked astronomically the site of its fall. The data appeared in the *Archivo de Indias*. General Juan Manuel de Rosas attempted to have the meteorite excavated, but it was impossible to do so because it weighed several tonnes. It comprised magnetic iron, and General Rosas had a fragment cut off and two pistols were made from it.

knew his whole life story well, and consequently so did Ernesto. He had immersed himself in the many hardships endured by my father and would later use the knowledge to good advantage.

In 1900 my father was head of the Fifth Borders Commission, which worked in the region of the Andean range to resolve an old frontier quarrel with Chile. The task was extremely tough and risky, as it was carried out high in the mountains.

In 1902 the survey of the province of Mendoza began and it took them fifteen years to complete the detailed census and register of property – years of penury, seeing their families only occasionally, enduring droughts, extreme heat, torrential rains, cyclones, altitude sickness, snow and snow-bearing winds. It was then that my father lost the young Swedish engineer Ebensen who, ignoring the advice of the experts, climbed Mount Los Tombillos, 6,900 metres high, to place a geodesic signal and was caught in a snowstorm. In spite of the intense search that was undertaken, using every resource available, Ebensen was never seen again.

We – my mother and my brothers – were always on edge because of the life my father led. The background I have outlined gave rise to a peculiar atmosphere at home, which nobody could ignore because somehow the life and exploits of our ancestors, for one reason or another, were always brought up in conversation.

I too learned how to escape the easy life of the big city. When I got married, our honeymoon trip was to the far-away jungle territory of Misiones[3] in north-east Argentina, where

---

[3] Misiones: this territory takes its name from the old Indian reservations founded by the Jesuits in the eighteenth century to convert them to Christianity. In fact the Jesuits were real colonisers who sought profit for themselves, but it is true that they left excellent sculptures, paintings and architecture, as well as teaching the Indians how to till the land.

we set up home and where I worked for several years. All these stories that my children were later to hear encouraged them, in my view, to seek a life on the edges of civilisation, surrounded by nature, with all the insecurities and dangers this brings with it.

At home, when we were together during mealtimes, we discussed life in Misiones over the years, as well as the events we witnessed or lived through ourselves.

The children could not fail to be emotionally involved and affected by the stories of those who attempted to escape the maté[4] plantations and building sites, with the police force always at the service of the landowners, the murderous bodyguards of the foremen known as *capangas* whose job it was to prevent the workers from escaping, the wild animals, the dangerous work, the jungle cyclones, the interminable rains and the tropical diseases.

This is a short summary of all that I believe may have had an influence on the make-up of Ernesto Guevara de la Serna. He grew up hearing these stories, which must have lodged in his subconscious mind, to come to the fore later on.

Both the region of Chaco, where my father had to work for a substantial part of his life, and the territory of Misiones, where I spent a couple of years with my wife, have a similar climate and vegetation to the Bolivian jungle, which is where my son Ernesto – by then known as Che Guevara – waged his struggle against enormous odds and eventually laid down his life.

Celia de la Serna – our marriage

My wife, Celia de la Serna (1907–64), lived with her family

---

[4] Maté: the evergreen tree *Ilex paraguariensis* is cultivated in South America for its leaves, which contain caffeine and are used to make tea. The word derives from the Quechúa *máti*, meaning gourd, the vessel in which the drink is brewed and served.

in the city of Buenos Aires. They were all good friends of the Echagüe family. The Echagües were like my brothers; however, I only met the de la Serna family several years after I had met the Echagües.

Celia's parents had died and she lived with all her siblings in a large house in Junín Street. They were four boys and three girls. Carmen, being the eldest, was in charge of the household. Later she was to marry the poet Cayetano Córdova Iturburu*.

I met Celia at their home and soon became good friends with her and her family. We used to meet regularly with the de la Sernas and the Echagües at either family home.

While Celia and I were only friends, all was fine, but when her family realised that there was something more than friendship between us, some of her brothers objected to our relationship.

Celia was underage, but she did not accept her family's impositions and said so outright. She went to live with an aunt of hers and not long after, in 1927, we got married. It was said at the time that I had been the cause of the family rift.

I had inherited some money from my father, and with it I bought 200 hectares of land in Puerto Caraguatay, in the territory of Misiones. Celia and I left for our estate.

She was the youngest of her family and never knew her father, who had died when she was only a few months old. Her mother, who had been brought up in a conservative home, sent her daughters to Roman Catholic schools and that is why Celia had attended the Sacred Heart School for her primary and part of her secondary education. When I met her she was contemplating becoming a nun. She was a true believer; so much so that she used to put pieces of glass inside her shoes to torture her flesh, as if it were a cilice. She never missed mass and, as she was very well-off, the nuns worked on her so that she would take orders and stay with them for good. But Celia was able to escape that trap by herself, and not much later we met and decided to spend our lives together. The flagellation, the sanctimonious prudery and the relatives and friends who tried to prevent us from marrying were left behind.

We were both young. She was twenty and I was twenty-seven. We decided that we would live our lives without taking any notice whatsoever of the idle gossip of bigots.

Celia, who was very intelligent, always tried to improve herself. She spoke French as fluently as Spanish, and she managed in English, too. We got on perfectly well and were, apart from husband and wife, true comrades, although sometimes we used to quarrel over unimportant matters, perhaps because our personalities were very similar. Discomfort did not exist for us. We sailed through every setback when we were striving for something we really wanted.

Social convention was the norm in Celia's family, but they had not managed to curb her spirit, and very soon she had dispensed with every convention. I – in spite of the fact that my family also accepted social conventions – had never bowed to them.

My background, from childhood, was Socialist, but I did not put any pressure on my wife. Little by little she came over to this new way of seeing the world, and after a short time she overtook me. She was impetuous and over-whelming and never did anything by halves – when she took up a cause there was no stopping her. We understood each other and together we defended ourselves from the attacks of our social equals, for whom we had now become 'the Communist Red Devils'. I was blamed for having taken Celia from the bosom of the Catholic Church to turn her into a Socialist miscreant.

At the time, in our country as well as in the greater part

of Latin America, the Catholic Church went hand-in-hand
with capitalists, who in turn were supported by the military,
who in time became the policemen of international capital.

The colonialist capitalists of the Argentine Republic
disapproved of those who departed from the orthodoxy
imposed by British and American imperialism. I had been
marked beforehand, and Celia was marked later. In the
meantime, her relatives did all they could to try to win back
the 'little black sheep', but the little sheep jumped the fence
and with time became a knowledgeable social leader, who –
next to me – had a decisive influence on the boy who was to
become Che Guevara.

Celia was very quick mentally and exhibited great
courage throughout her life, but never lost her femininity.
We shared happiness and wealth. We also went through
periods of great deprivation together. The ups and downs of
life did not affect her personality; on the contrary, they
accentuated her strength of character.

This was our early married life together, but the
international press, after the events that put Ernesto in the
headlines all over the world, used all means of communication at their disposal – newspapers, magazines, radio
and television – to concoct their stories and weave their lies.
Some commentators went as far as saying that my wife and
I sat down to dinner with the family and each one of us
carried a gun, so that any discussion could be resolved by a
shoot-out.

But those same commentators never mentioned the
support we were to each other in all matters to do with
social and political issues.

Celia's personality
Celia had become a great swimmer at a time when it was
rare in our country for women to swim. She had been taught

by her brothers, who were all expert swimmers. She used to train by doing 1,000 metres with no difficulty. She swam overarm style, which was not fast but was not exhausting either.

Not long after we were married I joined forces with my friend Germán Frers* at the Astillero Río de la Plata, a shipyard. The yard had built me a boat, a sort of sea glider, in which we used to sail the River Plate or the delta of the Paraná.

I recall that one day when we were at anchor in the middle of the Paraná de las Palmas, Celia appeared on deck in her swimming costume, determined to jump into the water. There were lots of guests on board, including my brother-in-law Martínez Castro, who was considered a great swimmer, and who tried to dissuade her by pointing out that there was a very strong current. I also tried to dissuade Celia, but it was useless and she jumped in.

As soon as she started to swim we realised that her speed was less than that of the current and that she was being dragged away by it. We set out to rescue her, but to do that we had first to raise the anchor, start the engine and only then go after Celia. It was going to take us too long. Without hesitation, my sister María Luisa threw a rope to Celia, which she just managed to grab hold of. We began to drag her; she was totally exhausted by the effort, and when she reached the boat several of us had to lift her because she could not climb aboard on her own.

We were surprised that Celia had grown tired so quickly. What had happened? At the time women used to wear rubber girdles, and she had jumped into the water without taking hers off. The rubber, in contact with the liquid, cut her circulation. Had we not acted so quickly, she would have been in danger of drowning.

This whole episode took place in front of our son Ernesto,

who at the time was five years old. He followed events from the deck, terrified. It was an experience for Celia, but she was impetuous from birth and paid no attention to past experience. For Ernesto it was also an experience and later on, like the rest of the family, he had to get used to this recklessness of his mother, who did not know what fear was.

Celia had a peculiar personality. She was not really irresponsible, but she was attracted to danger. When I was around she did not do dangerous things, but in my absence she amused herself by overcoming any difficulty that required daring and effort.

I could fill many pages with my wife's exploits, but I will only mention something that took place in Mar del Plata in 1935.

Celia was swimming with her brother Jorge, who was a swimming champion. The red flag indicating that the sea was dangerous had been hoisted, and this meant that nobody should go into the water. But Jorge de la Serna was in the habit of swimming when the sea was rough, so he dived under a large wave. Celia followed him.

Thousands of people, including the lifeguards, stood up to watch the two swimmers. Within a few seconds they were well into the sea. The difficulty was how to get back, since their attempts to return to shore were thwarted by the giant waves that kept dragging them back out to sea.

The lifeguards of several establishments along the beach had gathered, as they envisaged a difficult rescue. Celia and Jorge struggled against the waves for about twenty minutes. He would have been able to reach the shore on his own because he was an extraordinary swimmer, but Celia could not make any headway against the waves. Everyone was tense, and the lifeguards awaited the distress signal that those who are in danger use to ask for help: they raise an arm out of the water. Then the men would go to rescue them.

Finally both Jorge and Celia managed to reach the shore. They had given the holidaymakers a bad time and had incurred the wrath of the lifeguards, who grumbled about such recklessness.

Ernesto was present that day, as were our other children. Of course they were in anguish to see their mother fighting against the waves. But with the passage of time they would get used to their mother's recklessness. Fortunately I was not present during that incident. I had left the beach a little earlier, asking Celia very particularly not to go into the water in view of the circumstances. But the temptation to face the danger was greater than her prudence and she did exactly the opposite of what she should have done.

Celia as a mother and political activist

Celia truly loved all her children, but for Ernesto she had a special affection. She had suffered with him through all the different stages of his asthma. His asthma attacks were exceptionally violent and frequent. Celia never hesitated when it came to moving to a location where it was thought the climate would be beneficial to Ernesto's health.

When Ernesto was between four and six years old he endured the worst attacks. These were continual and prevented him from attending school regularly. He had to miss school frequently and over lengthy periods. Celia, with the patience of a saint, would teach him the lesson he would have been taught at school, and that was another way in which the companionship between mother and son developed.

Celia was also very affectionate with the other children, but she was more demanding and severe with them when they were naughty, and steered them towards their lessons.

When Ernesto was a grown man and began to travel, he used to write to his mother frequently. Ernesto's letters to

Celia, apart from being very funny, would narrate all the ups and downs of his eventful life, as well as showing clearly how he was developing as a political and social thinker.

Ernesto and Celia treated each other as equals. They teased each other, but their mutual affection was always present. Ernesto had no secrets from his mother and always confided in her, while Celia would ask his advice every time she had to face an important decision in her life.

Celia learned about her son's revolutionary politics as he developed his ideas and, as a result, knew his thinking in depth.

She would express her own ideas wherever she went, without stopping to think whether this would have unpleasant consequences or cause offence.

She travelled to Brazil and met several left-wing groups. She also lectured there, informing many people of the logic and justice of the Cuban Revolution. She also went to Chile and Uruguay and attended conferences of Socialist women, and took advantage of the opportunity to inform students about the political aspects of the Cuban Revolution.

At home in Argentina she spoke in public and lectured about Cuba and its government. At a lecture at the Faculty of Law of the University of Buenos Aires, some Fascists who opposed Celia's views began to taunt the students who were listening to her, and soon there were scuffles and shots were fired. Celia serenely continued speaking as if nothing had happened, but the police arrived and dispersed the crowd.

In 1961, when she returned from a trip to Cuba, she wrote a series of articles about Cuba for the Socialist newspaper *La Vanguardia*, in which she analysed the economic, social and political impact of the revolution. Celia launched herself passionately into a pro-Cuban campaign even after diplomatic relations between the two countries had been severed. She travelled to the northern provinces of Argentina, where she had to endure serious incidents and provocations from right-wing elements.

She worked very hard and was sometimes surrounded by opportunistic politicians who saw in her the means of promoting their careers. Celia always trusted people. She thought that all those who approached her were decent people, and would continue to think so until the person in question betrayed her, either materially or morally. There was more than one shameless 'friend' who was actually a member of the intelligence services of either Argentina or some other country.

On 23 April 1963, as she returned to Argentina from Uruguay, Celia was taken into custody in the city of Concordia with the excuse that she was carrying Communist or pro-Castro propaganda.

Her team of lawyers sprung into action immediately. They proved that she was only carrying personal papers and photographs of her son and grandchildren. The photographs were confiscated by the police and we were never able to retrieve them. She had been carrying two books, which were used as an excuse to detain her: one was *Agrarian Reform in Uruguay* and the other was a book sold in all bookshops in Buenos Aires.

In view of the lack of evidence, the presiding judge in the province of Entre Ríos ordered that she be set free, but the government put her 'at its disposal', a trick that supposedly-democratic governments avail themselves of to deprive citizens of their freedom.

Celia spent two long months at the Buenos Aires Women's Correctional Centre located at Independencia and Defensa Streets, for the sole crime of being the mother of Che Guevara. It was never proved that she had done anything forbidden under Argentine law.

She sued the government and a judge called Dr Kenny,

who was a rare exception among Argentine judges – he was honourable and courageous and was capable of ingenuity and initiative – one day set up a surprise tribunal inside the jail itself, and at two in the morning ordered that she be set free immediately. Only in this manner, and by surprising the security forces, did Celia manage to leave prison. Minutes later police cars were looking for her all over Buenos Aires. The case was much discussed, and I suppose it was one of the few in which a judge was able to successfully challenge the government's anti-constitutional behaviour, headed at the time by President José María Guido*. He held the highest office in the land, as if he were a worthy successor to Rivadavia*, but in fact he had been placed in that position by the military junta as their stooge.

Celia had suffered a lot during those two months in prison; her health had deteriorated. After she left prison she was forced to go underground in Buenos Aires and eventually crossed the border into Uruguay, having to avoid the police and military authorities as if she were a common criminal.

Once she was in Uruguay, Ernesto sent her a ticket so that she could travel to Havana, but she turned him down. She wrote to him saying that she would remain in exile in Uruguay and would continue to work for the freedom of the peoples of America. Prison had convinced her that only total revolution could bring about the freedom of the oppressed. Otherwise, by peaceful means, all those who opposed dictatorial rule would end up becoming pensioners while remaining in detention in all the jails that the dictators had at their disposal for precisely that purpose.

Many years have gone by, and those held in custody without trial and at the disposal of the authorities fill Argentine jails. Meanwhile the President of the day emphatically claims that he presides over a democratic government, at the same time launching wordy diatribes against those who are the enemies of public order – while the country is enduring a level of despotism never seen before.

When Celia returned from Uruguay to Argentina she had to remain in hiding for some time and avoid appearing in public, for fear of having to spend more time in custody. Her life was really full of incident. I remember she used to say that she would not reach old age and would die, like her mother, while still relatively young. And that is how it was; she died of the same illness as her mother at the age of fifty-eight.

Celia had been born into wealth and had received a conservative education, had attended a convent school and had even contemplated becoming a nun. She nevertheless managed to make a home and bring up her children in a totally different way. She struggled with the lack of financial security, and turned against her family circle and their friends, who saw her as a 'Red Beast'. She found in her son Ernesto the incentive that she needed to develop herself fully and to steer her life towards what she considered to be the truth.

She was intelligent, well informed and courageous, and she turned herself into what she wanted to be. And although she suffered while her son was involved in the violent conflict that was the Cuban Revolution, she had the good fortune of seeing him triumph not only as a soldier, but politically as well.

A few days before her death she learned of Ernesto's departure from Cuba, and this filled her with sadness and bewilderment because she was not aware of his reasons. Only months later did the family learn that Ernesto had decided to return to armed struggle in order to continue the fight against those who usurp power and oppress the so-called underdeveloped peoples.

Celia's family

My wife's family were extremely rich. Her father had inherited a vast fortune and had become a lawyer at a very young age. He owned several *estancias* or ranches, which he administered using modern methods, but he devoted most of his time to his professorship at the Faculty of Law of the University of Buenos Aires. He was a cultured man as well as an extremely intelligent one, and he widened his knowledge well beyond the confines of the legal profession. He joined the Radical Party, which at the time was a centre-left movement under the leadership of Leandro N. Alem*. In 1889 the conservative oligarchy felt the severe blow of a revolution by the youth of the Radical Party led by Alem. Among them was Juan Martín de la Serna, Che's grandfather. That revolution, labelled the 1890 Revolution, did not succeed at the time in toppling the President of the republic. Many of the leaders of the revolution were killed, wounded or incarcerated, but the government was forced to change direction and called an election.

Celia did not know her father, because he died when she was only a few months old. Her mother died when Celia was still very small and the household was then taken over by Carmen, the eldest sister, who in 1928 married the famous poet Cayetano Córdova Iturburu, who at the time was a member of the Communist Party. During the courtship, writers, artists, politicians and scientists met at the de la Sernas' home, and some of these guests were militants of left-wing parties. The de la Serna brothers were of a liberal tendency, but were totally apolitical.

Celia began to attend these gatherings at a very early age, gradually shaking off the influence of the Sacred Heart School where she had studied.

When we married she turned to Socialism and never changed her position throughout her life. I remember how we suffered at social events at the Hotel Sierras in Alta Gracia. For years we had to endure the aggression, whether direct or indirect, of many right-wing people who were annoyed by our way of thinking and behaving. Neither my wife nor I was ever affiliated to any political party, but we never abandoned our Socialist views.

The influence of the territory of Misiones on our lives

In 1926 I was studying architecture, but still had a long way to go. I wanted to marry the woman who then became my wife: Celia de la Serna. I did not get on well with her family, and neither did she. That is why we decided to cut loose and leave for wherever I could use my skills.

Quite by accident I got a contract to develop some 70,000 hectares in Alto Paraná, in the territory of Misiones. A close friend of mine and his brother were transferring this contract to me. Pedro León Echagüe became enthusiastic about the work to be carried out, and we agreed that we would go and colonise that area. I had some experience because I had been to the Argentine Chaco region and had the advantage of knowing how to carry out surveys, measurements and partitions, since I had worked as a surveyor.

I had received a little money as an inheritance from my father and thought that I would use it for this project. Echagüe asked me to wait for him for a week because he wanted to go to Alta Gracia in Córdoba to say goodbye to his girlfriend who lived there. The week turned into a month and then two. Between letters, telegrams and phone calls the time went by, and one day, realising that Echagüe was not coming, I decided to turn down the contract and look for another job.

It was then that Pedro León Echagüe was appointed deputy manager of a large establishment, owned by one of his uncles, which was also in Alto Paraná. It was called Caraguatay.

Echagüe and I had been friends since before we learned to walk. Once he settled in Misiones he wrote frequently asking us to visit him. It was following a trip he made to Buenos Aires that I accompanied him on his return there and went to see the place where he was working. This was in 1927.

I was attracted not only by the physical aspect of the place – it had a mysterious atmosphere that captured the imagination of the traveller. So much so that many visitors never left. The French doctor and naturalist Aimé Bonpland* travelled to Misiones in the nineteenth century believing that he would stay for a short visit, but the jungle won him over and he stayed for more than forty years; while there, he wrote one of the most thorough works ever published about that region of Argentina and Paraguay. The then-territory of Misiones (it is now a province) is situated in a huge wedge between Brazil and Paraguay, bordered by two large rivers, the Paraná and the Uruguay. The region has a central range some 2,000 metres in height and boasts the thickest jungle imaginable, with trees that are up to forty metres high, as well as an intricate and luxuriant vegetation of brushes, lianas and bracken. Within the region there are many deep rivers and streams. The temperature is subtropical, ideal for the most marvellous flora and fauna.

The area has always represented an inviting escape for those who wanted to leave the large cities in the quest for a little peace in these remote lands. Other travellers, explorers and scientists felt the attraction of this area, like Bonpland. Félix de Azara*, Martin de Moussy*, Alexander von Humboldt* and Moisés Bertoni* were also fascinated by the mysterious jungle of Misiones and wrote works that were read all over the world.

There, in mysterious Misiones, everything is excessive: the impenetrable jungle, full of enormous trees that prevent the sun from getting through; lianas and *icipós*[5] and *garabatos*;[6] the *yaguareté*, a native jaguar capable of splitting open a bull; the *onza* that resembles a panther; the puma; the *yacaré*, which is a South American alligator; the *anta* or tapir, and the anteater; the salty marshes where all the wild fauna go to drink; the streams that cut through the jungle and fall in great cascades reaching the currents of the deep Paraná; the pine forests and the ancient *lapachos*[7] felled by the construction workers; the wild maté plants and the vast plantations; the hurricanes that devastate all they find in their wake; and the rainstorms that last for months, making people fall into a sort of black mood; the red and sticky soil and the cesspool of the woodland; the sharp *tacuarembó*[8] and the tall *tacuara*[9] reeds . . . everything in the region of Misiones attracts and traps the visitor.

It is attractive like all that is dangerous, and it traps like all that is seductive. In Misiones nothing was similar to anything we knew: neither its soil, its climate, its vegetation, nor the jungle populated by wild animals, and far less the inhabitants.

I have probably described this region in too much detail, but it is because I am absolutely certain that climate creates an atmosphere that has an effect on the psyche, not only of

[5] *Icipós*: a creeper with very resistant stems that grows in the subtropical part of Argentina.
[6] *Garabatos*: a shrub of the leguminous family that grows in Argentina. Its branches end in a couple of thorns in the shape of a claw.
[7] *Lapacho*: a gigantic tree whose extremely hard wood is used in the construction industry.
[8] *Tacuarembó*: a species of reed that can reach a height of twenty metres.
[9] *Tacuara*: a strong but flexible reed, smaller than the *tacuarembó*, which grows on the banks of the rivers of northern Argentina. It is used in the construction industry and to make furniture. The local Indians, as well as the primitive Argentine armies, made their spears with this reed.

those who were born and lived there, but on those who remain in touch with the region after they have left.

In the beginning, the territory of Misiones was inhabited by the Guaraní[10] Indians. The famous Spanish Jesuits colonised the area and subdued the Indians, who took from them their organisation and religion. They learned from the hard-working priests how to toil and, when the Jesuits were dislodged by order of the Spanish Crown in 1777, the Guaraní Indians, who had become Christians, continued to live in the region, giving the territory a very special character.

The *mensú* – the word comes from *mensual* or monthly, which was how long their contracts lasted – is the descendant of the Indians who were enslaved for the protection of the Spanish Jesuit missions, and who has not been able to free himself from the notion that he is the property of his master. He carries the old heritage of Spanish colonisation in his blood as a stigma, but he also carries the indomitably rebellious blood of the Guaraní race. The new colonisers, under the novel guise of lumbermen or plantation owners, have imposed an even more servile yoke on this man of the soil, who continues to be the servant of the powerful landowners.

And this is how the life of the *mensú* goes by: nights of madness in the whorehouses of Posadas, the capital of Misiones, where they go to be hired and given an advance (which will enslave them); the journey to the jungle accompanied by armed guards; life in the forest, malaria, malnutrition; the lack of accommodation; the heavy and dangerous workload, always with his axe on his shoulders or cutting open up a path through the jungle for himself with

[10] Guaraní: an ancient indigenous civilisation whose descendants inhabit the area from the Amazon to the Río de la Plata. The population of Paraguay is mainly Guaraní in origin.

his machete, always increasing his debt and never being able to repay it.

At the General Stores, which were the property of their employers and the only place where they could buy supplies, they bought poor-quality food and clothing, for which they paid ten times what they were worth. The work was not well paid and the peon, or hired hand, got further into debt each day. The *mensú* thought that his only possibility of salvation was to run away through the forests, machete in hand. His obsession was to reach the River Paraná before the 'employer's justice' – in the shape of the *capangas* who searched for them in packs of armed men with dogs, paid for by the employers to kill anyone who tried to escape – fell upon him and sent him to the next world.

Only two social classes were known in the area: the employers and the peons. The extreme inequality and the exploitation to which the workers were subjected generated a climate of hatred that coloured the atmosphere of the place, made more sinister by theft and murder. One man chasing and shooting another by order of his employers, and the other who defended himself like a wild beast, just to have enough to eat, characterised the nightmare existence.

After the trip to Misiones with Pedro León Echagüe and our mutual friend Faustino Lezica, I returned home full of enthusiasm for the region. I thought there would be ample scope to survey and study the area.

And that is how, when I got married in 1927, we went directly to Caraguatay for our honeymoon, with the intention of settling there.

We lived for a while in that tense and attractive climate. I was twenty-eight years old then, and I had not travelled to the remote region of Misiones to join forces with those who exploited the poor workers, who had no alternative but to accept their impositions in order to survive. I made the irrevocable decision that I would not pay my workforce with vouchers, but with cash, and I would not accept the prices of the General Stores. That is how the landowners of the territory of Misiones came to nickname me 'The Communist'.

It was in Misiones that my wife Celia conceived our son Ernesto. I imagine that for a woman like Celia, born in the city of Buenos Aires, brought up in a sophisticated atmosphere of wealth and privilege, the move to that land full of mystery and implied terror – where, from the moment one set foot on its coast, one felt that one's life had to be protected by the gun or the machete – must have had a powerful influence. I often wonder if all that went through her head at the time could have had an influence on the child she was carrying.

Ernesto lived in the territory of Misiones for a little under two years. He did not remember living there, but my wife and I were intimately linked to that region, which he left in 1931, but which I continued to visit in order to manage our property there.

I had to leave Misiones for a while because the Astillero Río de la Plata, the shipyard of which I was co-owner, was in difficulties. One of the partners had left and I travelled to Buenos Aires to do his job. I did not expect this replacement to last long and, although I had left my maté plantation in order, I did not want to leave Caraguatay, as I had grown fond of the place. So we left Misiones believing that we would soon return. We took up residence in the area of San Isidro to be near the shipyard.

And it was then that Ernesto began to suffer from asthma. From that moment on, our return to Misiones was in question because the climate would not have been appropriate for an asthmatic child. But the fact that we left the area did not imply that we would totally disengage from it.

We never forgot the jungles of Misiones, which were always present in our minds. At home we often discussed the ups and downs of our life in Misiones; the insecurity of our existence there was a favourite subject of the Guevara children. They knew the names of the places, the trees, the animals and the birds of the region as well as we parents did. In addition, the maté plantation that I had started in 1929 was our main source of income, so it follows that the subject of Misiones was never far from our thoughts.

I am a curious man and I like to enquire and learn, so my bookshelves began to fill with the chronicles of travellers and with scientific books, as well as literary works about that enchanting place and its inhabitants.

My children listened attentively to the anecdotes my wife and I told our relatives about what we had seen, heard and felt in that remote region. Ernesto, being the eldest child, passionately embraced the cause of those men who were being exploited by other men. I believe this may have had an impact on his attitude towards exploitation later in life.

This description of the conditions in which men lived in that territory will help the reader to understand a little of the atmosphere of Misiones, where my son Ernesto spent his early years.

It is not possible to tell the complete history of this interesting region of our country, or of the people who inhabited it then and still do. The subject merits a separate book, but I will refer to many of the things that I learned there, because I cannot escape the influence those events had on me, on my wife Celia and consequently on our oldest children.

Ernesto's early childhood
These were difficult years, but happy ones as well. To live in the midst of the jungle in Misiones with a family, with all

the difficulties and upheavals that entails, was not advisable
for anybody, and far less so for us, who were used to life in a
big city.

From our house, built on a bend of the River Paraná on a
high bank, we could see a large section of the river and could
observe the barges and launches that came upriver, long
before they sailed past our home. The River Paraná is more
than 600 metres wide here. On the opposite bank one could
see the uninhabited and thick jungle of Paraguay, which
formed an impenetrable tangle of *tacuaras*, lianas and *icipós*
as it reached the river.

As happens in areas near the tropics, storms were pre-
ceded by total calm, which then turned into veritable
cyclones with lightning and thunderbolts and torrential
downpours. The spectacle was spellbinding. The force of
nature was remarkable and we could not keep our eyes away
from the marvellous sight. Nature's behaviour made us
forget the minor inconveniences that we had to face on a
daily basis in this isolated region of our country.

When the days were calm, flocks of thousands of wild
parrots flew over our heads travelling west just above the
trees, squawking loudly. It was here that Ernesto took his
first steps.

Because of the large number of insects, he wore a light
one-piece suit that protected him from the bite of the
mbarigüis, gnats, *uras* and mosquitoes that are the carriers
of malaria. His guardian angel, his nanny Carmen Arias, did
not let him out of her sight for an instant. She had come
with us from Buenos Aires and was one of the first persons
to hold Ernesto in her arms. She loved him dearly.

Few people from Buenos Aires visited us – we were too far
away. It took a week by boat from the capital.

One of Celia's sisters, Edelmira, arrived with her husband
Ernesto Moore and their two children, who were almost the

same age as my son Ernesto. They stayed with us for a long time. The house was set in a large open space, so all the children had plenty of room to chase around.

Carmen, the nanny, used to take the children for a ride in a small carriage pulled by a couple of mules and driven by a young boy from Paraguay. The children were ecstatic when they went out in that precarious cart with its awful suspension, which bounced up and down along the rocky roads of the jungle, and you could hear them screaming with delight in the thick of the forest.

I remember something that made us laugh a lot. Ernesto had started to walk. As my wife and I liked to drink maté, we used to send him to the kitchen, which was some twenty metres from the main house, to fetch the gourd with the maté that would have been prepared for us. Between the kitchen and the house there was a small ditch that hid a pipe. Ernesto invariably tripped there and fell to the ground with the maté in his hands. He would get up angrily and, when he came back with a newly brewed maté, would fall again. He kept going back for the maté until he learned to jump over the ditch.

One of Ernesto's favourite pastimes was to ride a horse with me. He would sit on the saddle in front of me and we would go round the house and then into the forest. He did not miss a single detail of what went on around us. The abundance of butterflies of the most varied colours, the birds that flew off and hid in the foliage, the brooks that crossed the paths, the mountain rats that ran for cover or some lizard that scuttled at full speed from the horse's hooves – all this must have made an impression on his young mind as he grew to have a profound knowledge of the jungle in later life.

We had a boat called *Kid*, which had a small cabin. In it I sailed the whole of the Paraná River from Buenos Aires to

Caraguatay (some 2,700 kilometres) and Ernesto became acquainted with the pleasures of navigation. We often sailed the Paraná looking for currents where we could fish for *dorado*, a large fish that can weigh up to 20 kilos and which is found only in the waters of the Paraná and its tributaries.

Most children like to fish or to watch others fishing. They are fascinated when the fish is caught by the hook and they can pull it out of the water still alive.

Sometimes we would go on the *Kid* to the streams that flow into the Paraná, crossing unexplored regions, and we could see virgin forests and wild animals that looked at us with curiosity, but without fear, probably because they had never seen a human being.

Towards the end of 1929 we went on an outing from Caraguatay to the River Iguazú. The famous waterfalls of this river are some 200 kilometres upstream from Caraguatay. In order to get there we sailed in the *Ituzaingó*, an old passenger and cargo riverboat that travelled weekly between Posadas, the capital of Misiones, and Puerto Aguirre on the frontier with Brazil.

The River Iguazú runs between Argentina and Brazil and, not long before it flows into the Paraná, forming a great semicircle some 3,000 metres long, it falls in a marvellous cascade of water fifty to one hundred metres high. Thousands of cubic metres of water per second fall into the abyss with a thundering noise, and millions of drops of water rise into the air.

My foreman Curtido and the insects

The *mbarigüi*, the gnat, the *pique* and the *ura* are the real enemies of man in Misiones.

The *mbarigüi* is a fly so small one can hardly see it, and it can pass through the fine mesh of a mosquito net. It sits on human skin and stings just like a bee. To begin with, it leaves only a small swelling, but the itch is so strong that one cannot resist scratching and this can cause infection. These insects arrive by the hundreds and, until one gets used to their sting and remembers not to scratch the affected area, they can be very unpleasant.

The gnat is smaller still and arrives in veritable clouds and can pass through every type of mosquito net. The people that gnats bite develop a fever and the area where they have been bitten feels like a burn.

The *ura* is a fly with a whitish abdomen, which is how you can tell it apart from other flies. It bites and leaves its eggs behind. These eggs produce a worm that cannot be seen to start with, but, as it begins to feed under the skin and grows, it comes out, leaving a hole in the skin. When cattle are slaughtered in this region one can see that they have countless marks from the bite of the *ura*.

The *pique* is almost invisible. It lives stuck to the floor of houses. If one steps near it with bare feet, it will crawl under one's toenails. Once it has been fertilised it becomes about two millimetres long and, as it grows, begins to cause pain. So far it is tolerable, but the fertilised *pique* explodes, producing thousands of minute *piques* that make galleries under the skin. This is not only extremely painful, but the affected area can become infected.

In order to protect Ernesto from contact with these insects, my wife used to dress him in long-sleeved overalls. This was sufficient protection against the *mbarigui* and the gnat. The *ura* was more dangerous, as it could be mistaken for an ordinary fly. But the most terrible one was the *pique*. Every evening Curtido, my foreman, would arrive at our house and, while Ernesto slept, patiently remove all the *piques* that had stuck to his feet that day.

It was a simple operation, but it had to be carried out without waking the child. Curtido would take Ernesto's foot while I held a torch to it, and he would hold his lit cigarette as near as possible to the black spot that indicated the presence of a *pique*. When exposed to the heat of the cigarette, the *pique* would loosen its grip and Curtido would pick it off the child's skin with a gold pin. This operation had to be carried out without letting the child feel the heat of the cigarette, which would wake him up and prevent the operation from continuing. Curtido would effect the extraction of the *piques* with such calm and composure – obviously the result of great experience – that there was nobody who could do a better job of it. This operation lasted about half an hour every single night, but it was considered absolutely essential.

The hurricane

We were at our home in Puerto Caraguatay on the River Paraná. It was midnight when a strong wind began to blow; its speed kept increasing. I had built the house myself, so I knew to what extent it would resist the wind, but I did not know if it could resist winds of more than 120 kilometres per hour, which threatened to become a very destructive spinning column of air. The pillars, the wall panels and the roof were all made of timber, but had no joinery or ordinary nails; they were held together by galvanised iron nails. Consequently, if one of those joints gave way, it was highly probable that the whole structure would give way and the house would collapse.

The wind was becoming more like a hurricane. The timber seemed to be about to break. The whole structure was shaking. I distinctly remember the roar of the wind in the trees that surrounded the house. I had the feeling that the structure was not going to hold – in which case we would slide down into the River Paraná, which ran some 100 metres from our bedroom. I had heard about cyclones in torrid areas, but I had never been at the vortex of one. Now I had the feeling that we could be in the centre of the cyclone.

We could hear the branches breaking in the forest and the roar of the wind in the thickness of the jungle, and every now and then we heard something like a long lament, which was the sound of a tree being torn from its roots and dragged by the storm.

Our son Ernesto was asleep in his cot next to our bed. At one point I thought I should leave the house with my wife and child and try to find cover in the forest, but then I thought that if the wind was so strong, it would drag us into the water as if we were feathers. I then remembered something that I had heard in my father's house: in 1891 there was an earthquake in Mendoza, which destroyed most of the city and killed two-thirds of the population. A whole family – father, mother and several children – having gone into the street as soon as the tremor started, went back indoors following the father who had run in to save the youngest child, who was in his cradle. At that very moment the house collapsed as the father flung himself on top of the child. The story goes that the fallen roof crushed the whole family except the baby, who survived because his father's body had protected him from the falling debris.

Without wasting a second, I flung myself on top of Ernesto in his cot. My wife, who was a fatalist, remained in bed awaiting the consequences of the storm. The house resisted it well.

The next day I saddled my horse and crossed the forest that separated us from the Administration Office of Puerto Caraguatay. Carlos Benson, an old English engineer, greeted me. He had travelled all over the world working on the railways and really knew the tropics, where he had spent a large part of his life. When I told him what a bad time I had

had the previous night, Old Benson replied: 'I didn't sleep at all, expecting my house to be blown away at any moment, and I assure you, Mr Guevara, that I had never seen such a hurricane in all my life.'

On my way there I had seen many broken and uprooted trees, and now I was beginning to understand how a well-designed and constructed building, by distributing the stresses, could withstand the forces of nature even better than nature itself could. That is why my modest house was capable of resisting the furious storm.

The mensú

One afternoon a peon arrived at my house. My foreman, Curtido, had sent him from the forest. He was a tall man and looked very fit. 'A professional axe-cutter,' I thought to myself. When he reached the covered area where I was drinking my maté, he took off his wide-brimmed straw hat respectfully.

'Good afternoon, master,' he said.

I asked him what brought him to the house. He said he had an order for the payment of almost 100 pesos signed by my foreman. I looked at it and was about to pay him when the man asked with some hesitation if I had a 100-peso note.

I replied that I did, but the order was only for ninety-five pesos. Without another word he produced a rolled handkerchief from his pocket in which he had five one-peso notes. He handed them over to me.

'Why do you want a hundred-peso note?' I asked him.

The man stood at attention and looked towards the forest and, with a solemn voice, announced: 'Master, I have never seen one.'

I brought a 100-peso note and handed it over to the man. He stared at it and turned it in his hands.

'One hundred,' he said, staring at it as if hypnotised. 'You know, master, we can never earn this sum.'

I asked him to sit down and, after sharing a few drinks of maté and chatting with him, he told me his story. It was the same dark tale of the men who were like slaves in the timber trade.

He told me how they were hired, how they spent their advance money on clothes and merchandise, how they were transferred under armed guard, and then . . . all there was left for them to do was to use the axe and the machete for years and years, while the General Stores took their money. He was unable to explain how he had arrived at Puerto Caraguatay, but he showed me his gratitude in his own way with the pleasure it gave him to own a 100-peso note.

Carmen Arias de Gabela

I could not tell exactly when Carmen Arias arrived at our home, but with time she grew to be like a member of the family. Many years have gone by, but I still remember her face when, having just arrived, she picked up Ernesto, who had not yet learned to walk. I can see her talking with my wife. She was a robust woman with very blonde hair and lots of freckles. She had blue eyes and was unpretentious and austere. She and Celia exchanged a few words and understood each other perfectly, so she stayed on as Ernesto's nanny. When the other children arrived she was like a mother to them.

Carmen was not interested in money or comforts, she had grown fond of us. There was a period when we lived with my mother in a flat on the corner of Santa Fe and Guise Streets on the first floor. It was forty years ago, and the building still looks just as it did when we lived there, except that now there is a huge sign across the balconies advertising a business school. Every time I go by, and I go by almost every day, I cannot help looking up and thinking that I am going to see Carmen with Ernesto in her arms, sunbathing.

Carmen – *Gallega*, as we called her affectionately – was in charge of Ernesto and did not leave his side until eight years later, when she left our home to get married to one of the nicest men I have ever met: Alfredo Gabela.

She loved Ernesto as if he were her own, and she then gave her affection to all the little ones who followed. When one of them did something very naughty and I wanted to slap him, the slap invariably fell on Carmen, who always managed to come between us. I used to tell her off and so did my wife; we thought she was spoiling our children. She never answered back, but carried on behaving in the same way.

Carmen was with us in Buenos Aires, where we lived in a nice apartment, but she also came with us on all our trips to the country. She came when we stayed at the *estancia* of the Moore family in the province of Entre Ríos, at El Socorro with the Echagüe family, at my wife's *estancia* in Villa Sarmiento, and at Puerto Caraguatay in Misiones. There life was that much more difficult because of the climate and the local landowners, with whom we had very little in common.

I remember her as a vision from the past, tanned by the strong sun, carrying the basket full of clothes on her head to wash them in the river, because that was how it was done in her native Galicia. She used to do the washing, the ironing and prepare Ernesto's food. She did the same for all the other children later on. She came to Alta Gracia with us, always in charge of the children. I am in no doubt that she was the most loyal person I have ever met. When I think of the past I cannot separate it from the image of Carmen surrounded by all the children, with Ernesto at the head.

One day Carmen had to travel to Buenos Aires and there she met Alfredo Gabela, who was also from the Galician port of La Coruña. Although they wanted to get married, Carmen postponed the wedding until Roberto, my third child, was a little older. When she finally told us she was leaving we were devastated. It was like losing a member of the family. I still remember her departure from the old train station at Alta Gracia. Leaning out of the window unable to control her tears, she kept asking my wife to look after little Roberto for her. Celia and I never forgot that parting.

After she married, Carmen lived in Buenos Aires. We kept in touch by letter. Through one of those letters she found out that I had had serious financial problems that year. The entire production of maté from my plantation in Caraguatay, which was my main source of income, had been stolen. It was nearing Christmas time when one afternoon a large packet arrived in the post. It contained all sorts of sweets, fruits and toys, as well as a note from Alfredo Gabela that read: 'I can't have you not celebrating Christmas properly.'

In 1962 Ernesto, who had by now become known as Che Guevara, travelled to Punta del Este in Uruguay as a minister of Fidel Castro's government. He led the Cuban delegation that represented that country at the conference of the Organisation of American States. Needless to say, the whole family took the opportunity, as it was so close to Buenos Aires, to travel there and spend a few days with Ernesto. Alfredo Gabela joined us there.

Carmen and Alfredo were always ready to receive Ernesto in their home. When Ernesto travelled from Córdoba to Buenos Aires, his first visit was always to them. Their friendship continued throughout his life.

Goodbye to Puerto Caraguatay

Just before the end of 1929 we decided to travel to Buenos Aires. My wife was about to give birth to our daughter Celia.

We decided to sail to Posadas under our own steam. We kitted out the *Kid* with all we needed, and we included an inflatable life raft similar to the one used by the Italian explorer Umberto Nobile* for his expedition to the North Pole. We needed to take these precautions because the River Paraná, which is very deep for much of its length, goes through mountainous areas that reduce both its breadth and depth and is only navigable by very good river pilots. We would travel without any. To be on the safe side, I went to try the vessel out with my foreman the day before we were to set sail. We were far from our moorings when we ran out of fuel. We had to moor her there and return on foot.

The following morning the time came to set sail on our journey. We would be away for several months. We went down the steep slope, which was about 100 metres long, to reach the spot where our boat was rocking graciously in the water. We loaded our luggage, baskets, utensils, foodstuffs, ropes, life-savers and everything else we would need for our two-day journey to Posadas. We would be sailing with the current, but in spite of that the *Kid* could only do twelve kilometres an hour, so it would be slow going.

We put the extra fuel where it would be protected, gave final instructions to those who had come to see us off, and I cranked the engine . . . but nothing happened. After a half-hour struggle with the handle I decided to inspect the engine. The coupling bearings had burned out. Why? The previous afternoon I had sent the foreman to put fuel in the tank and bring the *Kid* to her moorings. He did bring her, but he also burned out the engine.

It was seven in the morning, the sun was beginning to appear and soon the heat would be unbearable. My wife did not want to go up the steep bank back to the house. So Curtido, Emilio Skipposted (a Brazilian friend who was travelling with us) and I decided to sail two kilometres upstream to Puerto Caraguatay – which was no port, but a sandy bank where the dinghies of the larger boats moored. I knew that at eleven o'clock the *Iberá* would make its appearance. It was an old river boat that had sailed the Nile for fifty years and had been brought to Argentina some fifty years ago. It was propelled by a paddle wheel just like the ones in those old photographs of river boats sailing the Mississippi.

So we had to hurry. We were advancing slowly and it was getting hotter. Celia could hardly breathe inside the cabin, which was like a furnace. Ernesto was skipping about the deck under Carmen's watchful eye. Curtido was pulling like mad, and I was pushing with the beam and swearing profusely.

By eleven we still had not arrived, but Captain Congó, an old friend, saw us in the distance and waited for us. Not long afterwards we reached the sandbank. It had taken us four hours to sail two kilometres. We were tired, sweaty and dirty. We threw our luggage into the boats that came towards us to take us to the ship. At last Celia, Carmen with Ernesto in her arms and I climbed aboard the *Iberá*.

We bade farewell to Puerto Caraguatay. It was our intention to return a few months later, but Ernesto's asthma and the birth of our daughter Celia forced us to give up that idea. Neither my wife Celia nor Ernesto ever went back, and I travelled there only a few times to deal with the administrative matters of the plantation.

The Moore family's estancia

During the summer holidays we used to spend time at the *estancia* of my wife's brother-in-law Ernesto Moore. We loved the place. We were attracted to it because of its rural atmosphere, which was the complete opposite of city life. The Moore *estancia* in Galarza was the most authentic gaucho establishment in the province of Entre Ríos. It was a property that had a vast area of pastureland and a lot of livestock.

The province of Entre Ríos had the reputation of having the best horsemen amongst its hired hands. Twice a year the animals were rounded up and driven to the small farms within the *estancia* where the gauchos lived, in order to brand them. Once at the farms, the animals were lassoed so that they could be branded, castrated and treated. These gatherings always ended with the gauchos breaking in wild horses. As I always enjoyed these occasions, I never wanted to miss anything, particularly the horse-breaking and taming.

During those events we were able to see gauchos wearing spurs and boots made with the skin of a horse's leg, which covered the foot as well as the lower leg up to the knee. I have watched many a gaucho take off his jacket, his thick leather belt and his long double-edged knife and tie a band round his head to hold back his hair, then single-handedly knock down a wild horse, control it, saddle it and jump onto its back. The horse would arch its back, bucking, plunging and prancing, its mane flying in the wind and snorting furiously, while it clicked its hooves against the ground. And I have seen gauchos hanging on without grabbing onto the saddle, using the whip to control the animal and return to the farm, still on horseback.

All this technique known as horse-breaking is the preamble to teaching the horse to accept a rider, and this is a task frequently carried out in large country establishments such as the one owned by the Moore family, where my son Ernesto learned about these practices as a child.

Ernesto Moore, who had an English father and an Irish mother, looked like a typical Englishman, except that he had gone totally native. He was tall, slim and bony, had deep-blue eyes and was covered in freckles. He was the personification of kindness. He had always lived in his *estancia* and had learned how to work on the farm and become friends with all the local people of the area. He dressed like a gaucho from Entre Ríos: he wore baggy gaucho-style trousers, a knitted girdle round his waist, high boots, a shirt of fine cloth and a handkerchief tied round his neck. He spoke like the locals and drank as much maté as they did. He used to sit on a dead cow's skull and chat with his hired hands pleasantly and without affectation. Sometimes he would stare into the sky and say, as if pronouncing sentence, 'It will rain tomorrow.' If someone asked him how he knew that, he would reply, 'The cock crowed at midnight.' He was in tune with nature, but did not brag about it.

He was married to Edelmira de la Serna, my sister-in-law, and they had two children more or less the same age as ours: Ernesto Moore was a year older than our Ernesto and Juan Martín Moore was a year younger. The three were always running around together. They were inseparable friends, and ever since they were young children they used to argue and fight as children do over the most trivial matters.

Ernesto Moore Senior adored his children, but he wanted them to be brought up to be tough men, just as he had been educated. He did not want them to be mummy's boys. From a very early age the Moore boys dressed in gaucho outfits.

Ernesto, our son, used to get involved in fights with the oldest boy, and they would kick and punch each other relentlessly. The younger Moore boy would immediately join forces with his brother against our son. I used to try to split them up, but Moore Senior would say in an ironic tone of voice, 'Let them fight, that way they will grow up as men.' I did not mind the children growing into men by fighting each other, but what I did object to was that two should fight against one, and even more so when the one was always my son. Of course, the Moore boys always won and their father watched the scene with delight.

One day I decided that was enough. I was tired of seeing how the two boys took advantage of my son. So I said to Ernesto, 'Look, when two boys fight against you together, you must grab hold of the first one and hang onto him as best you can, and when the second one joins him against you, you can bite him and kick him to fend him off, because they are fighting as a pair.' And that was what happened.

As soon as they had a disagreement, the boys went for each other. Moore, as usual, said, 'Let them fight it out', and settled down to watch his children beat up my son. But this time the situation had changed: when Ernesto saw them charging towards him together, as they often did, he sank his teeth into the ear of the eldest. The boy screamed at the top of his voice, but Ernesto did not let go of him. Moore tried to intervene and separate them, but I said, 'Let them fight it out like men.'

The eldest boy continued to scream and his ear was bleeding. His father was desperate, but at last he understood the injustice of an uneven fight of two against one.

There was a great commotion in the house over this incident; my brother-in-law was not happy, but from that day on the Moore boys stopped taunting Ernesto, for fear of ending up minus one ear.

Portela, my mother's farm, where Ernesto spent many a summer

Our old house at Portela was built by my father on land that belonged to my mother and that had belonged to her ancestors. Construction began in 1910.

It was a large house with big rooms. It had a dining room that looked like a conference hall, as well as eleven bedrooms and several bathrooms. With all these bedrooms there was room for many guests, so in summer it was like a hotel.

My mother adored that farm, which was in actual fact part of the larger *estancia* that had belonged to her father. When she arrived in Argentina from California, at the age of twelve, she went to live on the *estancia*, which was called San Patricio. Her father Francisco Lynch, who had lived in exile in the United States during the dictatorship of General Rosas, took over the management of this property on his return to Argentina.

It was a large *estancia* with a lot of land and livestock: horses, cattle and sheep. In those days in Argentina, land was only cultivated to cater for the needs of the inhabitants of the *estancia*. Cattle, sheep and horses were bred in the country, and the landowners' job was to fatten them up and keep them healthy to sell to the abattoirs or at rural markets. The landowners' homes were rather precarious, and that of the hired hands even more so.

The work was in tune with the physical and social fabric of the country, which lived almost exclusively off the land. Industries were to be found only in the outskirts of the large cities where commerce flourished.

Cattle were exported either live or slaughtered. Leather was also exported in large quantities. All the materials required to build houses had to be imported.

Those were generally the features of our country by the middle of the nineteenth century. Our countryside had a formative influence on the character of the men who lived and worked there, and it was there that they acquired the physical strength and unique social attributes that in turn proved crucial to the development of Argentina as a nation.

My grandfather, who was of Irish descent, had great affection for the land of his birth. From a very young age he devoted himself to breeding livestock, and he became an expert on rural affairs.

One can understand the love he had for his property – a love my mother had inherited, and which I and my children also feel. That little bit of land we still own is, for us, a sacred place.

When he returned to Argentina, my grandfather went to live in the main house at San Patricio, which was some five kilometres away from Portela. My mother, who was twelve at the time, used to accompany my grandfather on his rounds of the property, inspecting the livestock and taking part in the daily running of the place.

These *estancias* and their people have been admirably described by the Argentine writer Ricardo Güiraldes* in his book *Don Segundo Sombra*, which is today considered a classic of gaucho literature. What Güiraldes describes in his novel are the country and atmosphere in which my grandparents, my mother and her children lived. The General Stores at La Blanqueada and the old bridge on the River Areco are only nine leagues from our house at Portela. My son Ernesto knew the area really well.

It was through this small farm that my family learned to love the countryside. This small oasis, where we took refuge every summer and where our children enjoyed themselves throughout the long season, had a particular charm. At that time the place was called *Granja Santa Ana*. I don't know if it was the old house full of mementoes and memories, or the fact that the atmosphere was so peaceful, almost monastic, or whether it was the affection that is handed down from parents to children, which meant that for us Portela was almost a place of veneration. It represented the continuity between our ancestors and ourselves and our children, and perhaps our grandchildren.

Those of us who lived in the capital city found in Portela

a refuge, a quiet place far from the hustle and bustle of the metropolis, far from the noxious fumes and the noise and the anxieties that life in big cities entails. As soon as one left behind the paved highway and turned onto the dirt roads, all responsibilities and concerns melted away.

The house that my father built is still there. It looks different today, desolate and sad. The plastering is damaged, the paint is cracked and it is empty throughout. Like all uninhabited places, the peace and quiet overwhelm the visitor and the silence seems more intense in the shade of the leafy trees that surround it. Today this house, so dear to my childhood, is like a museum and yet I love to return to Portela. It is as if I was returning to an earlier time and the present no longer existed.

As I have already mentioned, a lot of people came to my mother's *estancia* in the summer. It was a peaceful house most of the time, but when we had a houseful of guests it seemed more like a noisy tenement.

I remember how we went out riding together, ten to fifteen men on horseback, galloping over those fields. Sometimes in the corrals the livestock were being branded and then the day ended with a barbecue and lots of good wine.

On my mother's *estancia* they also farmed. The corn was harvested, the hay was cut and piled up. The mechanical rakes went by loaded with alfalfa, wheat and flax. Every year the large threshers harvested and bagged the grain, and the roads to the village were full of carts carrying the grain to the railway station.

The bars were full of people whose only amusement was to listen to a gramophone record while having a drink at the counter. The drinking sessions sometimes went on for too long and often ended in knife fights.

It was at Portela that, years later, my son Ernesto learned how the bitches fed their puppies, how to slaughter a pig, how to milk a cow. He learned how to make butter and cheese, how to care for a cow's sore udder. He also familiarised himself with the local customs: for example, to rid a horse of worms, a frog was hung around its neck and that cured it.

He also learned how to topple a bull in order to castrate it, de-horn it and brand it. He experienced the smell of burned skin and heard the moans of pain when the red-hot iron was set on the hindquarters of the animals. He saw the wild horses being lassoed, brought to the tethering post and tied. And he saw horses being saddled, starting with the *sudadera*, a small blanket to absorb the horses' sweat, and the saddlebags. He saw too the gaucho jump onto the back of a wild horse, letting it buck under his whip and run over the fields. Ernesto learned how to scrape down, brush and shear gaucho-style. He also learned how to take the nests from the dovecotes and how to handle the incubators and be able to tell one breed of poultry from another. And it was at Portela that he tasted the jams prepared by his grandmother with fruits from the forest in shiny old copper pots.

It was there that he became acquainted with rural life and discovered the soul of the gaucho, who is so close to the land. He was able to see the gaucho bent over the plough or engrossed in other rural duties, riding his horse across the pampas, always frugal and stoic, always severe with himself, his only pride being his manliness and his honour.

All this may now be in the remote past, but I have no doubt that it had an influence on the character of Ernesto. I have taken the reader on a detour, but it is because I believe that one could not understand his personality without understanding the milieu in which he was born and raised and matured.

From his earliest childhood Ernesto loved my mother's company, and the friendship between them lasted as long as she lived. Ernesto loved to listen to her stories about life in California, of how she went riding with her father over these same prairies – at a time when there were no roads and no wire fencing – across the country, often stopping for the night at the home of some hired hands.

In fact Ernesto knew more about my mother's early life than I or my brothers did.

She had always enjoyed life in the open. Whenever she spoke about California, it was never about the city of San Francisco, but always about the countryside covered in flowers, the hills covered in trees. She always had a passion for nature.

In Portela she liked to go for a walk along the rows of fruit trees, *paraísos*[11] or eucalyptus. She would go to the cornfields to collect the cobs or walk among the alfalfa or flax crops.

She loved being in the corridors of the house because from there she could see the vast fields all the way to the horizon. Her favourite treat was to go out in the evenings in her four-wheeled American carriage and drive along the stables full of animals.

Ernesto inherited his love of nature from my mother – that nature from which he learned so much when he tried to tame it, and which played such an important role in his life.

As a child, Ernesto used to run around the large rooms of the Portela house under the watchful eye of my mother and my sister Beatriz. Sometimes he would race down the corridors in his little car. Every morning a pony was saddled and brought to the tethering post for him. He loved riding,

---

[11] *Paraíso*: a tree that can reach ten metres in height, has a tortuous trunk and grey, thin, whitish and lustrous leaves, with flowers that are small and white on the outside and yellow on the inside, and ovoid and reddish-yellow fruits.

and he not only rode over our own land, but out to the neighbouring farms where he had made lots of friends.

It is understandable that Ernesto felt so drawn to that farm. When he was older he used to go to Portela with his friends to spend time quietly. When we returned to Buenos Aires, after having lived in Córdoba for many years, he was almost a grown man and he used to travel to Portela frequently. He considered a stay there a real need. He visited my mother's old farm regularly until he left to travel across Latin America. The people of the area remember him with affection to this day.

Ernesto's asthma

I had returned to Buenos Aires from Misiones to work at the Astillero Río de la Plata, which I owned together with my relative and childhood friend Germán Frers. The shipyard was in San Fernando, a neighbourhood not far from the capital city and near San Isidro, where I rented a small house from my brother-in-law Martínez Castro. He lived next door in a colonial mansion that was considered an architectural relic. It had a leafy park, and we, living next door, had the advantage of being able to enjoy his garden and trees, and our children played there with their friends every day. Ernesto used to play under a huge pine tree while his younger sister Celia was still in a pushchair. My sister María Luisa and her husband Martín had three daughters who were like three little mothers to my children. Menina, the eldest, was fourteen years older than Ernesto.

We also used to enjoy going for a swim in the nearby river, and in summer we were able to do this almost every day at the beaches of the San Isidro Nautical Club. One cold morning in May, my wife went to swim in the river with our son Ernesto. I arrived later at the club to take them to lunch and found Ernesto in his swimming gear trembling with cold. Celia had not realised that the weather had changed. In Buenos Aires such frequent sudden changes of temperature are common.

By the time we arrived at our house Ernesto was not well. That night he began to cough. I had never witnessed an asthma attack and, when I noticed he had bronchitis and was tired, I called an old neighbour, Dr Pestaña, who diagnosed asthmatic bronchitis without complications and related this attack to the pneumonia that Ernesto had suffered in Rosario, a few days after his birth. Now, two years later, maybe the sudden cold had brought about the attack. Dr Pestaña prescribed the usual remedies at that time: heat, an adrenaline syrup and poultices. Ernesto's general health improved, but his asthma never left him.

Yet another attack lasted several days. Dr Pestaña became concerned about its recurrence. At last Ernesto improved considerably, but as soon as he caught cold, the asthmatic attacks would return.

San Isidro is located on the banks of the River Plate, and consequently it is very humid. Maybe this is why the boy never recovered completely.

Ernesto's asthma was becoming chronic, and for us it was becoming a curse. We took him to Buenos Aires, where he was seen by various specialists. He was X-rayed and had many tests and all the results were negative. As far as the doctors were concerned, Ernesto had chronic asthmatic bronchitis and nothing else.

Our torture began. We would hear him hiccuping and – not having any previous experience of an asthmatic condition – my wife and I would despair. Apart from all the medicine we gave him, at night we used to burn Andrews papers in his room. These were very much in vogue at the time and used to fill his room with smoke. But they did not make any difference.

So we tried all sorts of remedies – pills, syrups, injections – and gradually we saw that, so far, all the doctors' remedies had not been able to stop the attacks.

Ernesto was growing with that fearful illness and this began to weigh on us. Celia used to spend the nights listening to his breathing. I used to put him to sleep on my chest because it seemed he could breathe better that way, but consequently I hardly slept.

Ernesto had scarcely begun to talk when he learned to say, 'Daddy, injection' whenever his asthma got the better of him. This gives an idea of his suffering; children on the whole are scared of needles, but he had realised that it was the only thing that helped him when he had an attack.

Anybody with any sensitivity who has to witness daily the suffering of a child from an illness that, although not fatal, is chronic must be affected. I never got used to the sound of his breathing – a noise not unlike a cat's purring.

Our lives changed in accordance with his needs. We had to find a climate that was suitable for an asthmatic child. Asthma is an erratic illness and each case has different characteristics. What is detrimental to one person may be beneficial to another. This is where the diagnoses fail. An asthmatic person might be affected by a certain food, but only for a while, and might then find that he has grown immune to it. But then it might be a different food that affects him. In the case of our son, we were running out of tests.

We could not return to Misiones, where my plantation was my main source of income. It was too humid, too hot and the weather too unpredictable. Having discarded Misiones, we would have liked to live in Buenos Aires, where both Celia and I had our families and I had an occupation. But we listened to our doctor, Mario O'Donnell, who used to say that we should look for a better climate instead of relying on medicines.

One feature of Ernesto's asthma was that it was acute. All the doctors who saw him said that they had never seen such an acute manifestation of the illness, and some even said they had never seen it in children. We had grown used to discussing asthma, and none of the asthmatic people we talked to had attacks of the intensity of Ernesto's.

We move home several times

We used to spend a lot of time with my sister María Luisa and her family in their old house. Everybody loved Ernesto and spoilt him. We were comfortable in our house by the river and I did not want to move, but as it was here that Ernesto had had his first attacks of asthma, we thought that perhaps the vegetation and the humidity coming from the river might have been harmful to him. In view of the fact that Ernesto's health continued to deteriorate, we decided to move to downtown Buenos Aires and rented an apartment on the fifth floor of a block on the corner of Bustamante and Peña Streets. This was the beginning of our lengthy pilgrimage in search of a better climate for our child.

We left San Isidro with a heavy heart. We had grown used to the area and to having part of my family near us.

But Buenos Aires was not good for Ernesto's health, either. He experienced a slight improvement, but his asthma was always present. There were many consultations with different doctors and different treatments. While Ernesto fought his illness, little Celia was growing healthy and, fortunately, without any hint of asthma.

Our son Roberto was born in our apartment in Buenos Aires. We were now five and had to think of moving to a larger place. The great advantage of this apartment was its location: it was near Palermo Park with its trees and walks and gardens, where Carmen used to take the children every day to spend some hours in the sun. Whenever I could, I would drive Carmen and the children to the forest and lakes of Palermo, where I rented a tiny bicycle and taught Ernesto how to ride it. It was a joy to see him pedalling away with his tiny feet, which could hardly reach the pedals.

Whenever the weather permitted, we used to take the children to the Gamas' country house near Morón. They were family friends of Celia's and in their home our children spent many happy hours enjoying the sun and the fresh air.

By now Ernesto's asthma was shaping all our decisions. Each day brought a new restriction to our freedom of movement and we were at the mercy of his cursed illness. I remember with pride the tenacity with which my wife and I tackled our problem. We hoped to find a doctor who would cure him or a medicine that would alleviate his attacks. We began to consider leaving Buenos Aires and looked at various alternatives: Mendoza, Tandil, Córdoba . . . our nomadic destiny had begun.

Cutting our moorings

One day we decided to make a dramatic move. I bought tickets for the whole family on the overnight train. We were going to Córdoba. I had never visited that province, but the doctors had recommended its dry mountainous climate.

The day we were supposed to travel I had not finished some urgent business, so I decided that my wife should leave with the children. I would join them a few days later. But when we were saying goodbye I saw that Ernesto was very ill, so I decided to board the train and travel with them. I had no luggage with me. I had bought myself a pair of shoes that day and had sent the ones I was wearing home from the shop. I only realised once we had left Buenos Aires that the shoes were too tight.

The next morning I could not put my shoes on. As soon as we got off the train we took a taxi and I went to buy myself a new pair of shoes. This is how life in Córdoba began for me: my feet hurt, my child was sick and I had my whole family with me. I was not a happy man.

The Plaza Hotel had been recommended to me, so there we went. I remember it as if it were today. I took an apartment in the hotel for all of us and opened the windows onto San Martín Square. The air was dry and the rooms were flooded with sunlight. The square had really old trees, and behind it one could see the old Jesuit cathedral of the city.

To my amazement, I saw that Ernesto was no longer suffering from his asthma. One could feel the change in climate; there was not a cloud in the sky. The previous night during the journey Ernesto had not been able to sleep because of his laboured breathing, and now he was breathing normally.

Many people asked me later why we stayed to live in the province of Córdoba, and I gave all of them the same answer: what else could I do, when I had found the place where Ernesto could breathe normally?

That same day we decided to look for a house in Córdoba city. The change in Ernesto's health had made us optimistic and we thought he would be completely cured in these new surroundings. I started to plan my own return to Buenos Aires, where I had left my job, my friends and part of my family. But it was not to be. It is true that Ernesto had long periods free from illness in the climate of Córdoba, but he had serious attacks of asthma as well.

In Córdoba, Ernesto was looked after by Dr Soria, who became his GP. He was an extraordinary paediatrician and a man for whom medicine was a calling. He said we should stay for some time in Córdoba before imagining that Ernesto was cured.

We rented a house in Argüello, where Ernesto had a really bad time because his asthma grew worse. An old friend, Dr

Fernando Peña, used to praise the climate of Alta Gracia[1], a small town near Córdoba city at the foot of the Sierras Chicas. He had lived there for many years.

We were demoralised. Ernesto's initial improvement had evaporated. The four months that had been set as the length of our stay in Córdoba had elapsed. Time passed and we did not know how long we would remain there. Our return to Buenos Aires seemed further and further away. We were disoriented and disillusioned. I felt unsettled and unable to plan anything.

In this climate of psychological upheaval we decided to carry on looking for a place that would be beneficial for Ernesto's health. We heeded the advice of Dr Peña and moved in 1933 to Alta Gracia, where we were to stay for eleven years.

[1] Alta Gracia: at the time this was a small town in the province of Córdoba in central Argentina, not far from the city of Córdoba, the capital of the province.

Part Three: Growing up, 1933–52

One cannot write a biography without describing the physical and social atmosphere around the subject of the biography.

Alta Gracia is a small town whose fine, dry climate attracted many people suffering from tuberculosis and other respiratory ailments. My son Ernesto lived there between the ages of five and sixteen – that is, most of his childhood and adolescence.

What I have written may seem a crazy succession of isolated elements, a description of landscapes, incidents, friendships, studies, struggles, amusements, illness, but all of it is part of a picture that I would be unable to express otherwise.

I leave to the reader the pleasure, or challenge, of giving structure to these untidy basic elements. They are essential for understanding Ernesto's background and hence how he grew up and eventually became Che Guevara.

We had had to leave Argüello in a hurry because Ernesto had suffered one asthma attack after another there. We arrived at Alta Gracia and stayed at the Hotel de la Gruta, in the foothills of the Sierras. Here, Ernesto enjoyed such a recovery that it encouraged us to rent a house in Villa Carlos Pellegrini, very near the mountain slopes. The locals used to refer to this area as *'el alto'*, while the area of the old city below was called *'el bajo'*.

Alta Gracia gave us a measure of tranquillity. Although

Ernesto continued to suffer asthma attacks, he would go through long periods during which the attacks did not recur and he was in good health. He could go to school and play with the rest of the children, which meant running around the neighbourhood and the woods that surrounded our house. When summer came, all the children went swimming in the nearby streams. This sport was very beneficial to Ernesto's health.

But we were sceptical and did not have many illusions about his complete recovery. Although it is true that in Alta Gracia he could join the other children to play in the open air, it is equally true that he had long spells in bed with attacks of asthmatic bronchitis, which, when they came, could be violent.

For Celia and me, life in that city had no other purpose than that of finding a cure for our son. I felt like a prisoner. I hated that life among sick people or people who were there to accompany the sick.

Both Celia and I dreamed of returning to Buenos Aires. For us – although it turned out not to be so – Alta Gracia was a temporary place of residence. But the fact is that it was the only place where, until then, Ernesto had been able to spend entire seasons without an attack.

I would gladly have given my life for him to be cured, and my wife felt exactly the same way. But I was becoming deeply depressed. My wife, who had a stronger character, never suffered from depression – or, if she did, never allowed it to show.

I was thirty-four years old. I was strong and healthy. I had always led an active life and practised many sports. I loved sailing. But all that now seemed very far away.

Both my wife and I enjoyed reading and keeping abreast of the latest news, but in Alta Gracia we had nothing else to do but read. When the sun set, everybody retired. There

was only a small group of night-owls who met at the main
hotel and killed time drinking and playing cards and
chatting.

For me, hotel life had no attraction, nor did club life. On
the contrary, I found the atmosphere generated by those
who had to live there because of their tuberculosis boring
and depressing.

I had always enjoyed night-time and felt better when the
sun went down. But in Alta Gracia I used to feel so lonely
that sometimes I would get into my little car and drive out
to see the countryside in order to feel alive. I was growing
more and more depressed, but there was nothing we could
do. We had to stay there for Ernesto's health.

Both Celia and I had become 'experts' on asthma. We had
read all there was to read and had tried all there was to try.
To begin with we had been told that Ernesto would
experience a change when he reached the age of seven, then
when he became a teenager, and this is how our lives went
by. He was to spend his childhood and adolescence in Alta
Gracia and the cursed illness would never leave him: not in
San Isidro, not in Buenos Aires, Córdoba, Alta Gracia or
Cuba, or in any of the other countries he went to.

I decided to overcome my depression by establishing a
plan for our stay in Alta Gracia. My wife and I resolved that
we would continue to give Ernesto the medicines he had
been prescribed, but we would also encourage him to
exercise in the open air, to swim, ride and climb the nearby
hills. Ernesto made great progress.

But the most important development took place when
one summer we decided to go to the seaside for three
months. Mar del Plata is a seaside resort to which half the
population of Buenos Aires goes during the summer months
to escape the heat of the capital. Ernesto having spent a long
period in a dry mountainous climate, found the sea air had a

beneficial effect on him as well as on the rest of the family, of course.

Alta Gracia: the city; its aspect; its evolution; its influence

Alta Gracia is an old town founded by the Jesuits in the seventeenth century. It has a prestigious past, of which its well-preserved architecture reminds us to this day. The buildings of the old Jesuit *reducción* – as they used to refer to the place where they lodged and trained the Indians – became the present town after the Jesuits were ousted. Alta Gracia's historic buildings boast many beautiful monastic cells, corridors, ample patios and a parish church, which today are the silent witnesses of a past of Jesuit grandeur.

The old parish church in particular – with its turrets, its bell tower and its friezes that create a perfect equilibrium – has an imposing air of mystery. In Alta Gracia it is difficult to escape the subtle influence of this lost era.

No matter how pressed for time the visitor is, no matter whether he is on horseback or on foot, when he travels past the old house of Viceroy Liniers*, which used to be a Jesuit *reducción*, he will feel the weight of the past on those stones.

At the Sierras Hotel – the most luxurious of Alta Gracia – the upper classes as well as some politicians spent their many hours of leisure playing bridge or canasta while musicians, writers, painters and critics gave the place an intellectual atmosphere. And while the Sierras Hotel imposed its presence as a 'continental grand hotel', below among the tangled vegetation of the woodland or in the ravines of the hills were the poor areas where the miners lived in a completely different environment.

The working class lived in badly built housing and survived by working the land, or by going down the mines where wolfram and mica were extracted or working in the marble or limestone quarries. The wages of these people were low and they were paid irregularly. They worked a lot and earned very little.

Factories paid their labour force a little better, but there were few of them. The peon or hired hand was paid even less than all the others.

The children of these workers were consequently malnourished, badly dressed, in poor health and did not attend school regularly. The working class was exploited, as is the case in all capitalist countries. They ate little, their housing was appalling, they worked more hours than the law permitted, there was no severance pay, they carried out insalubrious jobs without the proper level of compensation. At the time there were no laws to protect the workers and they in turn, feeling cornered, lived with their fists clenched in an attitude of self-defence and defiance.

Many of their children did not attend school for lack of adequate clothing. Many school-age children worked as shoeshine boys, or sold fruit, eggs or *alfajores*,[2] or hung around the station terminals and bus stops or places frequented by tourists to beg for a coin. These children developed an instinct for survival; they used their imagination and became quick at grabbing whatever they could lay their hands on. Many of them became petty thieves.

It was in the countryside where there were more illiterate children. Their underdevelopment was more acute, but, on the other hand, they were in a better position to find food.

It can be said that Alta Gracia at the time did not offer the working man many opportunities to earn a living. Poverty had crushed the lower-class neighbourhoods and there was

---

[2] *Alfajor*: a traditional Argentine snack consisting of two or more thin slices of pastry with a jam filling.

much unemployment. The government did little or nothing; they just talked. The conditions existed for easy exploitation of the working class.

At the time I was building the golf links of the Sierras Hotel in partnership with my brother Federico. We had a contract with the Land and Hotels Authorities. I was in charge of the construction and management of the project. I had experience in Misiones of working with timber yards and maté plantations and I was aware of how badly paid the workers were in general, as well as how insecure their social situation was. The men were poorly paid and, if they were taken ill, too bad – they could drop dead. If a man needed a rest, he had no pay while on holiday; if his wife was pregnant, she should be discouraged from having the child. The exploitation of the workers was not a situation that was exclusive to Misiones or Alta Gracia – it was the case throughout Argentina.

Resorting to strikes meant a beating and prison. This was the labour-market climate when I began to work in Alta Gracia, and it was then that Ernesto became aware of the injustices the workers suffered. He would compare their salaries to those who had the privilege of being employed by the golf club.

The majority of Ernesto's friends were the sons of miners, hired hands at the golf club, caddies or hotel waiters. He did have one or two friends from the middle classes who lived in the chalets of Villa Carlos Pellegrini.

I remember a family – the children were Ernesto's playmates – who lived all in one room: parents and six children. There was only one bed, and for covers they used old rags and newspapers.

This is how Ernesto discovered, at a very young age, how the poor lived and what few prospects they had of improving their lot. He had the opportunity of living among the destitute as well as among the wealthy, and he drew a lesson from it that he never forgot. It was in Alta Gracia that he learned from his friends what real misery is and was able to appreciate the injustices to which they were subjected by the official institutions that relegated them to a life of deprivation.

At home Ernesto lived in a household where all types of social problems were discussed. He was born listening to stories of the exploitation of the workforce by landowners in Chaco, Misiones, Córdoba and Buenos Aires, and he was in daily contact with human misery. But also, as luck would have it, he was in permanent contact with members of the 200 families that owned the country.

Villa Chichita and Villa Nydia

When we first arrived in Alta Gracia we stayed at the Hotel de la Gruta. After a lengthy stay we decided that we should look for a house so that the children had more room to play and we could settle down, as well as have more privacy. It was not difficult to find a house because Alta Gracia was going through a bad period, since the casino had been closed down and only people suffering from tuberculosis now came to live in the city.

My friend Fernando Peña found a house on the outskirts that seemed ideal for us. It was called Villa Chichita and it was the last house on the old road leading to the hills. A forest of wild shrubs grew around the house. Peña warned me that the house had been empty for many years because it had a ghost. Because of this superstition, I was able to live with my family in this house for two years paying a very low rent.

One night, as I was reading in bed, a strong tapping started that seemed to come from the kitchen, which was in the basement. The noise stopped and then started up again.

'This is the ghost,' I thought to myself, thinking that it must be a practical joke that Peña was playing on us. But I remembered our neighbours saying that they had heard a noise at dawn, as if someone was dragging chains. I jumped out of bed and grabbed my Smith & Wesson revolver. I went down to the kitchen and switched on the light. There was nobody there who could have made the noise. I went back to bed; the noise started again. I went back to the kitchen and switched on the light; again there was nobody there. I went back to my room and the noise started again. I went back to the kitchen and opened the door without switching on the light, and shut the door behind me. As soon as I had done so, the noise started again. I switched on the light and discovered that the noise came from two wooden lids that hung from two hinges. They were the access to the coal storage and they trembled when the wind blew and came in through the tiny kitchen windows, which had broken glass panes. The pressure on the lids made them shake and create the noise. If the kitchen door was open, there was no pressure so the lids did not rattle. It was a well-known fact that a wind from the north blew at midnight. So that was the mystery of the resident ghost!

Villa Chichita was a solid, well-built house and it was really dry. Because of this Ernesto, whose health had greatly improved during our stay at the Hotel de la Gruta, continued to enjoy better health than had been the case previously.

Our daughter Ana María was born in this house. The only disadvantage of Villa Chichita was that in winter it was really cold. It was too high and had too many doors and windows, which made it draughty. And it had no heating.

We left Villa Chichita for Villa Nydia, a large house surrounded by a hectare of land. It was a good house, but it was very run-down. We were going through a bad patch financially because it was difficult for me to find work locally and my maté plantation was in crisis, since the price of maté leaves had plummeted. My wife's *estancia* was enduring a lengthy period of drought.

However, at Villa Nydia our doors were permanently open to all-comers. In the afternoon the house would fill with children who ran through the dining room to go and play in the grounds at the back of the house. Members of the higher echelons of society had given the nickname 'Do as you please' to our home because of a film of that name that was very popular at the time. It was true that in our home everyone did as they pleased, provided family unity was preserved and the parents were addressed with respect. Rather than being a family home, Villa Nydia was like a youth club.

At teatime swarms of children would turn up: they were my children's friends. Although we were in financial straits, we never had to refuse anyone a meal. They all ate whatever there was and it was shared out among whoever turned up. This was true in the afternoons, but also at lunchtime. There was hardly a day when we did not have four or five 'guests'.

The group of children who turned up at Villa Nydia did not all come from the same social class; on the contrary, they were from very different origins a few came from the higher echelons of society, but there were also children whose families were so poor they did not even possess blankets for their beds.

They were my children's friends and there was no discrimination. They all sat at our table and were treated as equals, and this was something that made us really happy. My daughters, who mixed with the boys, were treated no differently and they jumped and ran and fought like Indians. We would allow our children to play in the back yard and preferred not to know what they were up to.

We knew that some of their games entailed a bit of danger, but we trusted that they would be able to negotiate it on their own.

Negrina

Negrina was a schnauzer-pinscher bitch. She had been given to us by a close friend of ours and had her papers in order: she came from a line of pedigree dogs.

She was only two or three months old when she joined us and was welcomed with joy by every member of the family. She had long, black, silky hair that fell over her eyes and her large ears covered the sides of her face. She had a bushy tail.

The younger children played with her all day long: they would pull her ears, curl her whiskers or roll over the floor with her. She grew up enjoying the wild life of my children. When she was fully grown she would accompany us everywhere. If we travelled in the car, the children always found a place for her, even if it meant travelling less comfortably. Negrina used to sleep at the foot of Ernesto's bed. But often, when my wife and I were not careful, she would curl up on our bed between the pillows and the headboard.

While we lived in Alta Gracia she would run after the children, who would throw sticks or golf balls for her to fetch. They were in charge of removing the ticks that she would pick up in the hair on her belly when she ran away to the golf club. Negrina knew all the children who used to visit, as well as our own. If she barked, it meant that a stranger was approaching.

The friend who had given us Negrina recommended that we find a dog of the same breed to pair her off with, for otherwise her pedigree would be lost. One day the bitch was on heat. Consequently all the dogs of the neighbourhood began to roam around our house, which was not far from the golf club where these dogs usually hung out. My wife wanted to 'marry her off' to the dog of a friend of hers of the same breed. Day after day Celia promised to take Negrina to meet the fiancé she had chosen for her, but she kept forgetting to do so.

The pack of dogs that surrounded our house grew larger by the day, and when I came home from work I had to chase them away by throwing stones at them. Fed up with this situation, I gave my wife an ultimatum. Either she took the bitch to her friend's place or I would let Negrina out of the house and she would encounter all the mongrels that were hanging around the house, in spite of my efforts to chase them away.

I came home one day and, as I opened the front door, Negrina ran towards me to greet me. My wife and children were all there. I opened the door wide, as I said I would, and let the bitch out. She disappeared into the open space in no time. I cannot help smiling when I recall the whole episode. My wife ran out to chase her in an attempt to save her from the marauding dogs. But Negrina had the advantage and, when my wife reached her, it was too late. The ugliest and most battered of the street dogs had covered her with one single jump.

My wife, in a fury, tried to split the dogs up while our children, led by Ernesto, were laughing their heads off. Celia managed to remove the bitch and take her to her friend's house. But some months later Negrina gave birth to nine puppies, which looked exactly like the mongrel that had first covered her.

Ernesto and Zacarías
One morning in Alta Gracia, Ernesto answered back when his mother reprimanded him. I was at my desk reading and got up to scold him. But my wife had already chased him out of the room. Ernesto, realising that he would get a good

spanking, darted out of the house. He jumped over some ditches that had been dug by municipal workers carrying out repairs in front of our house, and disappeared into the hills.

Celia's demands that he return immediately were useless; he was angry and would not listen. When my wife shouted that he should return home, he would shout back from the woodland that he would not.

At the time, the municipal workers were opening ditches and laying pipes to renew the drainage and sewage systems. The men were enjoying the incident and would tell my wife where Ernesto was hiding when she tried to reach him.

Celia could not catch him. Convinced of my physical fitness, I jumped over the ditches and ran after Ernesto right into the forest. To my surprise, whenever I caught a glimpse of him, he would disappear into the bushes.

Exhausted after several vain attempts to catch up with Ernesto, I saddled a horse and went after him. As soon as I saw him in a forest clearing trying to hide, I spurred my horse on and chased him. It was useless. He disappeared again. All I managed to do was tear my trousers, scratch my arms and legs against the thorns of the bushes and get more and more angry.

I had to accept that Ernesto had become a mountain animal and could run like a hare. The workers were having such fun watching the events that they were neglecting their work.

It was afternoon by now and I was beginning to worry. At that point, Zacarías arrived. He was a boy some fifteen years old, dark and skinny, who had become famous as a long-distance runner in the Córdoba marathon races. He had even competed in bigger events in Buenos Aires.

Zacarías was very poor. He earned a living selling *alfajores*. He would go out early in the morning with a basket full of them and return home in the evening. The financial situation of the people of Alta Gracia was such that not many could afford non-essential items. Only the rich could indulge themselves, and the majority of the inhabitants had to do without. Zacarías often went home with half his pastries unsold.

The pastries cost five cents each. They were not very expensive, but Zacarías knew that those who most appreciated his mother's cooking were the ones who could least afford it. He often gave some of the pastries to the starving children of his neighbourhood.

'Did you sell a lot today, Zacarías?' I asked him.

'Very little,' he replied, looking up with distrust.

'Would you like to earn five pesos?' Five pesos would have been the earnings from a full basket – that is, 100 *alfajores*.

'Of course I would,' he replied with inquisitive eyes.

I then told him that if he managed to catch Ernesto, who was hiding in the woodland, I would pay him five pesos. It was a deal. Zacarías, whistling happily, went into the bushes.

We had to wait for the results. I hid where I could see what was going on. An hour went by and Zacarías returned, sweating and panting and looking disconsolate.

'What happened?' I asked him.

He replied, 'I had almost caught up with him. I put the basket down and shouted that I was offering him an *alfajor*.'

Ernesto, a few metres away from him, replied, 'Throw it to me.'

But Zacarías insisted that Ernesto should come and get it. They negotiated for several minutes, then Zacarías decided to leave the basket behind and run after Ernesto.

'I ran as fast as I could,' he said, 'but whenever I caught up with him, he would run away, making fun of me.'

And that was how Zacarías had returned, with his basket on his arm, tired and demoralised and probably thinking that he had wasted his afternoon. Since he had not caught Ernesto he could not expect to be paid.

I paid him his five pesos and Zacarías ran off, his face lit up with delight.

I began to worry. It was almost dark and Ernesto, who was only nine years old, was still lost in the forest, which comprised at least 200 hectares of scrub. I did not know what to do, when my wife appeared and said, without showing any concern, 'I know him better than you. Don't attach too much importance to it. I am sure that tonight when he feels hungry he will come back.'

And that was exactly what happened. I went for a walk in the town and after dark I returned home. Celia came out to meet me and, while making a gesture that indicated all was fine, said, 'Ernesto came in through the back door, went to the kitchen and then hid in his bedroom. He is asleep now.'

This episode made me think. How could it be possible that Zacarías, a professional runner who was fifteen, could not catch up with my son who was only nine? I realised that Ernesto and his friends, who used to play together in the hills and go into the woodland, which they knew like the back of their hands, were not only extremely fit physically, but had also become adept at using the forest to escape and hide.

I do not know what Ernesto's friends of that period have done in life, whether they have forgotten how to hunt or how to follow a trail or how to hide in the bushes and ambush their opponents, but it is evident that this training put Ernesto in good stead when, as a guerrilla, he had to attack, hide and escape in the jungles and mountains where he chose to fight. Alta Gracia turned him into a real master of the forests and mountains.

The war between Paraguay and Bolivia

In our household we always discussed politics. Celia and I
talked about politics constantly with the many friends who
visited us at home.

At that time Latin America was shocked by the war that
had erupted between Paraguay and Bolivia. Between 1931
and 1934 Bolivia – encouraged by the United States' oil
companies, and full of arrogance because it had a powerful
army trained by General Kunt (one of the German military
commanders who had fought in the First World War) –
invaded the Chaco region of Paraguay with a vague excuse
and with the intention of annexing the region. The general's
strategy was not totally illogical and he nearly achieved his
aim.

Paraguay was very poor at the time and its army was ill
equipped. Bolivia had money from the US and advice from a
German general, and its troops were on top form. It was the
heroism of the stoic Paraguayan people alone that put an
end to the Bolivian invasion.

For Bolivia, this war had a double purpose. If it defeated
the Paraguayan army, it would force it to retreat as far as the
River Paraná and would then have managed to obtain the
coveted route to the sea using the river, as well as taking
over the Chaco region of Paraguay, an area rich in oil. Bolivia
would then be able to give the US companies the contract to
extract the oil.

The whole world was incensed at Bolivia's behaviour, and
so was I. Having lived in the Argentine territory of Misiones
on the border with Paraguay, I had many friends from that
country who lived on the Argentine side. I had learned to
love Paraguay and its people. I was so enraged by the
situation that I even considered taking up arms to fight on
the Paraguayan side.

Ernesto was a little boy at the time, but he followed with

real concern the events that so interested his parents. When he and his friends played war games, the war was the Paraguayan-Bolivian conflict.

We could only be on the side of Paraguay, as General Kunt represented the hated German military class, while the Paraguayan General Estigarribia, who led his country's troops, had fought against the Kaiser's forces with the French army in 1914. Everybody knew that behind the Bolivian aggression lay the might of American imperialism.

The war came to an end with the crushing defeat of the Bolivian forces by the Paraguayan people, who rose up in arms to defend their country. For once our hopes were not dashed, and at home we all celebrated the Paraguayan triumph against its mighty enemy.

The Spanish Civil War

When the civil war started in Spain, Ernesto was still a boy. At that time I had a close relationship with the Republicans. In Alta Gracia, as well as in other locations throughout the province of Córdoba and the Argentine Republic as a whole, committees to help the Spanish Republic were set up. We were convinced that the Spanish Republic was struggling against an imperialist coalition that supported General Franco, who had succeeded General Mola*, the head of the insurgents.

Britain was turning a blind eye, and the French went to the trouble of putting the Spanish Republican refugees – who crossed the frontier into France hoping to escape persecution – in deplorable concentration camps.

Italy and Germany helped Franco in various ways, since he wanted to install in Spain a Fascist dictatorship following the Mussolini* model.

The majority of Latin American countries included many supporters of the Spanish Republic, which also received assistance from the Soviet Union. The latter contributed fast hunter aircraft that fought fierce battles against the Messerschmitt of German manufacture, at the disposal of General Franco.

The committee we had founded in Alta Gracia to assist the Spanish Republic included many Socialists and liberals. We often joined forces with the committees of the provincial capital, Córdoba, and those of the national capital, Buenos Aires.

The Spanish doctor Juan González Aguilar was a personal friend of President Manuel Azaña*. He held the post of head of the Naval Health Service of his country. At the outset of the war he had sent his family to Argentina and they had settled in Alta Gracia, where they soon became close friends with those who were helping the Spanish Republic.

When the Republican resistance crumbled, Dr Aguilar crossed the frontier into France, where he was interned in a concentration camp. He then went into exile and came to Argentina. His home in Alta Gracia became a veritable Spanish Republican centre where the many exiles met.

We had made friends with the González Aguilar family and Ernesto became very close to their eldest children. It was at their home that he met many Republican combatants and that is why, although he was only a child, he supported the Spanish Republic with great enthusiasm. He never missed any of the rallies that were organised to obtain assistance for the Republic, and he followed the development of the war through the newspapers and other publications. Many liberal-minded people would also meet at our house in order to organise public gatherings to collect funds for the Republic.

Ernesto would cut out the news from the papers, and in his room he hung a huge map of Spain on which he followed the movement of the armies by pinning little flags on both fronts. He was of an impressionable age and I believe this was the beginning of his need to rebel and develop his combative character.

The Spanish exiles never imagined that the Franco government would last so long and, thinking that they would go back to Spain soon, developed an intense information campaign to that effect. It was in their company that Ernesto learned about the true reasons for that war. For him, the Spanish exiles were his brothers.

My brother-in-law Cayetano Córdova Iturburu had been sent to Spain by *Crítica*, an Argentine evening newspaper, as war correspondent to cover the conflict. During his year-long stay he sent all his articles to his wife, Carmen de la Serna, who at the time lived in our house in Alta Gracia. Not a week went by without news of Policho, as we had nick-named him. Carmen would read her husband's letters and then send them on to the newspaper in Buenos Aires. This was a precaution so that the articles were not stopped or censored by the authorities of those areas of Spain that had fallen to the enemies of the Republic.

Policho not only sent to his wife his articles for publication, but also newspapers that were printed and circulated by the Republican forces. I distinctly remember *Mono Azul*, to which many who were to become Spain's greatest poets and writers contributed. And some of them established themselves in Argentina as a result of the conflict. It was in *Mono Azul* that we read the poems of Rafael Alberti* for the first time, not long before we met him personally when he arrived in Argentina as an exile. By then Ernesto was already familiar with the new literature born of the trenches in Spain.

General Jurado
General Enrique Jurado, a Spanish Republican general, was

the hero of the battle of Guadalajara[3] in 1937 during the Spanish Civil War. He defeated the Italian troops under the command of the famous Italian General Mario Roatta. The Italian offensive ordered by Mussolini had the purpose of taking Madrid. It started on 8 March 1937 and, at the beginning, the Italians found very little resistance from Republican troops.

Encouraged by their initial success, they were celebrating their imminent entry into Madrid. Mussolini had already congratulated the Italian Fascist Brigades fighting in Spain, envisaging their total triumph as a foregone conclusion.

The command of the Republican army placed the then-Colonel Jurado at the head of the Fourth Army Corps, which had three divisions: the Lister Division, headed by Comandante Enrique Lister*; Division 12, commanded by Nino Nanetti*; and Division 14, under the orders of Cipriano Mera*.

The counter-offensive ordered by Jurado started on 12 March; on the 18th they counter-attacked on all fronts and defeated the Italian Fascist army, which retreated in disarray and disbanded.

General Jurado had arrived in the Argentine city of Córdoba, like so many other political exiles, and from there moved to Alta Gracia, where we lived at the time, in the hope of finding work. He had fought the entire war in Spain and, after the Republicans were defeated, he began, without losing his dignity, a new and arduous battle: the struggle for his livelihood in a foreign land. The General was unable to find work since at the time even Argentines found it

[3] Battle of Guadalajara: this battle (8–23 March 1937) saw the Spanish Popular Army defeat Italian and Nationalist forces attempting to encircle Madrid during the Spanish Civil War. It was a decisive Republican victory and boosted the morale of the troops of the Second Spanish Republic, who sustained 6,000 casualties, either dead or wounded, while Franco's forces suffered 2,500 dead, 4,000 wounded and 300 captured.

difficult to get employment. But he did not lose heart. After listening to many promises and waiting patiently in the anterooms of many executives, the poor General ended up working for an insurance company. He accepted his new position as an insurance broker with good humour. One day he said to me, 'I fought in the Spanish army since I was fourteen and I must have killed a lot of people; now, by a twist of fate, I am selling life insurance.' And he laughed at the irony of it.

We became very good friends and he told me many stories of the war in Spain. At the time Ernesto was about ten years old and he followed the stories of General Jurado entranced, and did not miss a detail.

The General was one of the people we had the honour of having round to supper often and, having understood the atmosphere of my home, he felt that he could discuss the Spanish Civil War with total candour. He was never the main character of his stories, and he told episodes of that struggle that were electrifying. He would only speak about himself when replying to questions, but he always stressed the fact that his successes were not personal, but due to the commitment of his subordinates. He gave the impression of being an unassuming bourgeois businessman rather than a man used to waging war. In Argentina we were accustomed to military men who followed the Prussian model, and although I did not see them at war, I could observe their stern attitude and their propensity to frown. General Jurado, on the other hand, seemed more like a civilian than a military man. He always smiled, spoke clearly and precisely and never bragged.

Ernesto could see the contrast, and I believe that he saw in General Jurado the model for a military man. He was full of admiration for him.

Once, over lunch, General Jurado told us how the battle of

Guadalajara had taken place. He told us of the reckless advance of the Italian Fascist forces, whose fanfares could be heard throughout the valley as they made their way to Madrid, imagining that the road was clear. He told us how his own militias, who had taken up their position on the summit of the hills surrounding the valley, allowed the enemy to advance. Then General Jurado ordered the attack. He described how the Republican soldiers came down the slopes, surprising the Italian brigades, who were trapped and surrounded. The result was their total defeat.

Then the General described how the Republican troops, in their eagerness to take prisoners, did not hear the orders from their superiors to halt, because a veteran brigade of Franco's Moors and Spanish Nationalists had arrived and were waiting for them. They shot at the Republican soldiers, who were climbing back up to the hills in pursuit of the defeated Italians and did not take cover.

We all listened to the General attentively, but Ernesto was mesmerised. We heard how, in that cruel war between brothers, both sides had shown great courage, and the General told the story without affectation or pretence.

It was not just General Jurado who told us about the Spanish Civil War. Many Republicans visited us at home and we met others in the homes of our friends, so we were able to hear many stories of that cruel struggle that shook Spain to the core. But it was General Jurado whom we saw frequently.

When I watched my young son Ernesto listening earnestly to General Jurado's stories, little did I imagine that he himself would one day command his own troops. I have often asked myself if the stories of this Spanish general turned out to be valuable lessons for Ernesto in his revolutionary struggles.

The motorcycle

I bought an old motorcycle for my sons Ernesto and Roberto. It had only one cylinder and it was really quite ancient. I took it home and explained to them how to ride it.

They knew that when I was in my teens I had indulged in all sorts of pirouettes on a motorcycle and that I also fancied myself as a racer. For me, it was the ideal sport and in my youth some friends and I used all our spare time to go on excursions on our motorcycles.

Once I was through explaining the theory to Ernesto and Roberto, I attempted to show them in practice what I had just described. I got on the motorcycle, started the engine and sped off with great confidence. But I had not noticed a pile of sand on the road. The front wheel got stuck and the motorcycle leaped forward. I flew into the air and ended up hitting my head on the pavement.

I shall never forget the laughter of all the boys who had come to take a lesson on how to ride a motorcycle. And the ones who laughed loudest were my sons. The episode became a joke, and each time I embarked on a theory they would remind me of the lesson on how to ride a motorcycle.

My fall was an experience for them and they were soon driving the contraption perfectly; with it they learned how to be in charge of the road as well as of the machine.

That small motorcycle gave Ernesto the opportunity to visit new areas, and some time later – when he was already a grown man – he had a small engine installed on his bicycle and went exploring the north of Argentina. He travelled more than 4,000 kilometres. It was the beginning of his curiosity for new horizons – a curiosity that never left him, and which later on he would complement with his scientific and social concerns.

That small motorcycle was no doubt the start of the

experiences that turned him into a master in the art of being on the road.

Instilling the will power to repress fear

From the time he was a small child, Ernesto felt deeply attracted to danger. He sought it and enjoyed overcoming it. He did this very often and had acquired real control over his nerves, which gave him great serenity so that he could act without hesitation.

His friend Alberto Granado* once told me that when Ernesto visited him in his house at Río Primero (near Alta Gracia in the province of Córdoba), they used to go out on walks with several friends and Ernesto would enjoy making them all very anxious.

There was a railway bridge over a stream. The bridge was more than twenty metres high. Ernesto used to balance himself on the ledge and would then hang on with his hands, with his legs above his head and his back to the abyss. Their friends would cover their eyes so as not to watch him falling and, if there were girls in the group, Ernesto would take even more risks and would exaggerate his prowess.

Not long ago Alberto Granado showed me a photograph of Ernesto in which he appears crossing a large ravine some forty metres above the ground, walking on a water pipe that was about forty centimetres in diameter. Although the pipe ran horizontally, it was extremely dangerous to walk on it because it was wet and slippery.

In Alta Gracia we used to bathe in the river basin below a rock face. A huge cliff about five metres high protruded from there, and the large rock faced the basin itself. Ernesto used to climb up the hillside, put his feet firmly on the ground and then, by means of a huge jump, he could cover the distance between the rock and the centre of the basin and would dive in head-first. Had he miscalculated or slipped, or entered the water at an angle, he would have had an accident. But he enjoyed overcoming such obstacles.

During the invasion of Cuba by the Rebel Army he had to face a variety of dangerous situations. Many anecdotes are told about him. I am going to tell you something that I heard from Joel Iglesias*, who is a *comandante* in the Cuban army today.

At the time of the story Joel was sixteen years old and had just joined the Rebel Army. He fought next to Che in many battles and had been made a captain. Che was very fond of him and always had him at his side.

The famous *comandante* Sánchez Mosquera, of Batista's army, was withdrawing with his troops from the heights, as they were being harassed by Che's men. When doing this, Sánchez Mosquera left behind a rearguard to cover his retreat. In these circumstances Che ordered Joel to harass the rearguard. Joel left with two rebel soldiers and ran into a small deforested area, which was surrounded by several large rocks. He was unable to see some men who were hidden in an ambush and who opened fire on him. They were Sánchez Mosquera's men.

Joel fell to the ground seriously wounded, having been hit by several bullets, and, in view of the surprise ambush, Joel's men took cover and started shooting back without seeing their enemy, who were behind the rocks. They were trying to prevent Mosquera's men from liquidating Joel, who was lying face-down, since to do so they would have had to abandon their protected position behind the rocks.

Che arrived, having been informed of the fall of his adjutant. He grasped the situation in a second and, without hesitation, decided what to do. There was no time to lose since, if he and his men withdrew, Joel would be killed. Che leaped out of the bushes and landed at the side of Joel. He had cleared several metres and was well within firing

range of the enemy soldiers. There was a moment of sus-
pense. Che's men were expecting to see heavy fire raining
down on him. But, to their amazement, they saw him
quickly lift up his wounded comrade, put him over his
shoulder and disappear into the woods. A second later the
soldiers' shots could be heard all over the jungle. But it was
too late.

Some hours later those very soldiers were taken prisoner
by the guerrillas. When asked why they had not shot at Che,
they said that his appearance was so unexpected – he had put
himself within reach of crossfire – that by the time they
recovered from their surprise, it was too late: there was
nothing they could do, for he was gone.

Acción Argentina

Not long after the defeat of the Spanish Republic, the war in
Europe began. Hitler's* doctrine represented a serious
danger to the countries of Latin America. In *Mein Kampf* the
Nazi dictator explained his thesis without reservation and
informed that Germany would conquer all the underdeveloped countries of Latin America.

The Argentine people were aware of Hitler's intentions,
but it was among the proletariat that resistance to Nazism
grew strongest. The proletariat placed itself without hesitation on the side of the Allies. They were not defending one
type of capitalism against another; they understood that
they were defending our country from falling under the boot
of German Nazi troops. The majority of the peoples of Latin
America understood the situation and rallied behind the
Allies.

The danger of an invasion grew daily in Argentina, and for
that reason Acción Argentina was founded by a group of
citizens from different political parties who shared
Nationalist anti-Fascist ideas.

In its declaration of intent, this organisation denounced attempts by foreign powers to invade the country and invited citizens to join forces and form groups to resist such attempts.

Hitler's government, with great foresight, had introduced Nazi cells in our country, which had been active clandestinely for some time in order to be in a position to surface at a given moment if the war reached our shores.

The German bombing of Guernica[4] was still fresh in the minds of the Argentine people. Those ruins pointed to Nazi imperialists as representing the gravest danger for the peoples of Latin America.

These were my thoughts, and those of the many people who also came forward, when I decided to join Acción Argentina to work for the Allies. I was put in charge of creating the committee of Acción Argentina in Alta Gracia. It grew quickly and became one of the most important committees of the organisation in the province of Córdoba.

Ernesto had started his 'revolutionary' activities when he was a mere child. He had supported the Spanish Republican government even before he fully understood why we should do so. When war broke out in Europe, Ernesto, who was still a child, joined Acción Argentina and went to work for the organisation immediately. All members had their identity cards, and his showed that he belonged to the youth section of the organisation. He would exhibit it with enormous pride.

Ernesto always listened to the discussions of the grown-ups within the organisation. The possibility of a Nazi invasion of Argentina and its consequences were discussed.

[4] Guernica: in 1937 the German air force bombed the town of Guernica in the Basque country, at the request of the Spanish Nationalist General Emilio Mola. The Republican government had granted autonomy to the Basques, and Guernica had become the capital of this independent region.

The young of the organisation went to work, and I would travel the hills of the province of Córdoba looking for evidence of Nazi infiltration. Ernesto used to come with me, and in spite of his tender years he participated enthusiastically in the investigation.

Many reports of possible Nazi infiltration in the province of Córdoba reached our organisation. They were beginning to constitute a serious danger. We were able to confirm that lorries had entered Argentina from Bolivia transporting weapons, and reached the valley of Calamuchita without the provincial government being aware of it. Coincidentally it was in that same valley that the ex-crew of the *Graf Spee* were training. The *Graf Spee* was a German pocket battleship, which, having caused great damage to the British merchant navy, had been scuttled by its own skipper off the coast of Montevideo, having fought a hard battle against the far superior forces of the British navy, during which it was rendered practically useless. Many members of the crew of the *Graf Spee* were interned by the Argentine government in the valley of Calamuchita. They were training with wooden batons in place of firearms.

Acción Argentina was able to check the reports alleging Nazi infiltration and found many of them to be true. I was able to verify that in the province of Córdoba next to every bridge there was a house inhabited by a German Nazi, who would stockpile dynamite under any pretext. We also discovered that a German photographer who was on the payroll of an Argentine so-called cultural fund had carried out an aerial photographic survey of the hills of Córdoba. I discovered stones in the valley of Calamuchita that had been painted white and indicated the reference points for the aerial survey. I also found out that in an isolated area of Calamuchita, on a flattened mound, a perfect access road had been built up to the top of the hill. Nobody was able to say who had built it or for what purpose, but the people of the region said that they had seen the swastika flying over the hill. The only possible explanation is that the Nazis intended to use the road to install long-range artillery, since from the hill one could see the entire valley of Calamuchita.

We also discovered that every night in a hotel in the vicinity of La Falda, in the hills of Córdoba, a powerful radio transmitter communicated with Berlin. A group of members of Acción Argentina travelled there to verify this report, and Ernesto was with us. He was twelve at the time. When we arrived we found the hotel under police protection. The provincial government knew nothing about this and ignored those allegedly 'innocent activities' without investigating them. Fortunately the national government under President Ortiz* followed up the investigation.

Concerned by the discoveries we had made, we informed the Central Committee of Acción Argentina in Buenos Aires. The National Chamber of Deputies of the Argentine Republic met in a secret session in January 1943 and drafted a report from the Commission for the Investigation of Un-Argentine Activities, which was not published.

This commission was presided over by Mr Juan Antonio Solari and was composed of several deputies of different political parties. The report made it very clear that some German outfits, under the guise of commercial firms or tourist organisations, were acting in our midst as commercial and military spies, carrying out activities that 'endangered the security of the State'. The Commission for the Investigation of Un-Argentine Activities concluded that:

The Information Office of the German Railways (RYD), an 'Office' headed by the Nazi agent Gottfried Sandstede, was mainly a front for Un-Argentine and

Un-American activities which were organised in con-
junction with the Central Organisation of Germans
Abroad (Auslands Organisation led by E.W. Bohle) and
with the leadership of the German National Socialist
Party in Berlin and the German Embassy in Argentina.

The Tourist Office was created as a cover and to hide the
espionage work being carried out by agent Gottfried
Sandstede – Press Attaché at the German Embassy in
Buenos Aires – and the advance of Nazi-Fascist penetration
in South America.

As a result of the report drafted by the commission, there
was an attempt to strip several 'attachés' at the German
Embassy in Buenos Aires of their diplomatic immunity. The
German government opposed this move, but Sandstede and
other officials left Argentina, having been invited by the
German government to travel to their own country, and the
Argentine government did not oppose it. The Argentine
government did not go any further than declaring the Nazi
Naval Attaché in Argentina *persona non grata*. He was one
of the most notorious German spies.

But all this did not undermine the activities of the Hitler
government in Argentina. The initial plan to occupy
Argentina militarily may have failed, but the work carried
out by the Nazis in our country came to fruition years later
all over Latin America.

It was evident that, at the time, Nazism had grown roots
in Argentina and that its adherents were able to work
without any hindrance. Unfortunately President Ortiz, who
had personally taken charge of the investigation into Nazi
activities, was forced to leave his post as he lost his eyesight
and was replaced by his Vice President, Dr Ramón Castillo*,
who was ousted by the military not much later, in 1942.
After several military strongmen held the position, General

Juan Domingo Perón* became president. Following the disappearance of Dr Ortiz from political circles and during the military governments, Nazis were able to operate in our country without interference.

Not long after the German army was defeated in Europe, many of the top Nazis arrived in our country and entered through the seaside resort of Villa Gessell, located south of Buenos Aires. They came in several German submarines and disembarked using rubber dinghies. The local inhabitants remember this event and have stated that the Nazis entered our country without anyone intercepting them. Some of them took up residence in Argentina, while others fled to Bolivia and Paraguay, where they were supported by the military governments of those countries and where some of them live to this day.

Ernesto not only heard about our activities at Acción Argentina, but he was also able to see the painted stones, the flattened hill, the houses of the Germans, the training with sticks and clubs and much else. All the time that he did not devote to his studies he spent with us.

My reason for describing all this, which today is past history, is not so much to attach importance to a frustrated plan of the Germany army, but rather to throw light on the development of Ernesto's character and the roots of his determination to fight for his ideals and for the defence of Latin America.

But also because today in 1977, in our continent, there has been a resurgence of Nazi-Fascism, which is supported by the colonialist capitalism that sustains dictatorial govern-ments, which are using the methods developed by the Italians and the Germans during the governments of Hitler and Mussolini. The United States' policies of direct inter-ference in Latin America, in order to avail itself of the natural resources of the underdeveloped countries of Latin

America over the last forty years, may have changed in
appearance, but not in depth. The United States needs the
natural resources of the Latin American continent in order
to continue to be the world's superpower – today more than
ever, in view of the military defeats it has suffered in Asia,
and the fear that these may repeat themselves in Africa and
the Middle East. The present scarcity of energy and proteins
is of great importance for this nation. The Latin American
continent possesses vast oil reserves and enormous mineral
wealth, as well as sufficient land to be able to become the
bread-basket of the world. These are valid reasons for the
United States to refuse to let go of its prey. Armed invasion
of underdeveloped countries is too risky today, as it could
elicit grave reactions from other world powers. The method
used will depend on which nation the United States wishes
to conquer. Generally, the first stage is that of peaceful
penetration: a flood of capital that replaces national capital,
ideological manipulation of the armed forces, corrupting the
politicians and trade unions. Having thus prepared the field
and after having produced economic chaos, it will then
instigate and support coups d'état so that power can fall into
the hands of the military, who have already sold themselves
to American imperialism.

The 'southern cone' of Latin America, already prepared
by the American intelligence service, has fallen into the
net of the United States. By mid-1977 the following
countries were governed by military men of Nazi-Fascist
ideology: Argentina, Brazil, Bolivia, Chile, Paraguay,
Uruguay, El Salvador, Ecuador, Guatemala, Nicaragua and
Honduras.

Haiti and Santo Domingo do not have military governments, but the men in power are backed by Nazi-Fascist
armies. And Peru is going in the same direction.

The fear of international Communism unites the military

jackals who are the Praetorian Guard of national and international capitalism.

But there is a minimum common denominator among all
these Nazi-Fascist military governments, and that is the
brutal repression of the people who attempt to rise against
them.

Once the armed forces reach power, massive and ruthless
repression begins and the military assumes the role of
torturers and uses the most sadistic methods imaginable,
the mere description of which would revolt normal human
beings. Thousands of people have gone through the torture
chambers and thousands of them have been assassinated.
There are thousands of people who have disappeared and
their corpses have never been found. Jails are full of political
prisoners accused of subversion, or simply detained 'at the
disposal of the authorities', and who are periodically
assassinated by applying the 'Law of Flight'.[5]

The lawyers who defend political prisoners who have not
been assassinated by the police force or the military have
had to leave their countries. Repression does not affect just
the opposition, but their families as well.

Forty years have gone by since the military defeat of Nazi-
Fascism in Europe, but it has not been eradicated.

In 1945 many of the leaders of National Socialism left
Germany. Some of them arrived in Argentina and its neighbouring countries. The seed they sowed is multiplying
throughout Latin America. The same United States that is
supporting Nazi-Fascist military governments in Latin
America was the nation that created the Nuremberg tribunals
and that jailed and executed Nazis for their war crimes.

What an incredible paradox: the nation that created the

---

[5] Law of Flight: the lynch law of Latin American justice is the law of flight,
which is supposed to empower police to shoot fleeing prisoners, but in practice often means that a prisoner is set free, then shot before he can get very far.

Nuremberg tribunals today supports governments whose crimes are far more sadistic and horrendous than those committed by the Nazi-Fascists in Europe.

Whenever there was a public meeting of Acción Argentina or an investigation was being carried out, Ernesto would accompany me. He was proud of his role within the youth of the organisation. One afternoon we were supposed to travel to the city of Córdoba to attend a meeting that would take place there. The highest national officers were meeting representatives of the provincial branches. I would be opening the public meeting at the central square.

But that morning Ernesto woke up with a violent asthma attack. All the medicine he took was useless. He was very upset because his mother did not want him to come with me, so he asked me to intervene so that she would relent. He did not want to miss an event at which I was speaking. I felt sorry for him and could not face leaving him behind, so we took with us all the usual medicines and left for Córdoba, taking him with us. Ernesto was happy. He would be complying with his obligations and would have a chance to listen to his father speaking in public.

This episode showed me two things: that Ernesto took his commitments seriously and that he was very fond of me.

We return to Córdoba

We had lived in the outskirts of Alta Gracia, where my children had got used to being out in the open, in contact with nature, running amongst the scrub that surrounded our home or in the rough hills nearby. They had nothing to envy the children who were born in the area.

We had many friends in that city and we were used to it, but as my son Ernesto had enrolled in the Deán Funes National College in the city of Córdoba and as my daughter Celia would be attending the girls' school there too, it

became necessary to move to that city to avoid the children
having to commute there by bus. On the other hand, I had
joined forces with a well-known local architect and had
rented offices in the centre of town, so for me too it became
heavy-going to have to travel daily to the city.

Once we decided to move to the city of Córdoba, I looked
for a house that was not in the centre of town, and the
location of which would enable my children to run around
at leisure. Nothing better for that than the house at 288
Chile Street. It was a new two-storey building, quite comfortable for the family, as it had a large living and dining
room on the ground floor and three bedrooms upstairs, as
well as a garage and a terrace.

We rented the house because it had great advantages: it
was next to a large park with enormous open spaces and
leafy trees. The Provincial Zoological Park was also situated
there, as well as some local sports clubs. For us, who came
from enjoying eleven years of sunshine, light and fresh air,
this meant that we would be able to continue to live out in
the open. And all this was only a distance of twenty blocks
from the centre of town.

We moved to the new house at the beginning of 1943 and
lived there for more than three years. Our son Juan Martín
was born in that house in May of the same year.

When we rented the house we did not notice something
that in time caused us some concern. The house had been
built on soil that was of very poor quality. It was unstable
when wet. In order to build on such land one had to reach
firm soil, and to do so you had to dig to a depth of more than
twenty metres. Because of this, the wall of the façade began
to slide away from its vertical position and became
separated from the floor of the first floor where the terrace
was situated, opening up a deep crack.

Our bedroom faced the façade. I remember that from our

bed, at night, I could see the stars through the crack in the ceiling. I pulled Juan Martín's cot away from the front wall, but left our bed in its place. The other children's rooms also had a crack, and I took the precaution of separating their beds from the wall for fear that it might collapse.

As we found the house so comfortable, we did not want to move and decided to put up with it as long as we could.

The grounds facing our house were in even worse condition. A large basin had formed there from the rainwater, and year after year it grew deeper. As those grounds were not fit for construction, they were considered to have no owner and therefore a population of extremely poor people began to settle there. It was a veritable shanty town with precarious constructions made from planks, tin and cardboard, without water or electricity.

The neighbourhood had several houses and chalets of good quality side-by-side with cheap housing that was on the point of collapse, and across the road there was a population of very poor people who lived in real hovels; such was the neighbourhood of our house in Chile Street.

The Lawn Tennis Club of Córdoba was opening in the park next to our home. We joined this club and my children, besides playing tennis, could swim in the pool, play ping-pong and meet their friends. Both Roberto and Ernesto became good tennis players. The man in charge of keeping the courts in good repair had a daughter who was just a little older than Ernesto. She would spend the day practising her favourite sport and, as she had become good friends with my boys, she would play with them. She soon became the ladies' champion for the province of Córdoba and later took part in national and international tournaments. Both Ernesto and Roberto learned how to play from her and thus both became good players.

The brothers Alberto, Tomás and Gregorio Granado (a

group who were inseparable from my son Ernesto) played rugby for a new team called Platense. They rarely managed to get together the fourteen players required to form a rugby team, but that did not concern them too much; they liked the sport and practised it as they could and really enjoyed themselves, and my son Roberto joined in occasionally. When we lived in Alta Gracia my two boys played football with teams of 'strays', turning any ground into a football pitch, but now they afforded themselves the luxury of playing rugby in their own grounds.

Even if one could not call it 'the house of the people' – as the one in Alta Gracia had been labelled – Chile Street had a friendly and popular atmosphere that almost matched it. Friends of the children who studied at the Deán Funes National College, friends from their sports activities and some of the inhabitants of the nearby shanty town all turned up at our house without warning.

The González Aguilar family, neighbours of ours in Alta Gracia, had also moved to the city of Córdoba and were not far from us. Carmen, Paco and Juan González Aguilar were close friends with Ernesto, Celia and Roberto. Pepe González Aguilar and my daughter Ana María were inseparable, so that the friendships that had blossomed in Alta Gracia continued in Córdoba. When the González Aguilar family were not in our house, our children were in theirs.

Ernesto was becoming a grown man. His natural inclination to study and read continued to develop. By now his own library was growing with the addition of serious books, and he always found time to be on his own in order to concentrate on his books. He had a rare quality that was a trait of his personality: an enjoyment of reading and studying, to which he devoted a lot of time; but these did not prevent him from practising sports, or from playing chess as he always had, or from meeting up with his friends or going on outings and excursions. He was a real magician when it came to making use of time. I often thought: where does he find the time to do all these things? And as he grew older his knowledge increased, but he never neglected any of the other things he loved doing.

Ernesto and his circle of friends
Our house in Chile Street continued to open its doors to the friends of my children, just like the one in Alta Gracia had always done. Ernesto, as usual, was the centre of all the gatherings. With his traditional loyalty he never dropped any of his friends in favour of those from a better social background. He always had the capacity to bond with the heterogeneous group who surrounded him, without ever making anyone feel overpowered by his presence.

When Ernesto began to frequent other social circles, he also started to enjoy the parties where young men and women danced or listened to music or chatted. He did not enjoy large social gatherings, as he was rather reserved; he only became more open when he was with his group of close friends. However, little by little he got used to this type of party. He did not care for music and was a very poor dancer, but when it came to mixing with intelligent and knowledge-able people, he mingled with them and showed how well read and cultivated he was.

In summer, when there was no school, we left the house in Chile Street and rented a house in Alta Gracia for the season, and there Ernesto could see his old friends again. I remember the Ripamonti house that we rented in Alta Gracia. The gatherings of old took place again in this house – only now the children had become grown-ups and their personalities were beginning to be defined.

I had bought a weekend house in a place called Villa Allende, very near its golf club. Villa Allende was one of the favourite places of the people of Córdoba for the summer holidays or weekends. Its main attraction was the golf club. As Ernesto had begun to practise this sport when he was just six years old, by the age of fifteen he was already a good player. At the club in Alta Gracia he could practise as much as he wished because he would do so at times when nobody was playing. At Villa Allende he could show off his skill in front of good players. He loved the sport.

Not long before we returned to Buenos Aires we rented a rustic hut – which looked like a dump – over two consecutive summers in the Córdoba hills at a wild area called Pantanillo. It had just two rooms with a zinc roof over them and it was near a stream. One could only reach it on horseback or on foot, the terrain was so rough. My sister-in-law Carmen de la Serna and her husband, the poet Cayetano Córdova Iturburu, also rented a little house very near ours, but hers was much more comfortable. Many artists and writers visited Carmen's house and she hosted numerous interesting gatherings. I have read somewhere that the great Argentine writer Ernesto Sábato* had corresponded with the man now known throughout the world as Che Guevara. Sábato was one of the many writers who visited the Córdova Iturburus in Pantanillo and that is where he met my son Ernesto.

In 1950, at the González Aguilars' daughter Carmen's wedding, Ernesto met a girl from Córdoba called Chichina Ferreyra. She was very pretty and charming and particularly graceful. As soon as they met they fell in love. All their friends thought their flirtation would lead to an engagement and that the engagement would end in marriage. As was normal, Ernesto began to visit the Ferreyra family, in whose house people from high society in Córdoba met, in sharp contrast to Ernesto, who continued to wear his unironed trousers and generally did not wear a jacket or a tie.

At weekends, Chichina met up with her friends in a

lovely place in the country called Malagueño, where her family owned a large quarry as well as some sumptuous houses. As was to be expected, Ernesto's presence did not please her parents when they realised that there was something more than friendship between Chichina and Ernesto. Ernesto continued to visit Chichina without taking into account the opinion of her parents, and he dressed as he always had and expressed his views, which were not in keeping with those of Chichina's family, who were used to a life of privilege and luxury. However, some members of the family saw his worth and became his friends.

Our family, who was really fond of Chichina, did not think that she was the right person to marry Ernesto. She had been educated in a totally different way from the way we had brought up our children and I could see that, if they got married, it would be very difficult for it to work, since for Chichina it would represent a sharp contrast with her own upbringing.

We left the city of Córdoba in 1947 and moved to the city of Buenos Aires, where we went to live with my mother. Córdoba, where Ernesto's girlfriend lived, was 700 kilometres away, but Ernesto would travel north whenever he could to meet up with Chichina. This lasted until 1952. At the beginning of that year Ernesto informed her of his imminent trip through Latin America with Alberto Granado. As was to be expected, Chichina did not relish the idea of the separation and, when Ernesto came home from that trip after nine months of travel, she was engaged to someone else.

Rugby

Ernesto loved playing rugby. When we lived in Chile Street in Córdoba, he and his brother Roberto and his friend Alberto Granado started playing for a club called Estudiantes. The club's field was rudimentary.

I remember that the three of them used to practise their tackles on the paved patio of our house in Chile Street, where they took some serious knocks on the hard ground. According to his friends, Ernesto was a very gifted rugby player and his tackle would demolish his opponents.

In Córdoba at the time there was only one rugby club and they rarely managed to put together the right number of players for a proper match.

When Ernesto returned to Buenos Aires, I enrolled him and Roberto as members of the SIC (San Isidro Club), of which I was a founder member. It was there that they began to play rugby seriously and regularly.

I was concerned that Ernesto – who continued to suffer from asthma attacks regularly – should have chosen that violent sport, but my complaints fell on deaf ears. He was stubborn and he loved playing rugby and continued to do so in spite of his affliction.

During matches, he always managed to recruit a friend, who would run along the line with his inhaler and hand it over to Ernesto when he asked for it. If he felt seriously out of breath, he would ask the referee's permission to stop for a moment and use the inhaler, and then carry on playing.

His doctor had told me that Ernesto should not be playing rugby as it was seriously detrimental to his health. The doctor said that his heart would not be able to endure it. When I said this to Ernesto, he replied, 'I like playing rugby and I will continue to do so even if it kills me.'

In view of his reaction I decided to use a different tactic. My brother-in-law Martínez Castro was the president of the club, so I asked him to remove Ernesto from the team. My brother-in-law obliged. Ernesto was furious, but he simply joined the neighbouring club Atalaya and continued to play rugby wearing different colours.

Ernesto, Roberto and their fellow players used to edit a

rugby magazine called *Tackle*, using my study as their office. They all wrote articles, which they signed with pseudonyms. Ernesto's was Chang-Cho, which he thought sounded Chinese, but was in fact a variation of the nickname Chancho that some of his friends had given him.

Ernesto's friendship with Carlos Figueroa

Carlos Figueroa and Ernesto had met in Alta Gracia when we lived there. Carlos used to spend the summers in Alta Gracia in a house that his parents owned, next to ours. Their friendship continued when Ernesto moved to Buenos Aires, where Carlos lived for the rest of the year.

In 1949 Carlos and Ernesto decided that they would travel to Córdoba. They had no money and knew that they would have to hitch-hike all the way and stop anywhere for the night. They often bummed hospitality from some casual friend, or slept in an abandoned railway carriage or out in the open. The important thing was to make progress towards their final destination.

After spending some time on the side of the road attempting to hitch a ride, a lorry stopped. The driver said he would take them, without asking them for any money, on condition that, when they arrived in Rosario, they helped him to dismantle the top of the vehicle, which was too high to drive under a bridge in the outskirts of the city. He also said that he would pay them for their help and feed them. It was a deal beyond their wildest dreams.

The three of them drove to the outskirts of Rosario and dismantled the trailer header. The operation took up to five hours and, when they had completed it, the driver kept his word. He paid them their wages and then invited them to a copious lunch at a roadside restaurant.

The next time that Carlos and Ernesto decided to travel to Córdoba they were not so lucky. They arrived in Rosario without a cent. They had not had a decent meal for some time and wanted to 'refuel' before continuing on to Córdoba.

They were wondering what to do when a man went by pushing a cart. They were in the outskirts of the city and the man was a fruit vendor of Italian origin. Carlos and Ernesto chatted him up and persuaded him to let them sell the fruit for him for a percentage of the profits.

Carlos was a law student and Ernesto was reading medicine, but they cheerfully learned a new skill. They set off with the cart and shouted at the top of their voices, putting their hands to their mouths to project the sound: 'Pineapples, fresh pineapples, we have pineapples.'

The vendor, who did not trust them at all, would follow from a distance and take cover behind some trees, pretending that he was not really observing them.

The boys soon sold the whole load. The vendor was overjoyed, and they in turn had some money in their pockets to buy themselves a meal. They bade the Italian farewell and went on their way.

According to Carlos, Ernesto was the most generous person in the world. Once, when they were both broke, Carlos told Ernesto that he had a debt of honour and would be in real trouble if he did not pay it. Ernesto went to get his savings book and gave Carlos all he had, saying, 'Here are all my funds. If you can return them, fine. If not, too bad.'

Another time Carlos knew that Ernesto loved playing golf, so he offered to sell him a battered golf club that had belonged to one of his old aunts. It was ancient and Ernesto paid him five pesos for it. Unfortunately Carlos' aunts discovered that the club was missing and demanded its immediate return. They would not budge, so Carlos was forced to confess to Ernesto that he had actually taken it without permission.

Ernesto was philosophical about it. He returned the golf

club, although he knew he would never see his five pesos again.

By the beginning of 1947 almost all my family were in Buenos Aires. Ernesto, on the other hand, was still employed by the Córdoba Provincial Roads Directorate in the department of analysis of materials. Later on he was promoted to foreman.

Letter from Ernesto from the province of Córdoba

This letter was written by hand. It does not say the year, but it was 1947.

21 January

My dear Viejo,

I got your bank transfer the other day and it came in very handy. I had not replied until now because my situation was still unresolved. The die is cast and they have now sent me to Villa María. What I do like is that I will now have to work as foreman/manager and I am going to make use of the time there to try and get a promotion. For the moment I will have a lot of work because the employee who worked in the lab was a first-class vagrant and I will have to carry out the overdue tests corresponding to ten kilometres of road, but after some ten days of work I hope to be able to improve my situation and have time to study.

I am awaiting news from Osvaldo Payer,[6] who travelled to Uruguay to obtain the exam syllabus. If it's

---

[6] Osvaldo Payer: a fellow student who travelled to Uruguay to bring back the syllabus, to see if they could study without attending classes and simply turn up for the exams (which you could not do in Argentina, where it was required that you attend some lectures). At the time Ernesto was considering a career in engineering, and the degree obtained in Uruguay would have been similar.

possible to sit the exams without attending classes I'll stay here for the whole winter, since I reckon I would be saving between 80 and 100 pesos per month. I have a salary of 200 pesos and lodgings, so my expenses are food and buying books to keep myself amused. My address is Vélez Sarsfield . . . Villa María.

I am some ten blocks from town.

Ciao and love from

Ernesto

He enjoyed his job in spite of the fact that his employers kept relocating him. They did so because the engineers who directed the works trusted him. He was even contemplating studying at the University of Córdoba, which gave us the impression that he intended to stay there for some time. However, he was not sure which career he would pursue. His friend Tomás Granado, Alberto's younger brother, who was his colleague at the Roads Directorate, had just enrolled in the Faculty of Engineering in Córdoba.

But at the beginning of 1947 Ernesto left his job and returned to Buenos Aires because my mother was very ill. He did not return to Córdoba, and one day he informed us that he would be studying medicine. I believe that his decision had a lot to do with his grandmother's illness. He looked after her without leaving her bedside for seventeen days when her illness was in its most critical phase.

As soon as he enrolled in the Faculty of Medicine of the University of Buenos Aires, he went out to look for a job. I found him a post through a close friend of mine in Buenos Aires Town Council's Supplies Division. He now had the means to support himself while studying. Later on he worked for the same town council, inoculating animals.

In spite of all his occupations, Ernesto managed to study medicine and in 1948 he sat his first exam. Later that same year he passed two more subjects. In 1949 he passed three more, and in 1950 another three. In 1950 he also joined the National Merchant Fleet as a male nurse. This new job enabled him to travel to Brazil, Venezuela and Trinidad by sea.

Around that time he met Dr Salvador Pisani, who specialised in allergies. Ernesto had initially met him as a patient because of his asthma. He experienced a marked improvement as a result of the treatment Dr Pisani devised for him, but the doctor also saw Ernesto's potential as a scientist and offered him a job in his laboratory.

Dr Pisani was beginning to be well known in Argentina as a specialist in cures for diseases caused by allergies. His theory was that people with allergies could be desensitised by means of injections that he prepared in his own laboratory and which included semi-digested foodstuffs. His theory was beginning to be discussed by scientists outside Argentina.

Ernesto had started to work with Dr Pisani in his clinic, where different anti-allergenic treatments and vaccinations were being tested. It was at Dr Pisani's side that Ernesto carried out scientific studies in relation to allergies, which he then continued in Mexico.

Ernesto had the greatest respect for Dr Pisani and believed that he was a talented scientist as well as an honourable professional. He devoted all his free time to working in Dr Pisani's laboratory.

Once, when Dr Pisani had received a modern electric apparatus made in Sweden to grind entrails, Ernesto decided to try it out. He collected from the Faculty of Medicine some entrails that had belonged to people who had died of infectious diseases, and prepared to use the new equipment. But the apparatus had arrived incomplete. There was a rubber cap missing – its function was to prevent the infected minced particles from coming into contact with the operator. Ernesto was impatient and did not want to wait until the cap was sent from Europe, as he already had the entrails in the laboratory. He decided to go ahead and try the equipment. The result was disastrous for him.

Two days later he had a very high temperature. I arrived home and found him in bed. He never went to bed unless he was feeling very ill. I stopped by and we chatted for a few minutes. Ernesto told me about the entrails, and I became very alarmed. I stayed on in his bedroom observing him and could see how his condition was worsening. I said that I would call Dr Pisani, and Ernesto asked me not to. I waited for a while by his side; he soon gestured to me to call a clinic and ask for a heart stimulant and to call Dr Pisani. I now knew that he was seriously ill. I rang the nearest clinic and asked them to send a nurse with the stimulant that Ernesto had asked for. I then rang Dr Pisani. 'I am on my way,' he said.

I stayed put and continued to observe Ernesto. His breathing was agitated and he had a high fever, but what most concerned me was the expression on his face, because you could tell that his heart was failing. I was never able to find out how high his temperature was, because he did not allow me to look at the thermometer. This episode was the result of Ernesto's imprudence.

A few minutes later a fat nurse came up the stairs. She was dressed in white and carried a syringe in her hands. Behind her Dr Pisani was climbing the stairs three steps at a time. Once in Ernesto's bedroom, Dr Pisani took the syringe and placed it on the table. He listened to Ernesto's chest. The nurse left and Dr Pisani remained in charge. He and Ernesto talked for a long time and several hours later the doctor left. His orders were that Ernesto should take some medicines that he had prescribed for him and have complete rest.

The whole family was up all night. By about six in the morning Ernesto had got much better and, to our extreme amazement, we saw that he had got up and begun to get dressed. I knew how stubborn he was, so I said nothing, but when I saw that he was putting on his jacket as if getting ready to leave the house, I asked him what he was doing.

'I am going to sit an exam. The examiners will be there by eight.'

'Don't be such a fool,' I replied. 'Can't you see that you are not fit?'

But it was useless to argue with Ernesto. He had decided that he would sit his examination that day and he was going to do it. And so he did.

It was November 1952. Ernesto had decided that he would finish his studies before March 1953. He had already planned to go on his second extended trip through Latin America in July and still had several exams to sit.

When he returned from his first trip around Latin America with Alberto Granado in August 1952, he had only fifteen subjects left to take before he could graduate, and he was preparing those when he caught the infection at Dr Pisani's laboratory.

This story reveals Ernesto's will power. When he had decided to do something, he had the tenacity to carry on, no matter what obstacles and hurdles he had to overcome.

The insecticide factory

When we lived at 2180 Aráoz Street, the house had a small garage. Ernesto had discovered a product called *gamexane*. At the time the Ministry of Agriculture used it against locust plagues as it had proved to be an excellent insecticide. Ernesto carried out some tests, with extremely good results. He decided to market a product that was 20 per cent *gamexane* and 80 per cent talcum powder, and used our small garage as his factory.

He needed a name for his product. When we all met round the dinner table we made our suggestions, and between much joking and leg-pulling he decided it would be called Attila. But when he went to patent the brand name he was told that name had already been patented. So he went for the name Vendaval – that is, windstorm.

As he embarked on his business I offered to introduce him to friends of mine who might finance it, since I had verified the efficiency of his product, but he did not wish to meet anyone and wanted to do it on his own. He said he would not allow any of my friends to take over his business. He did not realise that he would need some capital, as well as time to devote to his new enterprise. At the time he was studying as well as working at Dr Pisani's clinic.

He bought a large amount of talcum powder and *gamexane* and ordered some containers. These were little round boxes, which each contained 100 grams of the mixture. The product was tried out in our neighbourhood and the results were deemed to be excellent. The little round boxes left the garage very quickly and went to supply his clients. The next step was to manufacture large amounts of the product, so Ernesto began to look for someone who could help him.

He was working at the time at a hospital using Dr Pisani's method for allergies. A Paraguayan patient who had severe eczema that covered almost all his body had been entrusted to Ernesto, who had almost completely cured him. The patient was so grateful that he was willing to join Ernesto in the manufacture of Vendaval.

Gamexane has a strong, unpleasant smell. The two of them worked in that small garage covered in white powder. The revolting smell was now all over the house and even our food tasted of it, but Ernesto continued to manufacture his insecticide, unperturbed.

The business did not last long. Ernesto was poisoned due to working in such conditions, and his friend lasted even less time. And that was the end of the project. Today many firms that deal in chemical products use *gamexane* as an insecticide, but it was Ernesto who originally discovered its wider uses. Prior to his experiment *gamexane* had only been used to combat locusts.

Ernesto at the Faculty of Medicine

Ernesto had to take an oral test. The examiners had been at work since seven in the morning, and although it was after midday, the professors continued to examine the students.

Ernesto had sat down at a marble table and produced a penknife and started to peel an orange. The president of the board of examiners noticed him and, annoyed by this lack of etiquette, said to him: 'It seems the gentleman is hungry!'

'Yes, Doctor, we have been here since seven in the morning, I have not had breakfast and I am very hungry. That is why I am eating an orange.'

'Ah, the gentleman is in a hurry. I will call him first.'

Ernesto's friends and fellow students thought the professor would suspend him. Ernesto simply went on eating his orange. Word had got round and many students had come to watch the scene. Ernesto was called. The examiners began asking their questions and Ernesto gave his replies. He was doing really well.

The chairman of the board of examiners asked more questions and Ernesto continued to reply with aplomb and fluency. Some questions were trick ones and others were really difficult. More than an hour and a half went by. The board only devoted so much time to those students it intended to fail. But Ernesto resisted the onslaught and continued to give the correct answers. The professor realised he was in front of a brilliant student, so he got up and shook Ernesto's hand, saying: 'Doctor' – by which he implied that Ernesto would graduate – 'I can only give you a distinction.' Thus admitting that he had tried to suspend Ernesto. The exchange had been more a duel than an examination.

Adalberto Larumbe was Ernesto's friend and fellow student at the Faculty of Medicine. They often studied together at home. Once when they were studying anatomy, Larumbe had persuaded one of the assistants to allow them to remove part of a corpse from the morgue of the faculty to be able to study it at home. But once he had been given permission to take a human leg home, Larumbe realised that he could not carry it with him on public transport. Ernesto said that he would take it, so he collected the leg and, wrapping it up in newspaper, left for his friend's home. He took the underground to get there. Apparently, the leg was not properly wrapped up and the toes started to appear between the newspaper sheets. Ernesto arrived at Larumbe's place laughing his head off. He had managed to shock the rest of the passengers on the train without uttering a word.

Ernesto sells shoes
One afternoon his close friend Carlos Figueroa came to offer Ernesto a business deal. He brought with him a cutting from a newspaper that did not have a high circulation. It mentioned a remote address where shoes would be auctioned.

This was, according to Carlos, a great opportunity. Nobody would turn up at that auction and they would be able to buy several lots of shoes for very little money. It was not a bad idea. So off they went with the little money they had managed to put together between them.

Of course the first lots went for an amount of money they did not have. Towards the end of the auction all there was left was a lot consisting of several bags of unmatched shoes. So they bought it for very little money.

Our house in Aráoz Street became a shoe shop. The shoes had to be classified and paired off. Very few shoes had a matching one. Some of them could be paired off because the differences were minimal, but there were many that remained unmatched.

Carlos and Ernesto left with their merchandise. As they sold the shoes for very little, they soon managed to get rid of those pairs that were a near-match. But now the real difficulty began. They were left with single shoes that bore no resemblance to each other. But they were not disheartened.

I cannot remember which of the two had the idea, but they approached a man who lived round the corner who had lost his left leg and offered him a single right-foot shoe. He was delighted to buy it. So off they went to find other men who had lost a leg. They managed to place most of the shoes. The remaining ones, which were totally different in colour and shape, were worn by Ernesto.

Playing chess

I taught Ernesto the first moves in chess when he was very young. I remember that I would let him win and he would be furious. He kept saying that was not how he wanted to play. Little by little he learned how to play and, when he was studying medicine, he played with good players. I am in no position to judge him as a chess player because I am not at all good, in spite of having played a lot too.

I know that in Cuba he played against great players. Miguel Najdorf*, the Argentine champion, told me in 1962 that Ernesto was a first-class player. Later on, he gave an interview to a Buenos Aires newspaper in which he said that Che had a chess library of more than 500 volumes.

When he was asked how Che played, Najdorf replied that

he preferred an aggressive game and liked sacrifices, but he prepared them well and that is why Najdorf rated Che a first-class player. Najdorf also said that he had been invited to play ten matches simultaneously at a chess club in Cuba. Several members of the government participated, including Che.

'With Che I played well and offered him a draw,' Najdorf said. 'He rejected the offer, saying, "When I was a student of medicine in Buenos Aires I lost against you at a display in which you played fifteen boards simultaneously at the Provincial Hotel in Mar del Plata. Now I prefer to lose or to ask for a return match." I accepted the invitation to fight it out, but the match ended in a draw.'

Part Four:

Argentine travel diaries, 1950

I owe it to chance, to pure luck, that I recovered these diaries by my son Ernesto, which had been condemned to water and fire.

At the time [1972] I lived in Buenos Aires, in an apartment in Arenales Street. The city had just endured heavy storms and floods, and the basement of the building where I lived had not escaped the avalanche of water. My elder sister Beatriz, who lived with us and was bed-ridden, suffering from paralysis of the legs, called me to tell me that the concierge of our block of flats was about to burn in the boiler all the junk, objects, furniture and papers that had accumulated through the years and which the water had destroyed, and he needed our approval to do so. Without any idea of exactly what my sister kept there, I went down to the basement. Manolo, the concierge, was standing in the water, which covered his ankles, and, with the boiler on, was throwing into the fire all the damaged objects that our neighbours were indicating. As soon as he saw me arrive, he pointed to a couple of trunks on one side and said: 'Don Ernesto, your sister Hercilia was here and she went through the things and told me to burn everything. I waited until you came before doing it.' Dear old Manolo! He knew my younger sister well and was aware that she always got rid of everything. Among old clothes, letters, dried flowers, photos, newspaper cuttings, shoes, lace and a thousand absurd objects accumulated by Beatriz, I found a good number of books that I recognised as belonging to Ernesto, because of the subjects they dealt with. Intrigued, I poked into that crazy mixture and it was then that I found the notebooks with my son Ernesto's handwriting. I started going through them. The worn covers showed that they were well travelled.

These were Ernesto's travel diaries and he had written in pencil. The diaries had evidently accompanied him during the journey he was describing. I picked up these unexpected treasures saved from water and fire, overcome with emotion, and took them upstairs. The continuous friction between the pages had deteriorated the contents and it was almost impossible to read them – but I decided that I would save the contents of these diaries from oblivion. This arduous task took me several months and, although I have not been able to decipher every single word, what I missed was minimal.

How had these notebooks ended up in the trunk of forgotten objects? My sister Beatriz, who was like a second mother to my son, was the recipient of all that Ernestito, as she used to call him, wanted her to keep for him. So many books, papers, letters and newspapers must have proved too much for her at some point and she decided to send them all down to the basement. As she was over eighty years old and suffered from memory loss, she forgot the whole episode. She knew some of the details of Ernesto's travels, but she did not remember these diaries. In the letters Ernesto sent us he used to include stories and anecdotes, but now these pages spoke to me about his life, his adventures, his emotions, the way in which he captured what he saw, as well as the way in which he tackled the problems he faced while travelling. His handwriting, which I know so well, seems illegible to those who are not in the habit of deciphering it. The letters run into each other, entire words are sometimes left out and the writing is often unsteady; it reveals his passionate and emotional nature. I am used to studying personality through handwriting. In the case of my son, this labour saddens me and it becomes a painful task that evokes the past and each line reminds me of him.

In any case, I have been able to save these fascinating notes, whose main interest resides in the fact that this is when Ernesto began to note down his thoughts and observations in a diary, a habit that he kept up throughout his life. He was young then, and after this first trip within Argentina he made many more across America and always kept travel diaries, which clearly show the evolution of his thought and the direct style in which he wrote. One could say that these first writings are his initial attempt at literary essays.

Before transcribing the diary that takes Ernesto from Buenos Aires to the northern provinces, I want to give you an outline of the route that he travelled.[1] He left the capital and took the road that cuts across the province of Buenos Aires – without any doubt the richest of the Argentine provinces – and then crossed to the south of the province of Santa Fe. Both provinces share similar aspects: they cover huge areas devoted to agriculture where maize, wheat, sunflower, linseed, alfalfa and other crops are grown and where livestock is reared as well. The landscape is rather monotonous, with extensive areas covered by green and humid grasslands and some isolated trees. When one

---

[1] The route that he travelled: it appears that Ernesto arrived in Córdoba at the home of the Granado family (parents of Tomás, Gregorio and Alberto) and from there visited the González Aguilar home, where his sister Ana María was staying. He then travelled on with Tomasito and Grego. Alberto Granado was a pharmacist in San Francisco del Chañar, where they visited him.

reaches the province of Córdoba, the physical landscape begins to change; the further north one goes, the drier the earth and the scarcer the vegetation. Near the city of Córdoba one can feel the proximity of the blue hills against the limpid sky. The city was built in the valley of the River Primero. The foothills begin on the outskirts of the city; the hills, no higher than 2,800 metres, run from north to south and their names are the Sierras Grandes and Sierras Chicas. The main chain joins the hills of La Rioja, which in turn join the foothills of the Andean range, where there are peaks up to 7,000 metres high. These mountains reach into the northern provinces of Catamarca, Salta and Jujuy. The province of Santiago del Estero is characterised by its huge salt mines, its sandy swamps and the forests of the northern area; it has a torrid temperature in summer, and the lack of water is felt almost everywhere. The province of Tucumán is in the centre of the country and is crossed by streams, rivers, forests and mountains up to 3,000 metres high. I believe few cyclists can have travelled on their own along these peaks using such precarious means of transport. Ernesto's bicycle had a Micron motor attached to it, but it was still more a bicycle than a motorcycle and the foothills of the Andean range required a strong car or lorry engine in order to cross them.

The notebooks that Ernesto left with us end with a meeting with lorry drivers and the bet he makes with them. I am almost certain that he wrote others, but since I never found those corresponding to the return journey, I have been unable to find out whether or not he won his bet.

We learned about the rest of the journey from his letters, although he did not give so many details in them. From Tucumán he went to the city of San Juan, the capital of that province, crossing the east side of the provinces of Catamarca and La Rioja. The road, which is very rugged, is almost always uphill as it climbs the mountains that join the Andean range, which in the province of San Juan has peaks up to 6,900 metres in height. From San Juan, Ernesto informed us that he would carry on to the province of Mendoza to visit my sister Maruja. Once he arrived in the province, he travelled on to the farm where Maruja was spending the summer holidays. He enjoys telling us that she did not recognise him because he was covered in dirt and had long hair and a beard. His aunt took charge of him immediately, sent his clothes to be washed, gave him all he needed to get his bicycle repaired and, after a succulent and plentiful lunch, they said farewell. She put several peso notes in his pocket, which he did not want to accept, in spite of the fact that he had practically run out of funds. And that is how he left Mendoza for Buenos Aires, where he arrived after crossing the south of the province of San Luis and the north of the province of Buenos Aires. He had travelled more than 4,700 kilometres in preparation for his forthcoming long journeys across South America, the first one of which he announced towards the end of 1951.

Diary of a bicycle trip across fourteen Argentine provinces by Ernesto Guevara de la Serna, 1950
First notebook

Prior to setting out, I had planned my itinerary to cover two or three places in the province of Córdoba, including the stretch from Buenos Aires, but it has been extended in an overambitious attempt to reach Santiago, Tucumán, Catamarca, La Rioja, San Juan, Mendoza, San Luis, Buenos Aires and Miramar. I would leave out Salta, the north of Jujuy, and the two provinces that comprise El Litoral.

When I left Buenos Aires on the evening of 1 January 1950, I was full of doubts about the potential of the machine I had, and had the sole hope of arriving soon and

well at Pilar – the end of the journey, as some well-meaning
people at home said – and then on to Pergamino, another
possible final point they mentioned.

When I left San Isidro, passing the highway police, I
turned off the little motor and went on pedalling, and as a
result another cyclist caught up with me. He was cycling to
Rosario under his own steam, so we went on together and I
pedalled rather than used the motor to keep the same pace
as my companion. When we passed Pilar I already felt the
first inklings of achievement: I knew I would succeed.

At eight o'clock in the morning of the following day we
reached San Antonio de Areco, my companion's first stage,
and we had breakfast and said goodbye. I carried on and
reached Pergamino in the afternoon, my second symbolic
stage; I was by now a winner, encouraged by having forgotten my fatigue, and rode off in the direction of Rosario,
respectably hanging onto a fuel lorry, after which I arrived
in Rosario at eleven at night. My body was screaming for a
mattress, but my will opposed it and I carried on. At about
two in the morning there was a downpour that lasted about
an hour. I took out my raincoat and the canvas cape that
were in my backpack, thanks to my mother's foresight, and
I laughed at the storm and told her so at the top of my voice,
reciting a poem by Sábato.

At six in the morning I reached Leones; I changed the
spark plugs as well as filling up with petrol. My ride entered
a monotonous stage. At about ten in the morning I went
through Bel Ville and there I hooked onto the tail of another
lorry that dragged me up to near Villa María. I stopped there
for a few seconds and did my calculations, according to
which I would arrive in under forty hours. I still had 144
kilometres, at twenty-five kilometres per hour; there was
nothing more to be said. I did ten kilometres and a private
car caught up with me – at that time I was pedalling to

avoid overheating as it was midday – and stopped to see if
I needed petrol. I told him I did not, but I asked him to pull
me at sixty kilometres per hour. After some ten kilometres
my rear wheel had a puncture and, as I was not paying
attention, I fell off.

While investigating the causes of the disaster, I realised
that my little motor had been rubbing up against the rear
tyre and had left the inner tube exposed.

Without spares and being very sleepy, I threw myself on
the edge of the road, determined to have a rest. About an
hour or two later an empty lorry went by and agreed to take
me to Córdoba. I put the battered remains of my bicycle in
a cab and reached Granado's, the goal of all my exertions,
in forty-one hours and seventeen minutes. Then [illegible]
eating, taking a bath, eating and then sleeping. The good
things in life.

After the accident that I have already mentioned, I met
a tramp who was taking a siesta in a culvert and who woke
up with the noise I made. We started chatting and when I
told him I was a student he took me under his wing. He
produced a dirty thermos and made me a maté with enough
sugar to sweeten an old maid. After chatting a lot and
telling each other the catalogue of our misadventures –
some with a pinch of truth, but others lavishly embroidered
– he remembered his years as a hairdresser and, noticing
my rather long hair, got hold of some rusty old scissors and
a dirty comb and set to work. Halfway through I felt something strange on my head and feared for my physical
integrity, but I never imagined that a pair of scissors could
be such a dangerous weapon. When he offered me a tiny
pocket mirror, I nearly fell on my back with shock: the
number of the zigzags was such that no area was spared.

I took my bald head as if it were a trophy to the home of
the González Aguilar family, when I went to visit my sister

Ana María, and to my surprise they paid no attention to the haircut and marvelled at the fact that I drank the maté they gave me. There is no accounting for tastes and opinions.

After a few days of leisure waiting for Tomasito [Granado], we went to Tanti. The place we chose was nothing special, but it was near all the supplies, even near the water source. After a couple of days we embarked on our planned trip to Los Chorrillos, a spot some ten kilometres from here. The journey was not without incident, but in the end we reached a hut [illegible], two or three caretakers of the place. We laughed at their dreadful appearance. Grego [Granado] agreed with our opinion by saying: 'These are all a [illegible].' But when we saw the price of the wine, they did not seem so foolish to us any longer. Afterwards, with the bread, the cheese and the sausages, we realised that looks can be deceptive.

The spectacle of the falls at Los Chorrillos from a height of some fifty metres is one of those that are worthwhile in the hills of Córdoba. The water falls spreading out into rows of multiple little streams, which fall on each stone until they are spread into a basin below; then, in a profusion of minor jumps, they fall into a natural basin, the largest one I have seen in streams of this size. But unfortunately it gets very little sunlight, so that the water is extremely cold and you can only be in it a few minutes.

The abundance of water there comes from all the neighbouring slopes and makes the place very fertile, and there is a variety of bracken and other plants typical of humid places, which give the site a particular beauty.

It was in this area, over the cascade, that I made my first attempts at alpine climbing. I had got it into my head to come down the stream by the waterfall, but I had to give up and started to come down by a steep slope, which was the most difficult one I found, to get the taste of it. When I was *halfway down I missed my footing and rolled down ten metres in the middle of an avalanche of stones and rocks that came down with me. When I managed to pick myself up, after breaking several [illegible] I had to start to climb back, because it was impossible to continue further down through there. I thus learned the first rule of mountain climbing: it is easier to go up than to come down. The bitter taste of defeat lasted all day, but the following day I jumped from heights of four metres and two metres, more or less, into seventy centimetres of water, which washed away the bitter taste of the previous day.*

That day and part of the following one it rained a lot, as a result of which the camping party was getting too wet, so we decided to fold the tent. At about five-thirty, when we were leisurely wrapping up our pots and pans, we heard the first rushing sound of the stream that would soon roar. Out of neighbouring houses people came screaming: 'The stream is coming, the stream is coming.' Our camp became a circus, the three of us carrying things back and forth. At the last minute Grego Granado takes the blanket by the corners and carries all that was left, while Tomás and I gathered the tent pegs at full speed. The wave was almost upon us and people from the sides were shouting, 'Leave all that, you crazy guys' and some other not very polite expressions. Only one rope was still in place, and at that moment I was holding the machete so I could not control myself, and in the midst of the general chaos I shouted, 'Charge, my brave ones' and with a cinematic blow I cut the rope. We managed to get everything out to one side just as the wave went past, roaring furiously and showing its ridiculous height of one and a half metres, accompanied by an interminable series of thundering noises.

It was at Tanti that I conceived the trip through twelve Argentine provinces, but the definitive plan only included

Catamarca, La Rioja, San Juan, Mendoza, San Luis. I left at four in the afternoon on 29 January and, after a short stop at Colonia Caroya, carried on up to San José de la Dormida,[2] where I honoured the name by lying on the side of the road and having a magnificent night's sleep until six the next morning.

I pedalled from there some five kilometres until I found a small house where they sold me a litre of petrol. I started the final section in second gear up to San Francisco del Chañar. The little motor decided to take fright on a steep slope and left me pedalling for some five kilometres, all uphill, but at the end I found myself in the middle of the town, from where the hospital's stationwagon gave me a lift.

The following day we went to visit one of Alberto Granado's [illegible] with a Dr Rossetti, and on the way back I fell and broke eight spokes of the bicycle and was stranded for four days longer than planned until they were fixed and the wheels were realigned – a task carried out by a patient, a Mr Zeus, who knows a lot about mechanics, although to repair this you do not have to be a genius.

We had decided to leave on Saturday 28th after a cocktail party at the home of a Mr Loza, a senator for the department, head of the district, a sort of sheriff adapted to modern times. However, the mishaps with my bicycle did not permit me to leave earlier than two in the morning, when the party was over. In any case, I went with Alberto Granado to patch up a tyre that had punctured, in order to leave immediately, but Alberto stretched out on a mattress to have a little rest and we ended up sleeping until eight in the morning. We spent the whole morning trying to decide which was the quickest way to go, and in the end, in the

[2] San José de la Dormida: dormida means asleep.

late afternoon, we decided to leave: me on the bicycle and he with a colleague on his motorcycle. But before that we decided we would go and have some vermouth that we found there and which was special for the [illegible].

As there was no ice, Alberto went to fetch some, and when he could not find any he decided that I was ill and he asked for ice for an ice-pack at the senator's house. He brought the cubes and we started to do some serious drinking, but, as bad luck would have it, the wife of the senator suddenly remembered that she needed some medicine and came personally to get it from Alberto's pharmacy. When we noticed her august presence it was too late. In spite of it, I flung myself face-down on the mattress and grabbed my head as if full of pain and desperation, but I did it only to practise my skill as an actor because I knew beforehand that the result would be nil.

When she left with her purchase, which she got for free, not sufficiently happy with that she muttered between her teeth, 'And for that I was left without ice.' But it was obvious that the real loser was Alberto, the new pharmacist, who watched with a bitter expression on his face as his profit evaporated.

Second notebook

At four in the afternoon, when the sun was rather low, we left for Ojo de Agua. Since Alberto had reduced his expectations down to a modest fifty-five kilometres, the distance, full of incidents, took four hours due to the many punctures I suffered. At Ojo de Agua I was advised to go and see the director of a small hospital and there I met the administrator, a Mr Mazza, brother of the senator who invited me to dinner. His family was charming and made me very welcome, in spite of having no idea where I was coming from – they empathised with the idea of my tour.

*After I slept some eight hours, and having been well fed,
I embarked on my trip to the famous Salinas Grandes, the
Argentine equivalent of the Sahara. The unanimous
opinions of my unofficial informers told me that with the
half-litre of water that I was carrying I would be unable to
cross the saltpans, but the well-shaken mixture of Irish and
Galician blood that runs through my veins made me settle
for that amount, and with it I left.*

*The landscape of this area of Santiago [del Estero]
reminds one of the north of Córdoba, which is separated by
an imaginary line. To the sides of the road there are
enormous cacti almost six metres in height, looking like
enormous candelabra. The vegetation is abundant and one
can see signs of fertility, but little by little the landscape
begins to change, the road becomes dustier and rugged, the
vegetation begins to leave behind the* quebrachos,[3] *and the*
jarilla[4] *begins to appear. With the sun now directly
overhead and its rays reflecting up at me from the ground,
it feels as if I am in an intensely hot oven. I choose the leafy
shade of a carob tree to lie down in to sleep for an hour. I
then get up, brew and drink some maté and go on my way
again. The milestone on the side of the road welcomes me
with the words 'Kilometre 1000 of route 9'. One kilometre
later the total preponderance of the* jarilla *begins. I am in
the Sahara and suddenly – oh what a surprise! – the road
that so far has had the privilege of being one of the worst
I have ever been on turns into a magnificent cambered*

---

[3] *Quebracho*: the common name in Spanish for at least three similar
species of trees that grow in the Gran Chaco region of South America: an
evergreen that sometimes rises to thirty metres, with an erect stem and
wide, spreading crown. The wood of the species is very valuable due to its
hardness. The name comes from the Spanish *quebrar* (to break) and *hacha*
(axe).
[4] *Jarilla*: *Larrea nitida Cavanilles* of the Zygophyllaceae family, a shrub
found in mountainous areas of western Argentina.

1. The author Ernesto Guevara Lynch with his wife Celia de le Serna and their son Ernesto in Rosario, province of Santa Fe, in 1928.

2. Ernesto drinking maté in front of the house the author built in Puerto Caraguatay in Misiones on the Paraná river.

3. Ernesto as a toddler in the arms of a nanny at the Gamas' country house in Morón in the province of Buenos Aires.

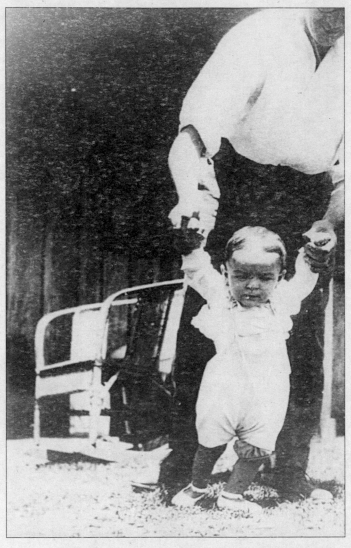

4. Ernesto learning how to walk with his father in Misiones in 1929.

(*Facing page*) 5. Ernesto as a toddler playing in the garden of the Gamas' country house in Morón in the province of Buenos Aires.

6. Ernesto as a toddler in the arms of Mrs Gamas, a friend of his mother, at the Gamas' country house.

7. Ernesto (in the middle) with his cousins.

8. Ernesto, looking like quite the little man, with his hat.

9. Ernesto on the balcony of the Guevara apartment in Aráoz Street with his brother Juan Martín, his uncle Jorge de la Serna, his brother Roberto, his friend Carlos Figueroa, and his future brother-in-law Luis Rodríguez Argañaraz.

10. Ernesto with his brother Juan Martín on his lap and his mother by his side in Córdoba in 1943.

11. The author, Ernesto Guevara Lynch, with his wife and children in Mar del Plata, 1945.

12. The author again with his wife and children in 1945.

13. Ernesto in Guatemala, admiring the ruins.

14. Ernesto's Argentine passport photo of 1955.

15. Ernesto on board a ship of the Argentine merchant navy when he worked as a male nurse in 1951.

16. Ernesto with his first wife, the Peruvian economist Hilda Gadea, and their daughter Hildita in Mexico City in 1956.
17. Ernesto with Hildita in his arms during a visit to the jail at Miguel Schultz Street in Mexico City where he was held in custody with Fidel Castro in 1956.

18. Ernesto as a guerilla in the Sierra Maestra during the
Cuban Revolutionary War in 1957.

19. Letter from Ernesto to his mother in Argentina written during the struggle in Cuba.

20. The author Ernesto Guevara Lynch in his office at the Astillero Rio de la Plata in the outskirts of Buenos Aires.

road, even and firm, where my motor delights in the easy ride.

But this is not the only surprise that the heart of the country has in store for me, because the fact that I can see a farm every five or six kilometres makes me wonder if I am really in that stark place. However, the ocean represented by the silver-stained soil and its green mane leaves us in no doubt. From time to time, almost like an ungainly sentinel, the vigilant figure of a cactus appears. In two and a half hours I cover the eighty kilometres of saltpans and then I get another surprise: when asking for some fresh water to fill my flask, I am told that drinking water can be found at a depth of only three metres and is abundant. Evidently the saltpans' undeserved reputation relies on superficial impressions if you don't know about the good roads, the many farms and the existence of water three metres below the surface. Not bad.

Well into the night I arrive at Loreto, a town of several thousand souls, which nonetheless is very backward. The police officer whom I encountered when I went to ask for lodgings for the night informed me that the town does not have a single doctor and when he heard that I am doing my fifth year of medicine, he gave me the healthy piece of advice that I should set myself up in the village: 'The doctors earn a lot and they are doing people a favour.' I told him that I would think about it, but I have not decided yet. I really don't know what to do.

I got on the road early, travelling over a dreadful section and then over some other sections that were paved and very good.

Here I bade farewell for ever to my water flask, which was swallowed up by a treacherous pothole – I reached Santiago, where I was very well received by the relatives of friends.

There I was interviewed for the first time in my life. It was for a newspaper in Tucumán, and the journalist was a Mr Santillán, whom I had met during the first stop I made in the city to quench my thirst (by the way, I owe him an invitation since, like the perfect boor, I let him pay).

That day I saw the city of Santiago, flat both morally and physically, and whose infernal heat frightens its inhabitants into staying indoors well into the late afternoon, when they come out into the streets for a walk: a way of socialising.

The village of La Banda seems prettier. It is divided by the River Dulce, which has a one-kilometre-deep ravine, but for most of the year no water runs through it. There is a blatant antagonism between these two towns, and this was apparent during the basketball match in which the two neighbouring towns faced each other. The team led by Lledo (from Santiago) [illegible] was stronger on the whole.

At nine in the morning the next day I continued towards Tucumán, where I arrived late at night.

On the road something strange happened to me: while I stopped to inflate a tyre, about a kilometre from a village, a tramp appeared from a nearby culvert and we started a conversation.

He was coming from the cotton harvest in Chaco and thought that, after doing nothing for a while, he would go to San Juan, to the grape harvest. When he found out that I planned to tour several provinces and that my motive was purely for the experience, he grabbed his head with both hands and said in desperation: 'Mamma mia, all that effort for nothing! My friend, come with me, we will do some business.' My timid protestations did not have any impact on his decision.

And as if I were following my mentor – me just a poor acolyte – I walked behind my new friend full of curiosity.

As soon as we reached the first shop in the town he went in with a decisive air and began his speech: 'This gentleman you see here is a young patriot who has set off to tour the fourteen Argentine provinces, collecting funds for a glorious enterprise. This young man intends to buy a bunch of Argentine flowers, as Criollo[5] as himself, and travel to Boulogne-sur-Mer, over there in France, to place them on the grave of the Great Captain* since this is the centenary year of the Saint of the Sword.' With that and other speeches, the shopkeeper was relieved of three pesos, but in the notebook bought ad hoc his contribution was entered as ten pesos 'so that people cannot say anything unkind about you'.

With varying degrees of success, we went into all the shops of the main street of the town and, as a result, we collected together 112 pesos. However, the tramp had such a deep scorn for the people that it all ended badly. He invited me to have a beer in a bar to toast all those who had been so easily fleeced. Not content with that, he invited two or three passers-by, who had stopped to stare or to make unsavoury remarks about my looks, and told them of the ruse. I don't know who the informer was, but I am sure there was one.

Not much later a policeman appeared to enquire about 'the young cyclist' and, after finding me among the five men who sat at the table, put me in the police station waiting room. 'The young cyclist', having followed the lead of the itinerant farm labourer, blamed 'the man with the checked gaucho trousers' – my friend who by now must have been comfortably back in his cosy culvert on the outskirts of the town. I spent four tedious hours in the nick

---

[5] *Criollo*: means born in Latin America of European ancestry, possessing the qualities of those native to the continent.

before they decided to let me go. Free at last, I ran to visit the charming promoter of the brilliant idea and found him calmly drinking maté.

During the harsh hours spent in detention I had examined my conscience, and as a result I reached the conclusion that he was really no more than a bum so there would be no difficulty carrying on with him, so as soon as I arrived [where he was] I proposed that he bought a bicycle to share the road with me; but, against my expectations, my suggestion did not amuse him in the least. 'No, my friend, I am no longer fit enough. I am almost old and getting tired and that does not appeal. Go on your way and take advantage of the ruse I taught you. But, you could leave me the remaining pesos for my vices.'

After complying with his just request and accepting ten pesos to help with expenses, I got on my way towards the capital of Tucumán.

Just like a fleeting spark that advances at thirty kilometres per hour, I left behind the majestic capital city of Tucumán and took the road to Salta immediately, but I was caught in a downpour so I ended up at the barracks, in the arsenal, some ten to fifteen kilometres from the capital city of Tucumán, from where I left at six in the morning for Salta.

The road that leaves Tucumán is one of the most beautiful of the north. Over some twenty kilometres of well-paved road there is on both sides luxuriant vegetation, a sort of tropical forest accessible to the tourist, with a multitude of brooks and such humidity that makes it look like a film shot in the Amazon jungle.

Advancing along those natural gardens, walking amid the lianas, stepping on bracken and observing how all of nature laughs at our lack of botanical knowledge, we expect at any moment the roar of a lion, or the silent movement of a serpent or the agile step of a deer. And suddenly one hears the roar, not loud but constant, and one recognises the whine of a lorry coming up the slope. The roar seems to demolish the castle of my daydreams with a noisy shattering of glass, bringing me back to reality. I then realise that something has matured in me, something that had been growing inside me for some time while surrounded by the din of cities: and it is a hatred of urban civilisation; the vulgar image of people moving as madmen to the tune of that enormous noise, which to me seems the hated antithesis of peace, that [illegible] in which the almost silent rustling of leaves is like melodious background music.

I return to the road and continue on my journey. At about midday I reach a police checkpoint and stop for a rest. At that point a motorcyclist driving a brand-new Harley-Davidson offers to tow me along.

I ask him at what speed and he says: 'I can take you at eighty or ninety.' But I have learned from experience that with an unstable load, poor road conditions and with deference to my ribcage, the tow must not be more than forty kilometres per hour. So I declined the offer.

After thanking the policeman who offered me a jug of coffee, I leave in a hurry, hoping to reach Salta during the day. I have 200 kilometres before me, so I have to get on with it.

When I reach Rosario de la Frontera, an unpleasant surprise awaits me. The Harley-Davidson, last seen at the police station, is being hauled down from a lorry. I approach and enquire after the driver. 'Dead' is the reply.

Naturally the minor personal tragedy of the obscure death of that motorcyclist does not touch the sentimental fibres of the masses, but to know that a man goes looking for danger without having even that vaguely heroic aura

*that the public would appreciate, and dies without wit-
nesses when taking a bend, imbues this unknown
adventurer with a vague suicidal 'fervour'. Something that
might make the study of his personality interesting. But I
digress and the subject is not the object of these notes.*

*From Rosario de la Frontera to Metán the paved road
offers me a rest because of its smoothness and prepares me
for the section Metán–Salta, and strengthens me with the
patience with which to face up to the uphill roads. All that
is bad in this area because of its roads is compensated by
the magnificent landscapes. I now arrive at a mountainous
area and at every bend there is something new to marvel at.
Near Lobería I have the opportunity of admiring one of the
most beautiful scenes of my entire journey: on the edge of
the road there is a sort of railway bridge, supported only by
a few timber crosspieces, under which the Juramento River
runs. The banks are covered in stones of every colour and
the greyish waters of the river run turbulently between the
steep banks covered in magnificent vegetation. I remain
gazing at the water for a long while and I do not know for
what strange reason, but every time I look at the sea or at
the rough torrents of water in their magnificent and
ceaseless struggle against the earth, I feel a violent, almost
lacerating need to have a woman by my side to wrap
around her a protective embrace – this is not specific, it
does not matter who she is, but someone in skirts who
attaches herself to me. It must be some kind of weak spot
in which to compare my strength, in order not to feel
intimidated by that infinite colossus.*

*The grey foam that jumps up like sparks when it crashes
against the rocks, and returns to the whirlpool in an endless
repetition, is like an invitation to jump in and be brutally
rocked by the waters and shout incoherently like a
condemned man.*

I climb the slope in a soft melancholy mood and the roar of the water that I leave behind seems to reproach me for my lack of amorous involvement. I feel like a confirmed bachelor. The largest goat of the pack laughs at my clumsiness as a climber, with my philosophical beard in the style of Jack London, and the rough roar of a lorry once again takes me out of my hermit's meditation.*

It is already dark when I climb the last slope and find myself in front of the magnificent city of Salta, to whose detriment one cannot help noting that it welcomes the tourist with the geometric rigidity of its cemetery.

With the shamefaced attitude that I am developing, I turn up at the hospital and introduce myself as a medical student, nearly broke – something of a touring cyclist and exhausted. I am put up in a vehicle with soft cushy seats and find it worthy of a king. I sleep like a log until seven in the morning, when I am woken up so that the vehicle can be used. It rains torrentially. I suspend my onward journey.

Around two o'clock in the afternoon the rain stops and I set out towards Jujuy, but at the edge of the city there is an enormously muddy area as a result of the torrential downpour and it is impossible for me to go any further. However, I find a lorry and discover that the driver is an old acquaintance, but after some kilometres we part. He is going on to Campo Santo to collect some cement and I continue along the road known as La Cornisa.

The water that had fallen collected into rivulets, which crossed the road coming down from the hills and proceeded to disappear into the Mojotoro, which runs along the edge of the road. This was not an imposing spectacle like the one at Salta on the Juramento River, but its cheerful beauty is a tonic for the spirit. After leaving this river behind, the traveller enters the real zone of La Cornisa, where one can appreciate the majestic beauty of the hills adorned with green forests. The gorges appear uninterrupted and, framed by the nearby greenery, one can see in the clearings between the branches the distant and green plain, as if through a tinted lens.

The wet foliage permeates the atmosphere with freshness, but it is not the penetrating, aggressive humidity of Tucumán, but something naturally fresh and soft. The charm of this warm and humid afternoon, tempered by the thick jungle and never interrupted by the roar of my eternal enemies, transported me to a world of dreams; a world far from my present situation, but whose return route I knew well and which was not cut off by those banks of fog that the realms of fantasy dreams usually display.

Sated with so much beauty, as if one had indigestion from too many chocolates, I reach the city of Jujuy, exhausted both inside and out and desirous of sampling the hospitality of this province – what better opportunity to visit the hospitals of the country than this trip?

I sleep splendidly in one of the wards, but before that I must give an account of my medical knowledge and, equipped with a pair of tweezers and some ether, I undertake the passionate chase of worms from the shaven head of a chango.[6] His monotonous groans lacerate my ears like a fine stiletto, while my scientific alter ego counts with careless greed the number of my dead enemies. I cannot understand how this dark little boy, who is only two years old, could be so full of larvae. If one wanted to do it on purpose, one would not easily succeed. When I finish my undertaking, the boy's mother regales me with one of those smiles that makes the frontier separating the sexes disappear, and I look one way and then the other as if searching for the good angel to shout my lack of dignity at

---

[6] *Chango*: an Argentine colloquialism for little boy.

me, but I only encounter the hungry peal of laughter of sex
that goads me on to take her. My hands stretch out, avid for
the delicious morsels of her breasts, but the appearance of
a nurse startles me, reminding me of my precarious
situation as a wanderer.

I get into bed and try to turn the insignificant episode
into the basis of my dream as a pariah. However, I still see
for a few minutes the bluish face that, from deep in those
eyes, sends me the obscure gaze of a vanquished race. But
then the pleasant dreams sweep away the yearning of the
flesh and I sleep the sleep of the just.

The next morning I unctuously imbibe a revolting sugary
beverage and take my leave. Without the rustic charm of
our previous encounter, the Indian woman is ostentatiously
insolent and I, a poor Quixote without a squire, find that
the delicious hands of Dulcinea that I clasp between mine
– under who knows what terrible spell – wound mine with
the thousand uneven spikes of their calluses.

The magnificent day fills me with light and invites me to
set forth; the affectionate purring of my bicycle is lost in the
solitude and I begin my return by the lower road that leads
to Campo Santo. Nothing worthy of mention happens
during this section and the only highlight is the marvellous
landscape of the Gallinato; even better, if possible, are the
views from La Cornisa, because from there your eyes have
a wider panorama and that gives it a grandeur that is lost
from the former.

I arrive at Salta at two in the afternoon and go to visit my
friends at the hospital, who marvel on learning that I did
the whole trip in one day, and one of them asks, 'What do
you see?' A question that was asked to remain unanswered,
because there is not an answer, because the truth is: what
do I see? At least I am not inspired by the usual tourist
sights, and I am surprised to see in the promotional maps of

Jujuy, for example: the altar of the homeland, the cathedral where the national emblem was blessed, the jewel of the pulpit and the miraculous virgin of Río Blanco and Pompeya, the house in which General Lavalle* was assassinated, the Chapter House, the museum of the province, etc. No, one does not know a people from this – a way and interpretation of life that is simply a glossy cover; the soul of a people is reflected in the sick in the hospitals, the men in custody at police stations or the anxious pedestrian with whom one enters into conversation, while the Grande River shows itself flooded and turbulent underneath. But all this would take too long to explain, and who knows if anyone would understand it. I thank them and leave on a visit of the city, which I did not see properly the first time round.

At nightfall I approach the police post in the outskirts of the city and ask permission to spend the night there. My plan is to try to do the mountainous part by lorry to spare myself those harsh climbs over bad roads, wading rivers and several flooded streams; but I am soon discouraged because it is Saturday and it is improbable that a lorry will drive by, as they go by early in the morning in order to reach Tucumán on Sunday morning.

Resigned to this, I chat with the policemen, who show me the famous female Anopheles *in the flesh; the longish mosquito, stylised and gracious, does not give the impression of being the carrier of the terrible malarial scourge.*

The moon shows its subtropical exuberance, sending out torrents of silver light that result in a very pleasant semi-darkness; its appearance enhances the garrulousness of the policeman, who launches into philosophical considerations, to end up telling a story.

This character heard the other day the gallop of a pack of horses and the barking of dogs, and went out with a torch and his revolver and positioned himself strategically. The pack galloped past again, to the sound of the barking dogs, and after all the noise, as an explanation, a black mule with huge ears appeared following the pack timidly. The chorus of barking increased in intensity and the pack again ran off noisily. The mule took a different direction and, when the moon could be seen between its ears, the policeman felt an intense cold down his spine. The older policeman interrupted with this wise pronouncement: 'It must be a soul from purgatory that is lodged in the mule.' And he prescribed the death of the animal in order to liberate the soul. 'And what can happen to me?' 'Nothing; on the contrary, it will thank you for liberating it, what else . . .'

Setting aside the humanitarian motive, I – educated with stories of justice, propriety, noises that disturb others, etc. – timidly made the objection that the owner and neighbours might not be very happy with the mule's exploits. They looked at me in a way that put me to shame. How could that mule have an owner and, even if it did, who would object to setting a soul free? My other objection they did not even bother to discuss.

The three of us remained deep in thought, gazing at the moon, which, in all its glory, spread silvery shadows over the hills. The cool night of Salta was filled with the music of the frogs and, lulled by their song, I took a short nap. At four I bade farewell to the policemen and started on my hard trip towards Tucumán. The brakes of the bicycle were causing me a problem, so I had to be very careful on the slopes, since I didn't know what I might find on the other side of a bend and my lights were not strong enough to show me.

At about seven in the morning I had a pleasant surprise. A long line of lorries, one behind the other, was stuck in the mud. The drivers were just waking up and they were conferring among themselves. I approached to listen in and

– oh! surprise! – my old friend Luchini the lorry driver was one of them.

The confrontation started, obscenities were shouted and the replies came thick and fast and the bets were quickly formalised: I would leave immediately and if they caught up with me before the asphalt road that leads to Tucumán, bad luck; but if they were unable to catch up with me, I would wait for them there and they would offer me a sumptuous meal with all the trimmings. That offered temporary relief from landscapes, faulty brakes, steep slopes, dangerous curves, exhaustion, thirst: I could visualise the splendour of a banquet and, with each step towards that goal, the vision of a juicy chicken surrounded by appetising roast potatoes grew ever more vivid.

Part Five:

Bolivia, Peru and Ecuador, 1953

In 1951 Ernesto sat several exams, travelled as a male nurse with the Argentine merchant navy to Brazil, Venezuela and Trinidad and continued to work with Dr Salvador Pisani.

On 30 December he set out with his friend Alberto Granado on a journey that would last eight months. They visited the south of Argentina, Chile, Peru, Colombia and Venezuela. Granado decided to accept a job in Caracas and stayed in Venezuela.

Ernesto was invited to return home via Miami in a cargo plane that had arrived in Caracas carrying racehorses. The flight was due to do an overnight stopover in Miami, then return for a brief stop in Caracas and fly south back to Argentina.

In Miami the captain ordered a check of the engines and it was discovered that one of them had a serious fault. The engine had to be removed and overhauled. The stopover lasted a month. Ernesto was thus forced to spend a month in the United States without any money. He managed to obtain lodgings at a boarding house, promising to pay his debt once he returned to Buenos Aires, which he did.

Because of his exaggerated pride he did not ask us for help. Once he was back in Buenos Aires he told us that he used to walk every day from his lodgings, which were in the centre of town, to the beach. He walked some fifteen kilometres a day to get there and back, and got to see a little of the US.

Once the aircraft engine had been fixed, the flight left to return to Caracas. The other passenger on board was the groom who had brought the racehorses on the flight north. The plane was now carrying a cargo of boxes of fruit. As soon as they took off, Ernesto fell asleep. He was woken up by the groom, who told him that the landing gear had got stuck and they were flying in circles over Caracas. Ernesto thought the groom was pulling his leg and went back to sleep. When he woke up he looked out of the window and saw the fire brigade in full force on the tarmac. Everything was in place for an emergency landing. Fortunately, at the last moment the landing gear was unblocked and they landed without incident.

We were told the date on which the flight was due to return to Buenos Aires. That morning the whole family went to the airport to await Ernesto's arrival. We had to wait for a long time because the sky was overcast and there was poor visibility. Finally the old Douglas cargo plane appeared on the horizon. Ernesto was home. During this trip he had managed to indulge his passion for archaeology, not only by visiting many sites, but also by reading about them in the local public libraries. He had practised what he had learned as a medical student when he and his friend Alberto had worked in a leper colony in Peru.[1]

Now, back in Buenos Aires, he was determined to obtain his medical degree before May 1953. He had fifteen subjects to sit. In November 1952 he sat and passed three subjects. In December he sat and passed more. By the end of December 1952 he had only one subject outstanding. He had not sat for

[1] Leper colony in Peru: Ernesto's experience of working in the leper colony with Alberto Granado is described in *Travelling with Che Guevara* by Alberto Granado, published by Pimlico, 2003.

it the first time that the examination board met, so he appeared before the board on 11 April 1953. When Ernesto began his studies, medicine consisted of thirty subjects. Towards the end of 1951 he had passed half of them, and between November 1952 and April 1953 he sat the remaining half and passed them.

He had also returned to work in Dr Pisani's laboratory, where he had been a member of a team that researched allergies. He had even been mentioned in some of Dr Pisani's published papers. Since he had already worked off and on for Dr Pisani for several years, I thought he would stay with him, as that way Ernesto would be able to carry on with his studies and research. This would not only give him the possibility of a brilliant scientific career, but would also afford him the opportunity of continuing to try and find a cure for his asthma.

After a brief period of three months during which he did not sit any exams, Ernesto obtained his medical degree. I was in my studio when the phone rang. I recognised the voice that said, 'This is Doctor Ernesto Guevara de la Serna.' The emphasis was on the word 'doctor'.

The family were very happy for him. But our joy did not last long. He soon announced that he was leaving again on a trip – this time with his old friend Calica Ferrer. He immediately began preparing for the trip. He collected his medical degree and had it legalised, got some money together and packed his bags.

Our illusions were shattered. We knew what he would go through: he would walk for kilometres and kilometres or he would hang onto an old lorry; he would sleep anywhere and eat whatever he could find. He would not pay any attention to his health or his asthma and he would be on the road, courting danger.

But we, his parents and his brothers and sisters, could do

nothing, nor should we. He was no longer a child, he was Dr Guevara de la Serna, and he would do as he pleased. All we could do now was learn to grin and bear it and try to help him as much as possible – something that he nearly always turned down.

Bolivia was their first destination.

Our house became a beehive. Young men and women came and went at all hours of the day and night until the date set for their departure came. Most of Ernesto's friends and many of ours gathered for a farewell party.

On a grey and cold afternoon of July 1953 we met at Retiro station to bid the travellers farewell. Ernesto's and Calica's friends and relatives came to see them off.

The international train for Yacuiba-Pocitos in Bolivia was due to leave at four in the afternoon. Ernesto had a crew-cut and was wearing green fatigues. He was carrying a holdall. As the train pulled off he shouted, 'Here goes a soldier of the Americas' a couple of times.

At the time none of us paid any attention to it, believing it to be another of Ernesto's eccentricities. Little did we know . . .

Bolivia: the very scene of the struggle

Ernesto and Calica Ferrer travelled north. They boarded the train that goes from Buenos Aires to Bolivia. It leaves Retiro station and belongs to the General Belgrano Railway Line and crosses the provinces of Buenos Aires, Santa Fe, Córdoba, Tucumán, La Rioja and Jujuy.

They were travelling to Bolivia because they wanted to witness the revolution that was allegedly in progress, and which was expected to topple the government of Paz Estenssoro*.

They had not planned their whole itinerary. To give you a better idea of this trip – which ended almost two years later in Mexico City – I have interspersed stories told by Calica Ferrer as well as letters, in full or in part, from Ernesto to members of our family. These are of interest because they reflect the objective aspects of the trip, as well as the political and social aspects of the countries they visited. They are mixed with anecdotes told imaginatively and spontaneously by both of them at the time.

Calica Ferrer was a friend of Ernesto's since his early childhood. With his brother Jorge they were part of the same gang. Their father had been our doctor when we lived in Alta Gracia.

The trip dreamed of for so long was at last about to become a reality

We had planned to go through Bolivia and Peru on the way to Venezuela, where I [Calica Ferrer] intended to settle. I preferred to go through Bolivia because I had never been there.

Between us we had saved a few bucks, not much, something in the region of 700 dollars. With so little money we would have to perform miracles to arrive in Venezuela without replenishment. The trip was long and the money short. We left Buenos Aires from Retiro station on the General Belgrano Railway Line on 7 July 1953. It was a very cold and sunless afternoon and as the train left the station it was beginning to get dark.

Family and friends had come to see us off – their clothing was in sharp contrast with those of the second-class passengers with whom we would share a carriage. First-class cost almost twice that of second-class, so we would be saving from the start. And although we would travel on hard wooden seats, we would be in the company of people who were much more fun. Besides, this type of ticket allowed us to take our own food, just as the rest of the second-class passengers did. We were well stocked. We had something like fourteen pieces of luggage; some were indispensable items, but the majority were farewell presents.

The passengers on the train seemed picturesque to us. A heterogeneous ensemble of people and objects, men, women, children, crushed suitcases, parcels, blankets, the indispensable kettle and maté. And to complete the picture, some little dog, cat or parrot hidden from the eye of the conductor.

They all were extremely humble people, many were hired hands from the Argentine north or Bolivians going back to their country after having earned a little money in Buenos Aires.

And thus, between the cries of babies, the chatter, the maté sessions and some singing accompanied by a bad guitar, sleeping off and on, reading whenever we could, chatting with our travelling companions and cramming ourselves full of landscapes, we travelled for two days. Leaving Humahuaca behind with its imposing view of high mountains, we made our entrance into La Quiaca, the last town on Argentine soil.

After some unavoidable paperwork we crossed the frontier and, once in Bolivia, we went on to La Paz.

Before boarding the train that would take us to the capital, a huge brute who acted as a porter came forward and attempted to take our luggage by force, but he was thwarted by the violent shove that Ernesto gave him to prevent him from touching the luggage.

We then travelled on across a mountainous landscape that we found rather monotonous, until we reached the city of La Paz, which neither of us had ever visited. I was impressed by its architecture, its steep and narrow streets full of twists and turns, and in particular by the

attire of the Coyas,[2] the native people who went everywhere very slowly. We were at an altitude of more than
4,000 metres.

La Paz was home at the time to a good number of
Argentine exiles and to some self-exiled politicians.

Among the exiles was Ricardo Rojo*, whom we also met
later on in other locations throughout Latin America.

In contrast with middle-class society, we were always in
direct contact with the working classes.

We wanted to know of their aspirations, their needs,
what they thought and how they lived. That is how we were
able to gain an insight into the misery into which this
ancient people have been plunged for centuries. Malnourished, sick and hooked on coca, they stoically and
silently, with clenched teeth, almost resignedly, put up
with this miserable existence they have suffered from
generation to generation and from century to century,
without ever having the means to remedy their misfortune.

The people live in such a state of backwardness that,
when the Coyas go to the city to obtain permits from the
authorities, the government employees, without any com-
punction or scruples, disinfect them with DDT.

For some of them this seems so natural that, after they
have been 'cleansed' in this way, they go out into the
narrow streets of the city, calmly walking around covered
in DDT powder.

Ernesto and I travelled inland to see the famous Bolivian
mines and we noticed that the workers were well armed
and possessed good organisation for their own defence. We
met a brigade of them who, armed to the teeth, went to La
Paz with the purpose of showing the Americans that they

[2] Coya: the Aymara and Inca population of the high plateaux of Peru, Bolivia
and Argentina (from the Quechua word *Kollasuyo* – the Bolivian sector of
the Inca empire).

were ready and able to prevent any attempt to topple the
popular government of Paz Estenssoro.

When these workers came back from that demon-
stration, they returned shooting their rifles and guns into
the air, delighted to show their strength in front of their
comrades. It was proof of great enthusiasm, but also of a
total lack of discipline and military training. The United
States were not happy with this 'popular revolution', which
supported the interests of the revolutionary workers and
had disbanded the professional army, replacing it with
popular militias who were preparing to carry out an
agrarian reform giving the land to the campesinos so that
they could grow crops.

This being a foreign country, all of us Argentines got
together, even if our convictions differed greatly. Our
patriotism, which at home lay dormant, awoke there.

Letter from Ernesto to his father

La Paz, July 24th [1953]

Dear Viejo,

I did not give any signs of being alive because I was
waiting for a job – which would be for a month – as
doctor in a tin mine, with Calica as my assistant. We've
now given up the idea because the doctor (who would
have given us the job) disappeared and we cannot be
here indefinitely eating up our reserves. I am a little
disappointed that I cannot stay because this is a very
interesting country and it is going through a particularly
effervescent moment. On August 2nd the agrarian
reform takes place and raids and commotion are
announced throughout the country. We have seen
incredible marches of people armed with Mausers and

piripipí[3] shooting just because. Shots are heard every day and there are people constantly being wounded and killed.

The government shows an almost complete inability to stop or even divert the masses of *campesinos* and miners, but these react in a certain way and there is no doubt that in an armed revolt of the Falange (the party in opposition), these would be on the side of the Movimiento Nacionalista Revolucionario (MNR).[4]

Human life is of little importance here and it is given or taken without much display of feeling. All this means that for a neutral observer the situation is very interesting, in spite of which, with one excuse or another, anyone who can gets the hell out of here, us included.

At this point of his stay in Bolivia, Ernesto was convinced that the government of Paz Estenssoro was there to stay. The newspapers of the period gave a right-wing coup against the government as a certainty because of the alleged agrarian reform that he planned.

People greeted us magnificently here, and there was not a single person, whether Argentine or Bolivian, who did not take an interest in our trip one way or another. We are trying to obtain our visas for Venezuela, but nothing is certain. If you can think of someone you more or less know in Ecuador, send me their particulars to the Argentine Consulate in Lima. I am in formidably good

---

[3] *Piripipí*: a colloquialism for machine guns in Paraguay and Bolivia.
[4] Movimiento Nacionalista Revolucionario (MNR): perhaps the most important political party of Bolivia in the twentieth century. Founded in 1941 by Víctor Paz Estenssoro and Hernán Siles Suazo, it began as a leftist/reformist party, but has moved considerably to the right since.

health in spite of not sticking to my diet as I should.
Please write so that I have fresh news in Lima. A hug for
all the family. Until the next. I'll stop here because I am
being collected to go to a party.

Ernesto in Bolivia

Ernesto and Calica had spent a couple of months in Bolivia.
President Paz Estenssoro was a military man with certain
Socialist tendencies. He had the support of the masses, but
it cannot be said that he was a true revolutionary. However,
large international joint ventures had already placed their
capital in this beaten-up country and they looked upon the
populist Paz Estenssoro with suspicion. If his support of the
masses of workers, especially miners, became really
effective, the said masses could become a battering ram
against foreign capitalism. The newspapers of developed
countries published their comments in this regard. In the
Bolivian capital there was a pre-revolutionary climate. Paz
Estenssoro, like all military demagogues, encouraged the
masses without knowing to what extent he could control
them.

And at that point Ernesto and Calica had arrived in
Bolivia. Ernesto needed only a few days to understand the
socio-political problems. He wrote to his mother telling her
that Paz Estenssoro was firmly in power, but he was
disappointed that he could not stay long enough to see an
armed revolt, as he had decided to head north to Peru.

Both Calica and Ernesto wrote to us from Bolivia with
many anecdotes of their trip. They went often to the home
of an Argentine millionaire from Tucumán who was against
the government of Perón and who lived in La Paz. There
they would discuss Argentine politics, and the government
of Perón was harshly criticised. Dr Ricardo Rojo, who had
met Calica and Ernesto in Bolivia, was also a regular visitor.

When they went north, Rojo took the same route, but used different means of transport – not on foot or hitch-hiking as they did – and met up with them in Lima, Ecuador, Nicaragua, Guatemala and later on in Mexico.

Che says clearly in one of his letters to his mother that he is in total disagreement with the political views of Rojo, in spite of which Rojo followed them throughout their trip.

Calica continues with his story:

Travelling by bus

We decided to go on to Peru. We arrived at Lake Titicaca and took the opportunity to visit the island where the famous Temple to the Sun is situated.

We hired an indigenous canoe and oarsman. Our destination was the island, which is rather far from the shore. When we left, it was very cold, but the weather was good. Not long after, waves began to form and a strong wind started blowing, turning the lake into a furious sea.

After visiting the temple and when we were returning to the shore, the oarsman, exhausted by his struggle against the waves, collapsed and let go of the oars. So we had to take the initiative by rowing ourselves. Without rest we finally reached the shore, with our hands totally raw and bleeding.

Not much later we crossed the frontier and started in the direction of the Peruvian city of Puno.

Again, to save money, we had decided to travel second class. When we reached the ticket office we asked for second-class tickets for Cuzco. The clerk raised his head in surprise and said, 'Gentlemen, you cannot travel second-class.'

'But we want to travel second-class,' I replied.

'But you would be in danger travelling like that,' he insisted, while pointing at a second-class carriage.

It was an overcrowded cattle truck packed with waiting Coyas.

'You see,' said the clerk, and then he added to reinforce his argument, 'sometimes the peon in charge of opening the padlock forgets to do so and the passengers have to return on foot to the previous station.'

The carriage was indeed locked with a padlock.

'Can't you see, sir, only animals or these Coyas travel that way?'

Near the window there were a couple of people who were listening to the exchange as the tone of our voices rose. One of them courteously intervened, saying, 'Gentlemen, please do not be offended, but you cannot travel second-class.'

By now I was fed up with the clerk's insistence, so I shouted at him, 'Well, that's enough, we bloody well want to travel like this, and you stop . . .!'

'One moment,' replied the man who had intervened, 'no swearing, I was only trying to help, we are . . . (while saying this he took a document out of his pocket) policemen', and he ostentatiously showed us his police identity card.

That was the end of the argument, we decided not to travel second-class. We invited the policemen to have a few drinks and very soon it was as if we had been old friends and we continued on our journey with our new acquaintances. After several hours on the train we arrived at the city of Cuzco, where we went to a tavern for a meal.

Letter from Ernesto to his mother

Cuzco, 22nd [August 1953]

Look at the letterhead, Mummy.

I have the great pleasure of being here for the second time and this time in semi-luxury, but the effect is different. When I was here with Alberto he used to dream of marrying Inca princesses and recovering long-lost empires. Calica, on the other hand, curses the filthy ground each time he steps on one of the countless turds that litter the streets. Instead of looking to the sky or at some cathedral soaring into space, he looks at his dirty shoes. Instead of taking in the essence of the surroundings and the almost palpable dramatic history, he smells only stews and shit: it is a question of philosophical outlook.

All that apparent incoherence of 'I am leaving', 'I left', 'I have not gone' corresponded to our need that you knew we were out of Bolivia because a revolt was expected from one moment to the next and we had the firm intention of staying on to witness it closely. To our disappointment it did not materialise and we only saw shows of strength from the government, which, contrary to what is said, seems to be solid.

I nearly went to work in a mine but, as I was not prepared to stay for more than a month and the minimum on offer was three, I did not accept.

We then went to the shore of Lake Titicaca, also known as Copacabana, and spent a day on the Island of the Sun, famous sanctuary from the time of the Incas. Here one of my most cherished hopes as an explorer was fulfilled: I found – at an ancient indigenous cemetery – a small female statue the size of one's little finger, but an idol nonetheless, made from the famous chompi, the alloy of the Incas.

When we reached the frontier we had to walk about two kilometres because there was no transport, and I had to carry my suitcase full of books, which was as heavy as a bag of explosives. The two of us and two hired hands arrived with our tongues hanging out down to our ankles.

At Puno we had a row at customs because they took a Bolivian book from me, saying it was Red. There was no way I could convince them that it was a scientific publication.

In this letter Ernesto describes his two close friends, Alberto Granado and Calica Ferrer, their personalities and their way of seeing things. He had been to Cuzco with Granado in 1952 and with Ferrer in 1953.

Letter to Tita Infante*

Lima, September 3rd

Dear Tita,

I am sorry to have to write to you in my 'beautiful' handwriting, but I could not find a typewriter to solve this problem. In any event, I hope that you have a free day in which to read this letter.

In La Paz I forgot all about the diet and all that nonsense, in spite of which I was fine during the whole month and a half that I spent there. We visited some of the nearby surrounding areas, such as Yungas: a region of beautiful tropical valleys. One of the things we did was observe the political landscape, which is very interesting. Bolivia is a country that has given a really important example to America. We saw the site of the struggles, the impact of bullets and even the remains of a man who died in the last revolution and was found in a cornice where his torso had been blown, as the dynamite he had strapped to his waist had exploded. In brief, there has been a serious struggle. Revolutions here are not like those in Buenos Aires – two or three thousand dead (nobody really knows how many) were left to rot in the fields.

The struggle goes on here, and almost every night there are men with bullet wounds from either side. But the government is supported by the people in arms, so there is no chance that an external armed movement can threaten it; it can only succumb because of internal strife.

The Movimiento Nacionalista Revolucionario is a conglomerate in which three more-or-less well-defined tendencies can be seen: the right, represented by Siles Suazo*, who is the Vice President and a hero of the revolution; the centre, represented by Paz Estenssoro, more slippery, but probably as right-wing as the previous; and the left by Lechín*, who is the visible head of a serious revolutionary movement, but who on a personal level is an upstart, a womaniser and a hell-raiser. It is probable that power will finally remain with the Lechín group. It has the powerful support of the armed miners, but the resistance from his colleagues in government may be serious, especially now that the army is about to reorganise.

Well, I have told you a little of the Bolivian scene. I will tell you about Peru later when I have spent some time here. In general it seems to me that the American domination has not brought Peru even that fictitious financial well-being that can be seen in Venezuela, for instance.

Of my future life I know very little as to direction and far less as to time. We had thought we would go to Quito and from there to Bogotá and then Caracas, but we do not know the roads in between. I came back to Lima via Cuzco.

I do not tire of recommending it. As soon as you can, you must visit there, in particular Machu Picchu. I assure you that you will not be sorry.

Ernesto

Calica Ferrer continues with the story

Ernesto had the most infectious laughter I have ever heard. When we reached the frontier between Bolivia and Peru we had an old trunk full of books. We hired two Quechúa[5] Indians and one of them offered to carry it. We had to walk a long way, something like two kilometres, to reach customs. The man carrying the trunk was a small skinny Indian who could barely move with it. He kept dropping it and Ernesto and I had to help him because his companion was carrying the luggage.

This march had turned into something rather comic. The trunk travelling up and down, spending more time on the ground than on the shoulders of the man. We all got the giggles and I remember that Ernesto laughed so heartily that the man also started laughing and, as he could no longer hold onto the trunk because he was laughing uncontrollably, he threw himself on the ground with his load. It was the first time I had seen an Indian laughing so much.

When we were in La Paz I decided to have a good bath. I was filthy and dreamed of a bath. As Ernesto was more austere than me, he was in charge of the money. He was on a diet because of his health, so he could not succumb to temptation – that is why I accepted that he should be in charge of our funds.

When I asked him for some money for my bath, he said

[5] Quechúa: the native language of the peoples of the old Inca empire, spoken extensively in Bolivia.

that he would not go to the baths with me because he considered it a superfluous expenditure. Food was more important than cleanliness and we were really skint.

I insisted, so Ernesto gave me my share.

Soon afterwards I was coming back very pleased with myself, having taken a good hot bath. Ernesto was having café-au-lait and crackers at a nearby coffee shop.

The hot bath had given me a voracious appetite. I went up to my friend and looked at him. I was no longer entitled to the extra expenditure. But he took pity on me and shared his meagre meal with me.

When Ernesto was in good health, by which I mean when he did not have asthma, he was capable of devouring any amount of food. In those instances he turned into a caveman. Ernesto behaved like camels do: he carried his reserve on him. It is said that when camels are about to cross a desert they drink a lot of water, which they keep in their hump. As Ernesto was not always able to eat abundantly, when he did eat he ate enough to keep him going for several days.

We were travelling in the high plateau of Bolivia, accompanied by an Indian, when we reached a store in a shack by the road and Ernesto bought a tin of sardines. When he opened it a jet of oil squirted out. As he was preparing to eat that rubbish, I intervened telling him that what he was about to do was sheer folly. They both ignored me, and he and the Indian devoured the contents of the tin.

I put my head in my hands. As the son of a doctor, I knew how dangerous it was to eat something that could be toxic in that desolate region where there would not have been any medical assistance.

But neither of them suffered any consequences, while I went hungry. Ernesto was as aware as I was of the danger he was in, but he was hungry and he just ate the sardines.

In Lima, the capital of Peru, we made friends with a nurse who had a brother who was a novillero, one notch below bullfighter in the bullfighting scale. We soon made friends with him. Ernesto and I had several pictures taken dressed as bullfighters.

One afternoon we were with the nurse's brother, who had to fight a bull that day, and Ernesto decided to put on the bullfighter's hat and, after parading himself arrogantly with it on his head, threw it on a bed. The man leaped to his feet. It is well known that people in that profession are very superstitious, and the hat on the bed is a sign of bad luck. The poor man screamed like a madman, swearing his head off and assuring us that he would not enter the bullring that afternoon. And it seems that in fact he did not face the bulls that day.

With little access to transport (little money and a lot of hitch-hiking), Calica and Ernesto continued travelling on to Guayaquil in Ecuador, where they arrived on 2 October. There they met up with Ricardo Rojo – who seemed to have followed the same itinerary, but using means of transport more in accordance with his finances. He had met up with some occasional friends from Argentina and was sharing lodgings with them in a derelict boarding house. The Argentines were Andrews Herrero, a law student at the University of La Plata; Eduardo (Gualo) García, a fellow student of Andrews; and Oscar Valdovinos, another student. With the arrival of Calica and Ernesto, the quartet became a sextet.

In Guayaquil, Ernesto's friend and travelling companion Calica Ferrer left the group and travelled on to Venezuela.

Ernesto's letter from Guayaquil

Guayaquil, October 4th [1953]

Dear Viejo,
   Our trip, of course, was very slow, but kept getting
more interesting. In Bolivia we met Ricardo Rojo, a
politician from the Radical Party who famously
absconded from the police station where he was being
held in Buenos Aires some four months ago. Later on,
we ran into him in Peru, and we met him again in
Guayaquil with three law students who are going to
Guatemala to seek their fortune. The six of us have
formed a tight-knit student colony; we live in the same
boarding house and consume litres of maté per day. As
a result we were held up at the port for a few days, but I
think we may be leaving the day after tomorrow for
Quito, where we intend to approach Tato Velazco or his
stooge.
   Here there is a good climate of personal freedom,
which is in contrast with that of Peru, where a totally
unpopular government is in power, thanks to the
bayonets of its friends – a service granted in exchange
for all types of concessions.

   Ernesto had understood the government of General
Odría* when he said it was a totally unpopular government,
in power thanks to the bayonets of its friends – by which he
meant the USA. In two lines he demolishes the government
of Peru, which was not unlike that of many other Latin
American countries – all yes-men of American power.
   The whole world knows that the US does not bestow
favours on slave governments for free, but always charges
for them, and it is the people who pay with blood and sweat.

Ernesto and Calica did not learn anything new in Peru: they had experience of that sort of government.

Another letter from Ernesto addressed to his mother

Guayaquil, 21st October 1953

I am writing you this letter – which you will read who knows when – from my new guise as a 100 per cent adventurer. Much water has passed under the bridge since my last epistle. It goes like this: we were walking, Calica, García (one of our acquisitions) and I, dreaming of our beloved country. We were talking about how well the two members of the group who had succeeded in leaving for Panama would be getting on, and we were commenting on the marvellous interview with the guardian angel that you sent me, about whom more later. The fact is that García, as if in passing, invited us to go with them to Guatemala and I was in the right frame of mind psychologically disposed to accept. Calica promised that he would reply the following day and he replied in the affirmative, as a result of which there were now four new candidates for American opprobrium. But at that point our misfortunes started with the consulates: pleading daily to obtain visas for Panama, which is the requirement that is still missing, and after a variety of alternatives, with their corresponding psychological ups and downs, the answer was no. The suit you made me, your work of art, the pearl of your dreams, died heroically at a second-hand shop and the same happened to all the unnecessary items of my luggage, which has greatly decreased, to the benefit of the financial stability achieved (sigh) by the threesome.

What I can say specifically is the following: if a
captain who is a kind of friend decides to get it sorted for
us, García and I will be able to travel on to Panama, and
then, thanks to the joint effort of those who reach
Guatemala, plus that of those who have reached
Panama, we will haul over he who has been left behind
as security for the existing debts. If the captain in
question does not play ball, the two chums will
continue on to Colombia, the security remaining here,
and from there they will leave in the direction of
Guatemala by whichever incautious means Almighty
God may put within reach of their claws.

Guayaquil 24th: after many comings and goings and
much calling, plus telling some seriously tall stories,
we have visas for Panama. We leave tomorrow Sunday
and we will arrive on 29th or 30th. Write to me quickly
care of the Consulate.
   Ernesto

Part Six: Guatemala, 1953–4

As Ernesto says in his letter to his mother, he and Gualo [Eduardo García] arrived in Panama between 29 and 30 October 1953.

There they hoped to meet Oscar Valdovinos and Ricardo Rojo, who had left Guayaquil before them in a ship of United Fruit's White Fleet. But they missed them and nobody had any news of them. Thinking that they might turn up, they waited for several days, but as time elapsed and they ran out of money, and fed up with waiting, they decided to travel on to San José in Costa Rica in the hope of finding them there. Their lack of funds forced them to leave a suitcase as guarantee of future payment at the boarding house in which they had lived.

Gualo García and Ernesto arrived in San José in Costa Rica with almost no money and did not find either Rojo or Valdovinos and, tired of waiting, they left for Guatemala, both hitch-hiking and on foot.

Letter from Ernesto to his aunt

10 December 1953
San José de Costa Rica

Auntie-auntie-mine,
    My life has been a sea of conflicting resolutions until I valiantly abandoned my luggage and, with a rucksack

on my back, I started out – with my companion García
– on the tortuous road that led us here. At El Paso I had
the opportunity of crossing the domains of United Fruit,
thus convincing myself once more how terrible these
capitalists are. I have sworn in front of an image of the
old and much-lamented Comrade Stalin that I will not
rest until I see these capitalists crushed. I will perfect
my skills in Guatemala and I will achieve what I still
lack in order to be an authentic revolutionary.

Besides being a doctor, I am a journalist and a lecturer,
which will give me some – although not many – dollars.

Receive a hug and a kiss from your nephew, the one
with the iron health, an empty stomach and shining
faith in a Socialist future.

Ciao

Chancho

This was the usual tone in which Ernesto addressed his
aunt. As she was not at all a Communist sympathiser, he uses
language that will alarm her, but also, between jokes, tells her
that in Guatemala 'I will achieve what I still lack in order to
be an authentic revolutionary', and he ends the letter by
reminding her that he does not always have a full stomach,
but instead has a 'shining faith in a Socialist future'.

And he signs himself Chancho, a nickname that some of
his friends had given him to tease him. In this letter he no
longer mentions medicine, archaeology or ruins. What
interested him at the time was the social and political
situation of the poor and oppressed peoples, which he was
beginning to understand. Here, for example, United Fruit, a
powerful banana company and sugar producer, dominated
the economy. The might of the dollar and full backing of the
United States government gave total power over the people.

During his stay in San José de Costa Rica he had met and

chatted with two well-known men: Rómulo Betancourt*
and Juan Bosch*, who were later to become the Presidents of
Venezuela and the Dominican Republic respectively.

At a later date Juan Bosch caused an international
commotion when he was ousted by means of a coup, led by
the general of the day supported by an invasion of 42,000
American marines.

Not long ago, in 1982 in Cuba, I met ex-President Bosch,
who remembered in detail his meeting with the then young
Argentine doctor Ernesto Guevara de la Serna. He
mentioned the impression that the conversation made upon
him, as it proved that Ernesto had a deep understanding of
the social and political situation of the Americas.

Letter from Ernesto to his mother

Guatemala City, 28 December 1953

Dear Vieja,

At last I have reached my goal and find myself at the
crossroads. Many of the Argentines who are here have
not received what they expected and many are unhappy.
If things go well, I will stay here for a couple of years, or
about six months if I see that there are no substantial
possibilities.

After we left San José we hitch-hiked as far as the road
permitted and from there we walked on some fifty kilometres to reach the Nicaraguan frontier, since the Pan-
American Highway is but a beautiful illusion in this part
of the world. My heel was in poor condition because of
the accident I told you about in a previous letter,[1] so I had

---

[1] 'The accident I told you about in a previous letter': while travelling with
his friend García, Ernesto sprained an ankle (or maybe fractured a bone)
when the truck overturned.

a tough time after crossing a river some ten times and getting drenched by the constant rainfall. When we finally reached the frontier we waited a whole day for a lorry or other vehicle that could take us north, since in Nicaragua there are no good roads. We had already lost hope and had decided to continue on foot (my heel had improved, thanks to the care of an old woman who fixes bones; I could not have cured it better even by chance) when a car appeared with whopping great licence plates from the University of Boston. In spite of it and with great anxiety, we were about to ask the gringos[2] for a lift when the huge moustache of Fatso Rojo, the exile from the Radical Party, emerged. He was trying to get to Costa Rica with the Beberaggi Allende brothers[3] – Father must have heard of him because his name was mentioned a lot politically when Perón withdrew his citizenship. Of course, they gave up their trip immediately, since it was impossible due to the condition of the roads, and we celebrated with one of those barbecues with maté that make you miss your homeland.

We reached Managua, where I found the stupid telegram[4] from Father, who always has to have that sort of attitude. I think you ought to know by now that even if I am about to die, I will not ask you for money, and if you fail to receive a letter, just be patient and wait – sometimes I don't even have enough for stamps, but I am perfectly well and I always manage. When you feel any sort of anguish, just take the money that you

[2] Gringo: a colloquialism that is used in Argentina to refer to someone from the USA.
[3] Beberaggi Allende brothers: Domingo and Walter Beberaggi Allende were from Argentina and were travelling around South America together.
[4] Stupid telegram: Ernesto's father had sent him a telegram asking Ernesto to let them know how he was and whether he needed any money.

were going to spend on a telegram and have a drink or something along those lines, but from now on I am not replying to any telegram of that sort.

From Managua we went on immediately in a car belonging to the Beberaggi brothers, who were bringing it to sell it in Guatemala, but as we were running out of money we ended up selling the jack, torches, tyres and anything else we could.

I am negotiating to see if I get a job at the leprosarium here, with a monthly salary of 250 quetzals and free afternoons, but nothing has been confirmed yet. However, I am going to manage somehow, because the people are helpful and there is a shortage of doctors. If I cannot do this I might go to the countryside with the same salary, but to some place with ruins of ancient civilisations, which, as you know, is what I am interested in.

This is the only worthwhile country in Central America, even if its capital is no larger than Bahía Blanca[5] and as sleepy. Naturally, all regimes lose credibility at close quarters, and to confirm it there is an authentic climate of democracy and of cooperation with all the foreigners who, for different reasons, end up marooned here. I am under the impression that I will be able to practise my profession here without problems since there is not a single allergy specialist in the whole country, so I am told. I am not very keen on this because it renders one more idiotic and bourgeois.

[5] Bahía Blanca: an Argentine city in the province of Buenos Aires, situated south of the federal capital and the main seaport for the area.

Well, a very all-embracing hug for all the clan, a
special one to the birthday girl and until we meet again.

The letter does not have a signature.

Ernesto in Guatemala

As can be appreciated from the letter dated 28 December
1953, Ernesto had at last reached the city he longed to see.
On or around 20 December he entered the Guatemalan
capital with Rojo, Gualo García and the Beberaggi Allende
brothers.

A few days later he met the woman who was to become
his wife. Hilda Gadea, a Peruvian, worked at the time for the
Guatemalan Institute for the Promotion of Production
(Instituto de Fomento de la Producción). She was a political
exile who belonged to the APRA Party[6] of Peru, led by Víctor
Raúl Haya de la Torre*. She had to go into exile as a result
of the military coup by General Manuel Odría, who became
President of Peru, following the well-known custom of so
many military men of Latin America.

Hilda had been a university student leader while studying
at the Faculty of Economy of the Universidad Nacional
Mayor of San Marcos and later, once she had joined APRA,
had been one of their leaders.

Hilda was Ernesto's *compañera* for a long time in
Guatemala and knew well the comings and goings of his
agitated life, especially when he found himself involved in

---

[6] APRA Party: Alianza Popular Revolucionaria Americana (American
Popular Revolutionary Alliance), also known as the Partido Aprista
Peruano (Peruvian Aprista Party). Founded in Mexico City by Peruvian
politician Víctor Raúl Haya de la Torre, who aspired to turn it into a
continent-wide party, it influenced other Latin American political movements such as Bolivia's Revolutionary National Movement (MNR). It
originally espoused anti-imperialism, pan-Americanism, international
solidarity and economic nationalism.

the political and social storms of that nation – for example, after the traitor Castillo Armas*, with the support of the USA, invaded the country from Honduras, toppling the Socialist government of President Jacobo Arbenz* and unleashing a cruel and brutal repression.

Hilda in turn suffered the consequences of her friendship with Ernesto and was jailed. She managed to leave Guatemala because she was Peruvian, but only after much suffering.

Ernesto met many revolutionaries in Guatemala, among them Professor Edelberto Torres*, a notable Nicaraguan writer, and his daughter Myrna, who became very good friends of his. They accompanied Ernesto and Hilda on many excursions and their friendship grew.

This Nicaraguan revolutionary, who not only shared much with Ernesto in Guatemala but also in Mexico, later on wrote a book about Sandino*. In its appendix he includes a short history of the life of Che, evidence of his high opinion of him.

The following is one of the first letters Ernesto wrote from Guatemala to his Aunt Beatriz.

5 January 1954

In any case, money for me means nothing, because I am following the way of the donkey (I eat six straws a day). This is a country in which one can open up one's lungs and fill them with democracy. There are newspapers supported by United Fruit that, if I were Arbenz, I would have closed down in five minutes, because they are shameful and yet they say what they like and contribute to the atmosphere that the USA likes, purporting that this is a den of thieves, Communists, traitors, etc. I cannot tell you that it is a country where there is any luxury or comfort at all, but there are opportunities to work honestly in decent jobs. And if they manage to overcome their tendency to bureaucratisation, which is a bit uncomfortable, I will stay here for some time.

In a letter dated 15 January 1954, addressed to all the family, Ernesto says to his sister Ana María:

I am exchanging ignorance with a gringo who does not have a word of Spanish and we already have our own language and we understand each other perfectly. Of this gringo they say that he exiled himself in Guatemala because the FBI is after him; others say that he is from the FBI. The thing is that he writes the most irate anti-American articles and reads Hegel*, and I do not really know whose side he is on. I am still dreaming of a square meal. I end here, wishing you a happy birthday.

This is the first letter in which Ernesto shows his distrust of someone he has met; it is mistrust of a political sort. Surely during his travels in Latin America he must have met agents of the FBI and the CIA. Thousands of them have been strewn all over America for many years and carry out their task with some efficiency.

And talking about the climate of Guatemala, he says:

As this climate is not good for me, I have to follow my diet to the letter (at the boarding house they starve me, but I still follow my diet).

Referring to a post he was seeking in the government, he says:

I went to the Ministry of Public Health and asked for a

position, but I demanded a categorical reply, either yes or no. The man I saw was very polite and took all my details and asked me to return two or three days later. The days went by and the Minister did not let me down because his reply was categorical: NO.

In any case, I have something good in mind for the first period and to settle down, since in order to practise, one must join a medical circle that is closed and very oligarchic. I am going to cross swords with them.

For the moment I sell, in the streets, a beautiful image of the Lord of Esquipulas,[7] a black Christ who does the most fantastic miracles. The one I am selling is illuminated using a system like Adolfo's,[8] but even worse. I have by now a rich collection of anecdotes of miracles performed by this Christ and I constantly add to it, and between one joke and another, I ask him for something, just in case. The climate is magnificent, and that is all.

In this same letter he sent me a little paragraph in which he calls me 'Chancho Padre Burgués' (Bourgeois Pig Senior). The origin of the joke was the following: a close friend of Ernesto's used to refer to him as El Chancho (the pig). I, annoyed by the nickname, told him off. So he stopped calling Ernesto that in my presence, but called me – behind my back – by the nickname Chancho Padre. Ernesto always included this sort of joke in his letters to the family.

And his letter goes on with a graphology tease:

. . . your letters, very Guevara, big handwriting, generous characters and pages filled quickly.

[7] Lord of Esquipulas: a statue of the crucified Christ commissioned by the Spanish conquistadores in 1594 for the town of Esquipulas in Guatemala.
[8] Adolfo: a friend of Ernesto who was a photographer in Buenos Aires.

Later on Ernesto adds:

The only thing I can tell you in advance is that I do not
want to leave the area without seeing Mexico. The way
I see things, in the whole of America 'and I know
about these things', there is no country as democratic as
this one (Guatemala). The two extremes and all the
shades in between say whatever they feel like with no
fear.

I should clarify that when he says 'and I know about these
things', he is pulling my leg affectionately, because
whenever we were having a discussion and I felt that he was
pressing me, I always used to say, 'I know about these
things' and the phrase remained in the family as a boast.

From my personal point of view I think that there is one
thing that has to end, since United Fruit (which grows
bananas, but has greenbacks in quantities) can spend a
lot of money on propaganda. The newspapers of the
opposition carry on a daily basis entire transcriptions of
the speeches of the company's representatives and US
government officials, and the real trouble seems to be
brewing at the Caracas Conferences, where the
Americans will use every trick to attempt to place
sanctions on Guatemala. It is true that all governments
kneel before them, but their most devoted lackeys are
Pérez Jiménez*, Odría, Trujillo*, Batista, Somoza*; that
is, the reactionaries, the most Fascistic and unpopular.
Bolivia was an interesting country, but Guatemala is
even more so because it has stood up against whatever
may come, without having even the slightest financial
independence and having to put up with armed
attempts against it of every type (President Arévalo*

resisted forty of them) and without even attacking freedom of expression.

At the end of this letter Ernesto said to his brother Juan Martín, who was then eleven:

Eat well and think of me when you swallow, because Argentine steaks are nothing but a distant and never sufficiently lauded dream; take advantage, my brother, of being in the country where people get more to eat than in the whole of Latin America.

The letter ends full of affection as usual and with a thought for each member of the family and friends.

On 2 February Ernesto writes to me saying:

Dear Viejo,

I am sending you my heartfelt condolences in advance for your new birthday, among other reasons because letters take a long time, because one has to have letters ready for when there is a spare coin, and because I am afraid I might forget the date.

The situation here is exactly the same as in my last letter. I earn enough running errands for my daily existence and I am in excellent spirits. I think that during this six-month trial period things will improve. Politically things are not going so well, because there is a constant fear that there could be a coup under the auspices of your friend Ike*. The other day a conspiracy was discovered in which all the heads of Central American democracy were implicated, whether by the sponsorship of the United Fruit Company or the Department of State, that was not clear.

The documents published are incontrovertible and the whole world recognised it [. . .]

The daily grind of struggling for grub has not permitted me to see Guatemala as I would like, but whichever of the two prospective jobs I have in mind I would be able to do it with relative ease.

Ernesto analyses his life

On 12 February he writes to his Aunt Beatriz:

My very dear, always adored and never sufficiently praised aunt,

I was pleased to receive your last letter, the culmination and complement of the two previous capitalist ones, of which only one reached me, meaning that the democratic post-office employee made a just distribution of wealth. Do not send me any more money, it costs you a lot to do so, and I find dollars on the pavement here; I should tell you that in the beginning I got lumbago from so much bending down to pick them up. Now I only pick up one in every ten, just to keep public places clean, because so much paper flying around or lying on the ground is a danger.

My plan for the next few years: at least six months in Guatemala, unless I find something financially rewarding that enables me to stay for two years. If the first option is the one, I will go to another country to work, and that could be, in a decreasing order of probability, Venezuela, Mexico, Cuba, USA. If the two-year plan happens, after a period of visits to the three latter countries as well as Haiti and Santo Domingo, I will go to Western Europe, probably with the Vieja, where I will remain as long as I can. If there is any time and money left I will visit you using some cheapo means of transport, such as flying for free or by boat, working as a doctor, etc.

This whole plan has two highly variable aspects that can direct it one way or the other. The first one is money, which for me is not of fundamental importance, but makes one cut short one's stays or modify itineraries, etc. The second and most important aspect is the political situation. My position is in no way that of a dilettante who chats and nothing else. I have taken a clear position next to the Guatemalan government and within it, in the PGT[9] group, which is Communist, meeting with intellectuals of that tendency who publish a magazine here, as well as working as a doctor for the trade unions, which has made me clash with the medical college, which is totally reactionary . . . I can imagine all that you are going to say and comment, but you will not be able to complain that I did not make myself clear.

Ernesto then refers to his scientific work, saying that he is putting together a bibliography in order to work on hyaluronidase,[10] and tells his aunt that she may know the effects of it from *Reader's Digest*. And then:

In the field of social medicine, and helped by my limited personal experience, I am preparing a very pretentious book, which I believe will require two years of work. Its title is *The Function of the Doctor in Latin America* and I only have the general plan and the first two chapters. I think that, with patience and methodology, it could be good.

[9] PGT: Partido Guatemalteco de los Trabajadores, the Workers' Party of Guatemala.
[10] Hyaluronidase: an enzyme that degrades hyaluronic acid.

A steel hug from your proletarian nephew.

An important P.S.: Tell me what you intend to do with
your apartment and whether I can send you some books
to keep for me. Don't be scared, they're not in any way
incriminating.

This letter is really important when one is analysing the
life of Ernesto Guevara de la Serna. In it he declares openly
for the first time that he has taken sides with the government of Guatemala, which for the rest of the world was a
Communist government, although in truth it was only
Socialist.

But what is significant is that he has definitely joined in
with the political left. He is aligning himself with the
Communist Party of Guatemalan Workers, associating with
radical intellectual groups, as well as working as a doctor for
the left-wing trade unions.

On 28 February we received a letter, part of which I
transcribe here:

Dear Daddy and Mummy,
    A plot was discovered here which had conspiratorial
ramifications. Somoza, Trujillo, Pérez Jiménez.

He then goes on to write about Mexico and says:

The situation there is growing more complicated and
that is accompanied by a serious financial crisis.
Nonetheless, I would like to have the address of Petit
(de Murat)* in case I go there (yesterday I was invited to
go for ten dollars, but you need thirty dollars to return,
which of course I do not have).

Thirty dollars was not a lot of money for a doctor, but Ernesto never took any money from any patient; he considered medicine to be a sacred profession and that the doctor should devote himself totally to the patient. During his travels and stays in Bolivia, Peru, Ecuador, Panama, Guatemala and Mexico he practised medicine, but he never profited from it. When medicine gave him enough to eat, it was because he had a scholarship that included room and meals or because his work was paid for by the government.

He then goes on to tell us how he earns his living:

A daily peso for giving Spanish lessons to a gringo and 30 pesos per month for helping with a geography book that an economist is preparing here. Helping means typing and collating data (a total of 50 pesos), which if you take into account that the boarding house costs 45, that I do not go to the cinema and that I do not need medicines, is one hell of a salary; the only drawback is that I already owe two months, but I hope to find a more permanent job in the next few days. [. . .]

To my failed work projects you have to add four more, which went by like meteorites without leaving anything more than a slight trail of boredom. This is the first time that I need to work and cannot find a job. In general in America, you have to dodge work. This is all relative since I have a firm offer to work as a painter in a workshop that makes placards, which is of interest because I could turn out to be a Hitler (an interior decorator) instead of a Rockefeller* (a newspaper boy).

I got a letter from the vieja, who tells me to learn from my little brother[11] who earns $750 working as a

[11] 'Learn from my little brother': Ernesto's brother Roberto worked as a plumber for the Argentine navy, although he had already graduated as a lawyer.

plumber, but I beat him because I earn $1,500 as a painter, so it's worth one's while to go out and see the world and make one's fortune.

In this letter dated 28 February one can see that Ernesto is a bit disorientated with regard to his future activities, so he says:

My future activities are a mystery even for God the Father himself: for the moment I would like to have a bit of peace and quiet because I am classifying the material for a book . . . but the struggle for our daily sustenance does not allow me to devote too much time to the matter, which in any case is not something you can do in one day.

It seems that the best of the opportunities will fail because the cooperatives do not want to pay a doctor, in spite of the fact that, in my case, they would have the unique possibility of being able to show off the title (which I have) of a doctor specially imported from Argentina. The place was ideal, 98 per cent of the inhabitants have parasites and 107 per cent are illiterate. The truth is that the guild is shit. I am referring to the medical guild. I went to work for a banana company and it was the same thing (the matter of incorporation), but somehow or other it will be resolved, and if it is not, on to another place and that is that. But not for four months, which is the time I need to pay off my debts, visit the Maya[12] ruins and see the country (so much time at work prevents me from doing so at the moment).

[12] The Mayas: have been considered the most civilised of the ancient indigenous populations of the American continent.

Daddy and Mummy, loving love, send news and until the next one.

As with so many of his letters, this one was not signed.

Letter from Ernesto to his mother and father

March 1954

Dear Mummy and Daddy,
I had not written all this time because I was waiting to be able to give you definitive news of my employment, if not as a doctor, at least as a male nurse. Unfortunately people here take their time to decide and nothing has been resolved. The job would be in Petén,[13] the jungle region of Guatemala, a splendid place where the Maya civilisation flourished. It was later the scene of the epic conquest by Alvarado*, Cortés'* captain. Because there are a hell of a lot of illnesses there, one can learn a lot (if one so wishes, naturally).

During this period of time Ernesto's passion for medicine ran side-by-side with his passion for archaeology. Petén would cater to both.

I forgot to tell you that the job pays 120 pesos per month plus food, so that the first month would go to pay back what I owe at the boarding house.

And he continues to make remarks and calculations about what he can earn, which in reality are about what he will be able to eat.

[13] Petén: a region of Guatemala. Descendants of the Mayas, Itzás and Lacandones still live there today.

In many of his letters Ernesto discussed the book he was planning to write. I never managed to read any of it, and I never knew what became of the part that he did in fact write. When he had decided to leave Guatemala, he sent me a large number of books that belonged to him, but he did not send the manuscript in question.

His writing was sometimes illegible and we used to spend hours deciphering his letters.

Letter to Tita Infante, written on letterhead paper from the Instituto de Fomento de la Producción de Guatemala

Guatemala City, already in March of 1954

In spite of everything, my dear Tita, we grow old: almost a year from the date of my departure and I have not made much progress in anything, but I am assuming that you like exotic adventures, so I will now tell you about my projects, travels and misadventures.

The first thing is an apology for not having replied earlier; several things happened that prevented me, because I wanted to send you a decent chronicle of Guatemala and did not have the time, then I tried to find an indigenous writer to do it for me, so that it could be published somewhere over there. But this also failed, as the man who invented work came here to die many years ago, but then I was asked for an article about Guatemala for a magazine over there, and do not know what it is called, and I thought that I would send you a copy, but I have not finished it and I don't think I am going to be able to for some time, due to the fact that I want to do it properly.

I am telling you all this because I believe that Guatemala is a country that deserves to be well known and well understood. I think that your fears are not unjustified, given the belligerent and, up to now, triumphant situation of that country. On 1 March President Arbenz in his annual message to Congress announced unequivocally the cooperation of the Communist Party with the government and the need of the same government to defend the members of that political group against any type of sanction. On the whole, the Communists take positions with caution, and if it were not for the hullabaloo made by the national press against 'the intrusion of exotic doctrines', the party would go unnoticed, but it is the only political grouping in Guatemala that joined the government in order to comply with a programme in which personal interests do not count (maybe there is a demagogue amongst its leaders), in frank contrast with the other three groups of parties, which are a veritable snake-pit; so much so, that each of them has been split up into at least two opposing wings and they go as far as making deals with the opposition in order to obtain the Presidency of the Congress (it needs to be passed by both chambers). For your information, if you do not know the problem better than I do, I will tell you that the influence of the PGT is great in sections of the other three parties, by means of elements that have moved to the left and are prepared to help in the total socialisation of Guatemala – a very difficult task, among other reasons, because there is not a lot of quality in human beings inspiring the revolution (I am referring to the word in its intellectual sense, above all).

This is a country with a typically agricultural economy, which is only now leaving behind the usual handicaps of feudalism, whose only card in the pack is a single-crop economy that weighs on the international

scales: coffee. Without being too pessimistic, one can
say that a big decrease in the production of this product
can topple the government unless emergency measures
are taken, which would only be possible when facing an
international boycott with the blessing of the gringos. I
believe that the most difficult moment for Guatemala
will come in three years' time, when they must elect a
new president. The names bandied about until now are
not very worthy of trust when it comes to the
continuation of the revolution in the magnificent way
in which it is being carried out. If you are interested and
are not afraid that you might be harassed over there, I
can arrange to send you some interesting publications,
but I will not do so until I have your reply.

I meant to write only one page because my financial
situation is rather precarious and the new page will
make the letter slightly more expensive, but I am
interested in learning a few things:

First, how is your student life in this month of March
(and the months that will go by before you reply), what
are your plans or non-plans? I am asking you this
because your letter indicates to me that you are in a
very romantic and very desperate and dangerous
situation. As a piece of advice, I will tell you that one
must be a fatalist in the positive sense if one wants to
be a fatalist, and not concern yourself so much with the
useless passage of time and any failure of any type; the
difficult thing is to stop the days from passing, and that
is what you are doing in crying for them one by one. If
you look back one or two years you will see the progress
that you have made. Please forgive the doctoral tone.

Second, what of your intellectual group and of the
magazine – I bet they went bust; how is Paz and how is
your health?

Third, what about Montenegro? I wrote him a letter
to which he did not reply, and then I wrote to Dickstein
and he did not reply either, so that I know nothing of the
life of the tiny group I knew there in the dives
frequented by medics. When you decide to write to me,
read the questions and answer them, please.

Now, about me. I must tell you that my efforts to
work as a doctor were a total failure due to the hermetic
spirit of the law, made to satisfy a group of oligarchs in
all its prerogatives. All of them are the heirs of those
who wanted the revolution – typically bourgeois – of
1944 and who now do not want to let go of the booty
under any circumstances. Among my occasional occupations I attempted to work in your field, with
frightening results when it comes to statistics: 98 per
cent of children are infected by Ascariasis or Necator.[14]
I also devoted myself to breaking open the backside of
the *vinchucas*[15] (*triatomes* as they call them) to look for
Trypanosoma cruzi and *T. rangeli*, which are also
present in abundance. That's it, in the area of health,
because beyond it I have worked in whatever allows one
not to die of hunger, in the end to make the great leap:
it seems that I will be going to Petén, the jungle of
Guatemala, hired as a male nurse and with a very
meagre salary, but I will go into the woodlands with
those who extract gum and timber in an area of the old
Maya culture (since the one in Yucatán is a modernised

[14] Ascariasis or Necator: ascariasis is a human disease caused by the
parasitic roundworm *Ascariasis lumbricoides*; perhaps as many as a
quarter of the world's population are infected. *Necator americanus* is the
human hookworm and the second most prevalent helminthic infection
(after ascariasis) in the world; it is found mainly in moist, warm climates.
At the time of the letter Tita was researching parasites, hence Ernesto's
reference to 'work in your field'.
[15] *Vinchuca*: an insect of northern Argentina, Paraguay and Bolivia – its bite
is lethal.

version of this culture lost in the jungle) and with the opportunity to study properly tropical diseases of every type. Still pending – because here there is always something pending – is that the trade union approves my appointment, since it is an important job in the employer–trade union give and take. I hope to persuade them that I am not as bad a guy as they imagine, as I am being recommended by the boss, and if this goes ahead, in a fortnight's time mosquitoes will take up residence on my body and I will commune with Ma Nature. The only thing that makes me a little sad is that in Venezuela I would have done the same job, but instead of earning 125 I would earn 800 dollars. What a curse!

Tita, brotherly vibes, I await your news by the same consular route. Do try to put an end to your ordeal. Until we meet.
Ernesto

Letter from Ernesto to his mother from Guatemala

This letter came without a date, and instead it says: 'First Month of Hope' and could be from the end of April 1954.

Vieja, my old vieja,

Don't think that the heading is just to keep the Viejo happy; there are signs of improvement and the prospects are not so desperate in relation to the financial outlook. I mention the peso tragedy because it is true, and I assumed that the Viejo considered me sufficiently macho to put up with whatever befalls me. Now, if you prefer fairy tales, I can tell you some really nice ones. During my silence my life went as follows: I went with a backpack and a briefcase, some on foot, some hitch-hiking, some (shame) paying, as I had ten dollars that the government had given me. I reached El Salvador and the police confiscated some books I had brought with me from Guatemala, but got through. I obtained a visa so that I would be able to return here to Guatemala, and then I went to see the ruins of the Pipiles.[16] They are a branch of the Tlascaltecas,[17] who went to conquer the south (their centre was in Mexico) and stayed there until the Spaniards came. This has nothing to do with what the Mayas built and far less with the Incas. Then I went to spend a few days at the beach while I waited for a visa that I had requested, in order to go and visit some ruins in Honduras, which are really splendid. I slept in the sleeping bag I've got, by the seashore, and did not follow my diet strictly, but I was fine leading this healthy life, except for the blisters from the sun. I made friends with some chaps who, like everyone in Central America, are powered by alcohol and, taking advantage of the extroversion caused by the alcohol, I socked them a little Guatemalan propaganda and recited a few little verses which were deep Red in colour. The result is that we all ended up in the nick, but were released immediately, after a decent-looking officer gave us the advice that we sing to the afternoon roses and other beauties. I chose a sonnet to turning into smoke and vanishing. The Hondurans refused me a visa for the simple fact that I am resident in Guatemala, although I need not tell you that I had every intention of catching a glimpse of a strike that has been unleashed there and to which 25 per cent of the total working population is adhering – a figure that is high in any place, but extraordinary in a country where there is no right to strike and the trade unions are illegal. The fruit

[16] Pipiles: an ancient indigenous tribe of Mexico.
[17] Tlascaltecas: a tribe of the Chichimeca Indians from southern Mexico, who lived there until the arrival of the Spanish.

company is roaring and of course Dulles* and Co. want to intervene in Guatemala for the country's terrible crime of acquiring weapons from whoever, since the US has not sold them even a round of ammunition for ages.

Of course I did not even consider the possibility of staying there. I started back through half-abandoned roads and with empty pockets, because here a dollar is little more than one peso, and with twenty cents there is not much you can do. Some days I walked around fifty kilometres and after many days I ended up at the fruit company's hospital, where there are some small but beautiful ruins. Here I became totally convinced of what my Americanism did not want me to know: our forefathers were Asian (tell the viejo that they will be claiming their paternal rights soon). There are some figures in bas-relief that are the personification of Buddha and all the features prove it, as they are totally identical to those of ancient Hindustani civilisations. The place is beautiful, so much so that I committed the crime of Silvestre Bonnard[18] against my stomach and spent more than a dollar on film and renting a camera. Then I begged for food at the hospital, but was able to fill my hump only to half its capacity. I was left without money to be able to reach Guatemala by rail, so I went to Puerto Barrios and worked there unloading barrels of tar, earning 2.63 pesos for twelve hours of really heavy work, at a place where there are clouds of diving mosquitoes in unbelievable numbers. My hands are a mess and my back, I cannot tell you, but I confess that I was quite happy. I used to work from six in the evening to six in the morning and slept in an abandoned house

[18] Silvestre Bonnard: protagonist of the novel by Anatole France (1844–1924), *The Crime of Silvestre Bonnard*. France was awarded the Nobel Prize for Literature in 1921.

by the sea. Then I left for Guatemala, and here I am with better prospects.

And he ends as follows:

Next time, more calmly, I will send you news if there is any . . . A big hug for all.

Again he does not sign the letter.

April 1954 letter from Ernesto to his mother from Guatemala

April 1954

Vieja:

As you can see, I did not go to Petén. The son of a bitch who was supposed to employ me made me wait for a month, to then tell me he could not do it. [. . .]

What I want to do in any case is visit the ruins of Petén. There is a city there, Tical, which is marvellous, and another one, Piedras Negras,[19] which is far less important, but where the art of the Mayas reached extraordinary levels. At the museum here there is a lintel, which is in really bad shape, but which would be revered as a work of art anywhere in the world.

My old Peruvian friends lacked the artistic sensitivity of their tropical brothers, so that they could not do

---

[19] Tical and Piedras Negras: admirable stone constructions, temples, pyramids, palaces and sculptures built by the Mayas and the Quichés. It is believed that they were religious centres and that the population lived in the surrounding areas. Not all these constructions were contemporary; according to indigenous traditions, the people abandoned them when they had built new ones. When the Spanish arrived the main buildings had been in ruins for some time.

anything similar, in addition to not having the cal-
careous stone that there is in this area, which is so
easily carved.

Here Ernesto tells us clearly that he is more unhappy at
not being able to see the ruins of Petén than at having lost a
post as a doctor. His passion for archaeology is greater than
his interest in medicine.

I am so happy that I left. My medical knowledge may
not grow larger, but in the meantime I am assimilating
knowledge that interests me far more than that.

What was this knowledge that he was interested in? We
already knew of his passion for archaeology. The other
knowledge was, beyond doubt, social and political. Ernesto
had just entered Guatemala and was already foreseeing a
coup d'état in the making. The approaching tempest was
already engulfing him.

In the midst of his financial difficulties he did not forget
his country, and he says to his mother:

I want to go for a visit, but I have no idea of when or
how. Making plans in my situation is like telling you of
a web of dreams. In any case if – and this is an express
condition – I get the job with the fruit company, I intend
to pay all the debts I have here, the ones I left there and
buy myself a camera, visit Petén and leave for the north
– that is, Mexico.

And in reply to a question from his mother, he says:

I am glad that you have such a high opinion of me. In
any case it is improbable that anthropology becomes

the only occupation of my mature years. It seems to me that investigating that which is dead beyond repair, as the aim of my life, seems a little paradoxical. I am sure of two things. The first one is that if I reach an authentically creative stage by around thirty-five, my exclusive – or at least main – activity will be nuclear physics, genetics or a subject of that sort, which brings together the most interesting aspects of the subjects I know. The second is that our America will be the scene of my adventures in a much more important way than I could have imagined. I feel that I have really learned to understand it and I feel American, from that America whose character is distinct from all other people of this earth.

Naturally, I will visit the rest of the world. [. . .]

Of my daily life I can tell you little that will interest you. In the mornings I go to work at the lab for a few hours. In the afternoons I go to the library or to a museum to learn something about this region. In the evenings I read medicine or any other subject, write a letter – you know, domestic chores. I drink maté when I have some and I get into interminable discussions with *compañera* Hilda Gadea, a girl who is an Aprista and whom I, with my characteristic gentleness, try to persuade that she drops that shit of a party. She has a heart of platinum at the very least. Her help can be felt in all aspects of my daily life (in particular at the boarding house).

It was the first time he mentioned Hilda Gadea, who later became his wife.

This is a typical letter from Ernesto. In it he tells his mother, in any order as if he were talking to himself, all that he does, thinks and plans to do. He thinks and writes, and his thoughts are a projection of what he plans for the future. He is involved in so many things, and his interest is so great, that he even has difficulty finding time for them. He says that at the age of thirty-five his main occupation might be nuclear physics, genetics or a similar subject – and he managed to bring to fruition some of these projects in Cuba, when he was already a minister; he devoted his attention to these subjects as well as studying higher mathematics. And with reference to the fact that America would be the scene of his adventures, he really understood it and therefore felt deeply American.

For us, his letter was very amusing and at the same time very worrying. We mistook his ideological development for lack of direction. Today, thirty years from the time he wrote them, besides being very funny, his letters are deeply interesting. From them one learns about the maturity of his thoughts, and one can glean his decision to become a man totally devoted to the liberation of the oppressed.

May 1954 letter from Ernesto to his mother from Guatemala

10th May 1954

Vieja:

[. . .] Besides looking towards a future tasting of *asado*,[20] my residency is going forward, although with all the sloth typical of these lands, and I assume that in a month's time I will be able to go to the cinema without latching on to some kindly neighbour. I have been promised something that I think I already told Father and I also told him about my projects, but

---

[20] *Asado*: a barbecue or Argentine roasted meat.

superficially. I have decided to leave this boarding house
with a sleeping bag I inherited from a fellow national
who travelled through these places. That way I will be
able to see all the places I want to – except Petén, where
one cannot go because it is the rainy season – and I will
be able to climb some volcano, since I have wanted to
look at the tonsils of Mother Earth for some time (what
a pretty figure of speech). This is the land of volcanoes
and there are some for every taste; my taste is very
simple, neither too high nor too active. In Guatemala I
could become very rich, but through the base procedure
of revalidating my degree, set up a clinic and devote
myself to allergies (this place is full of colleagues). To do
that would be the most heinous treason to the two that
are already at war inside me, the sort of socialistic and
the traveller.

Warm and wet hugs because here it rains all the time
(while there is maté it is very romantic).

In May 1954 Ernesto was in Guatemala, but as his visa
had expired and his residency request had been turned down,
he travelled to El Salvador to get a visa there, in order to
return to Guatemala.

In another letter he tells us that in Honduras there was a
fantastic strike, with 25 per cent of the workforce on strike,
and the newspapers of the opposition were inciting the
people to revolt; there was a revolutionary climate.

About the situation in Guatemala, Ernesto thought that
the government of Arbenz would be respected, in spite of the
blows against the government that had taken place.

On 20 June he writes to his mother telling her what was
going on in Guatemala when the attack by the Honduran
forces commenced.

June 1954 letter from Ernesto to his mother from Guatemala

20 June 1954

Dear Vieja,

This letter will reach you a little after your birthday, and you may be a bit concerned about me. Let me tell you that for the moment there is nothing to fear, although the same cannot be said of the future, even if personally I have the feeling of being inviolable (maybe not the right word and my subconscious played a trick on me). The situation along general lines is as follows: some five or six days ago a pirate light aircraft that came from Honduras flew over Guatemala for the first time, without doing anything.

The next day, as well as on successive days, various military installations of the country were bombed, and two days ago an aircraft bombed the lower neigh-bourhoods of the city, killing a two-year-old girl. The incident has served to unite all the Guatemalans behind their government as well as all those, like myself, who have felt attracted by Guatemala. Simultaneously, mer-cenary troops under the orders of an ex-army colonel, discharged for treason long ago, left Tegucigalpa, the capital of Honduras, from where they were transported to the frontier and are already deep inside Guatemalan territory. The government is proceeding very cautiously to avoid the United States declaring Guatemala the aggressor, and has limited itself to protesting to Tegucigalpa and to sending the complete file of events to the United Nations Security Council, allowing the invading forces to penetrate sufficiently into the country so that nobody could pretend it was one of the alleged boundary incidents. Colonel Arbenz is a man with guts, no doubt about that, and he is ready to die in his post if need be. His last speech did nothing but reaffirm this, which we already knew, and it gave us peace of mind. The danger is not in the number of troops who have entered the country at present, since it is infinitesimal, nor in the aircraft that do nothing but bomb the houses of civilians and machine-gun some of them; the danger is in how the gringos (read here the Americans) manage their puppets at the United Nations, since a declaration, no matter how vague, would greatly help the invaders. The Americans have totally dropped the good-guy mask that Roosevelt* had given them and they are committing an outrage and a half around here. If matters reach a point where it is necessary to fight against planes and modern troops sent by the fruit company or the USA, there will be a fight. The morale of the people is very good and the shamefaced attacks, added to the lies of the international press, have united all those who were indifferent towards the government and there is a really combative mood. I am already registered with the urgent medical-assistance service and have also joined the youth brigades to receive military instruction or whatever else. I do not think it will go any further, but we will know that after the meeting of the Security Council, which I believe is tomorrow. In any case, when you get this letter you will know how things have developed.

Other than that, I have no news. As the Argentine Embassy has been closed over the holidays, I have not had any fresh news after a letter from Beatriz and one from you last week.

They say they will give me the job with the Ministry of Health any minute now, but since everyone has been very busy with all the mess, it seemed a bit imprudent to go and pester them about a little job, when they are all involved in more important matters.

Well, Vieja, I hope you had as happy a birthday as possible in this year full of tragedies; as soon as I am able to, I will send further news.

Ciao

There is no signature.

Nervous tension grew in our home. We knew that Ernesto was not going to miss the opportunity of taking part in the defence of Guatemala if there was an invasion, so we were all hanging on every word of the wires that arrived constantly in Buenos Aires. We knew from his letter that he intended to take part in the struggle, not only through the Red Cross, but also as a combatant in the Youth Militias.

July 1954 letter from Ernesto to his mother from Guatemala

4 July 1954

Vieja,

It has all gone by like a beautiful dream that one is bent upon continuing after one has woken up. Reality is knocking on many doors, and retribution is being meted out to the most ardent adherents of the old regime. Treason continues to be the preserve of the army, and once more the aphorism that says that the cancellation of the army is the true beginning of democracy is verified. (If this aphorism does not exist, I am creating it.) [. . .]

The naked truth is that Arbenz did not rise to the occasion.

This is how it all happened:

After initiating the aggression from Honduras, and

with no prior declaration of war or anything along those lines (still protesting about alleged frontier transgressions), the planes came to bomb the city. We were completely defenceless since there were no aircraft, no anti-aircraft artillery, or shelters. There were some deaths, not many. Panic, however, took over the people and above all the 'courageous and loyal army of Guatemala'. A US military mission met with the President and threatened him with bombing Guatemala properly and reducing it to rubble, as well as with the declaration of war by Honduras and Nicaragua, which the United States would make its own because there were mutual-assistance treaties in existence. The military shat themselves and gave Arbenz an ultimatum.

He failed to see that the city was full of reactionaries and that the houses that would be lost would be theirs and not the people's, since the people have nothing and it was the people who were defending the government. He did not remember, in spite of the examples set by Korea and Indochina, that an armed people is an invincible power. He could have armed the people and he chose not to. This is the result.

I already had my little job, but I lost it immediately so I am back to the beginning, but without debts, as I decided to cancel them because of *force majeure*. I live comfortably because a good friend returned a favour, and I do not need anything. Of my future life I know nothing, except that I may go to Mexico. I am a little ashamed to admit that I had the most marvellous time during these past days. That magic feeling of invulnerability that I was telling you about in a previous letter made me relish seeing people running around like mad as soon as they saw the planes, or at night, during the blackouts when the city was filled with bullets. By the way, I'll tell you that light bombers are quite imposing. I saw one launching itself against a target relatively near where I was, and one could see the aircraft growing larger by the minute, while from its wings little tongues of fire escaped intermittently. And the noise of its machine guns, as well as that of the light machine guns shooting at it, was deafening. Suddenly it was suspended in the air for a moment, horizontally, and then very quickly it dived very fast and you felt the earth shaking due to the bomb. Now it is all over and you can only hear the fireworks of the reactionary lot, who crawl out of the soil like ants to celebrate their triumph, to try and lynch the Communists – as they have labelled all the members of the previous government. Embassies are full to capacity and ours, together with the Mexican one, is the most overcrowded.

If you want to have an idea of the politics of this government, I will give you some information. One of the first villages taken by the invaders was a property of the fruit company in which the employees were on strike. When they arrived they immediately declared the strike over, took the leaders to the cemetery and killed them by throwing grenades at their chests. One very dark night, when a plane was flying over, fireworks came out of the church. The first thanksgiving was by the bishop, the second by Foster Dulles, who is the lawyer of the fruit company. Today, 4 July, there is a solemn mass with all the scenic apparatus, and all the newspapers congratulate the government of the USA on their national day in exaggerated terms.

Vieja, I shall see how I send you these letters, because if I send them by post it will ruin my nerves (the President said – up to you to believe it – that this is a country with steady nerves). A hug for all.

Letter from Ernesto to his Aunt Beatriz from Guatemala

July 22nd 1954

Dear Beatriz,
[. . .] Here it was all great fun with shots, bombardments, speeches and other events, which interrupted the monotony in which I lived.

I will be leaving in a few days, I don't know how many, for Mexico, where I intend to make a fortune selling whalebones for shirt collars.

In any case, I will be on the alert to go to the next flare-up, since there certainly will be one, because the Yankees cannot live without defending democracy somewhere or other.

Big hugs from your adventurer nephew.

He always wrote to Beatriz with jokes in order to counter the nervous tension in which he kept her. When he writes to her he seems to be treating the revolution as a joke, but later on he says that he 'will be on the alert to go to the next flare-up'. It is evident that Ernesto had by now become aware that underdeveloped countries could only liberate themselves from the exploitation of imperialism by means of armed struggle.

Letter from Ernesto to his mother from Guatemala

7 August 1954

Dear Vieja,
[. . .] From my life in Guatemala there is nothing left to tell, since its rhythm is that of any dictatorial American colony. I have tidied up my affairs here and I am leaving for Mexico. [. . .]

He ends with an affectionate 'until the next one' and does not sign his name.

This letter is full of memories and family news, which I have left out. We were always waiting for his news. At the time, anyone who was not with the government of Castillo Armas was not safe in Guatemala and far less those who, like Ernesto, had shown that they were militants on the left.

In this letter he tells his mother that he is leaving for Mexico, but does not know where to go from there. It is evident that the catastrophic fall of Arbenz had disoriented him.

Letter from Ernesto to his parents from Guatemala

August 1954

Dear Viejos,

[. . .] I asked for asylum at the Argentine Embassy, where they treated me very well, but I did not appear in the official list of those who had been given asylum. The storm is all over now and I will leave for Mexico in a few days, but until I tell you otherwise, please write to me here. [. . .]

I think you sent me too many clothes and spent too much on me, and maybe I am a bit prissy, but I feel that I do not deserve it (nor are there any indications that this might change in the near future). Not all the clothes will be useful because my latest motto is: travel light with strong legs and the stomach of a fakir.

Give my regards to the gang from Guatemala. Please treat the young woman who will arrive with you as well as possible.

When all this calms down and things take on a different rhythm I will write to you more precisely. For all of you a hug from the first-born, the request that you forgive me for all the shocks received and that you forget about me; whatever comes has always fallen from above. In America nobody dies of hunger, and I suspect that neither do they in Europe. Ciao.

Ernesto

This letter was written in an almost illegible hand. It was one of the last from Guatemala. Now we were convinced that Ernesto would not return to Argentina, as we had asked him to and as we thought he would do when we sent him clothes and money. By now, we had a new definition of our son: Ernesto would carry on 'on foot' with his backpack, eating whatever he could and on the path he had decided for himself. He was now beginning to fit the description of himself[21] that he had given when he was leaving Buenos Aires for Bolivia with Calica Ferrer.

Political asylum-seekers from Guatemala

General Juan Domingo Perón, President of the Argentine Republic, gave political asylum to the people who had sought refuge at the Argentine Embassy when Colonel Castillo Armas took over the government of Guatemala with the support of the United States.

In order to comply with this decision, several military aircraft took off from the airport of Palomar, in the province of Buenos Aires. They would return to the Argentine capital carrying more than 100 asylum-seekers.

The captain of one of those planes, an acquaintance of mine, offered to take letters, clothes, food and money to Ernesto.

[21] Description of himself: this refers to Ernesto's parting comment: 'Here goes a soldier of the Americas.'

It was July 1954. We already knew that Ernesto would not travel with the exiles, but we went to Palomar anyway to pick up his letters. The captain who had brought the flight back told me that Ernesto had rejected the invitation to return to Argentina and would travel on to Mexico.

All the exiles who arrived in Buenos Aires were lodged at the Immigration Hotel and, by order of Perón, around thirty of them, branded as Communists, were taken to jail to await trial at Villa Devoto. This way Perón saved face in front of the United States. They were kept in detention for several days and then set free.

Responding to a request from Ernesto made in writing, we found jobs in Buenos Aires for many of them, within our capabilities.

Guatemala

Ernesto had arrived in Guatemala towards the end of 1953 and stayed there until after the fall of President Arbenz. During his stay he carried on reading, studying, sometimes practising medicine and embarking on his usual excursions to the ruins, thus nurturing his passion for archaeology.

When he left for Mexico he sent us a box containing more than 100 books that dealt with subjects such as statistics, economics, geography – the majority dealing with political and social aspects. All this proved that he was taking a greater interest in those subjects. His letters offer us today an interesting insight into his life, but they are not a complete guide to his aspirations and projects. Those chatty, amusing and juicy letters lacked something, and that was precisely the turn that his life had taken: he had decided to study the peoples he was encountering and their financial destitution, the product of American imperialism.

In his letters he had not spoken of Professor White*, but simply of a gringo who had become his friend. We learned precisely who White was after Che had left for Cuba, and the same happened with several of the important people whom he met in Guatemala and Mexico.

One of those people was Dr Alfonso Bauer Paiz*, who at the time was President of the National Agrarian Bank, and who was also a member of the political commission of the Revolutionary Party of Guatemala (PRG).

Professor Bauer was a friend of Ernesto and Hilda Gadea. In 1977, while in Cuba with the post of advisor to the Ministry of Justice, he gave an interview to the journalist Aldo Isidrón del Valle, for *Granma*.[22] The interview was published on 29 October 1977 and the following paragraphs referring to Ernesto are from said article.

He was a young doctor, but did not look like one, but rather like a student, restless and cheerful. [. . .]

Ernesto had told Hilda Gadea that he wanted to meet me, as he knew that I worked for the Arbenz administration and that I knew the politics of Guatemala in depth.

However, I was surprised that Ernesto, who was a doctor, should take an interest in me, a lawyer who dabbled in economics, instead of being interested in my brothers, who were doctors. Later I realised that what he sought was not a professional. [. . .] The natural talent, simple, frank and jovial, of Ernesto contrasted with the doctoral pose of the other visitor.[23] [. . .]

The meeting was animated not just because of Ernesto's conversational skills, but because of the subjects broached as well. That afternoon we began a long discussion about political matters in our America, which lasted well into the night.

[22] *Granma*: Cuban daily newspaper named after the motorboat in which Fidel Castro and his comrades landed in Cuba for the invasion.
[23] Other visitor: this refers to Dr Ricardo Rojo.

So many years have gone by that it is impossible to remember in detail that conversation, but broadly we discussed, among other subjects, Peronism, the Venezuelan Movement for Democratic Action, APRA and the currents that run along similar lines. We analysed the situation in Guatemala. [. . .]

If I am to speak with total candour, the degree of political awareness of the three participants in that friendly encounter was as follows: Ricardo (Rojo) was a liberal who was a member of the Argentine Radical Party, while Ernesto and I, although quite influenced by Marxist* ideology, still had certain political ideas that were populist, something that was in vogue during the forties and early fifties.

What Dr Bauer says here is correct in relation to himself, but I believe – and I reinforce my belief when I reread his letters – that Ernesto had already gone beyond the populist line and had made a move towards Marxism.

And Dr Bauer continues:

This explains the fact that in the spontaneous dialogue that took place, people like Juan José Arévalo were mentioned with affection. I remember that we also agreed in saying that Víctor Raúl Haya de la Torre, Rómulo Betancourt, José Figueres* and others were adopting opportunist stances, which became more and more evident and which would unavoidably reduce them to having to give in to the political interests of Washington.

As Bauer himself says, too many years had gone by since that discussion to remember the details, and for that reason I believe that he was unable to gauge the full weight of Ernesto's socio-political ideas.

According to my calculations, this meeting must have taken place around March 1954. By then it was already possible to glean Ernesto's Marxist ideology through his letters, in which he refers to Karl Marx as St Charles.

Bauer goes on:

Ernesto criticised the lack of unity of the political parties that supported Arbenz – Acción Revolucionaria, Partido de la Revolución Guatemalteca, Renovación Nacional, etc. – and the PGT or workers' party of Guatemala, with a Communist ideology, which had been infiltrated and divided. [. . .] In this alliance of the parties, the PGT, although a minority party, preserved the hegemony of political decisions in relation to agrarian reform and important aspects of the economy, matters concerning the workers and international policy. Their unity was more apparent than real. These were details that Ernesto pointed out, while also emphasising the threat of a much-anticipated American imperialist coup. Ernesto believed that it was necessary to organise the defence by the people and to be ready to fight. [. . .]

How could I have imagined that evening that fate had given me the most honoured distinction in my life: to establish a friendship with the man who, through his momentous deeds, would become the archetype of the hero, the revolutionary and the liberator. How could one have had the intuition to predict that that young man, Ernesto Guevara, Che, would become the Heroic Guerrilla?[24]

I did not see a lot of him in Guatemala since the

[24] Heroic Guerrilla: in Cuba, 1968 was declared the year of the Heroic Guerrilla in memory of Che Guevara.

country was undergoing a period of agitation caused by the daily aerial bombardment launched by the imperialists to harass the capital city.

The statements about Che by this well-informed politician gave us an idea of the true sense of Ernesto's journey, through which he was becoming a soldier of the Americas.

The precautions that he took in his correspondence to leave out names and details of places, disguise locations and omit dates were an attempt to divert our attention from the possibility that he was taking an active part in any revolutionary struggle. Our spirit crumbled as we began to realise the absolute truth of his decisions.

Part Seven: Mexico, 1954–6

What had happened in Guatemala had given Ernesto experience, and now in Mexico, having entered with his papers in order, it would not be to his advantage to be noticed as a man who had been politically in agreement with Arbenz, who had just been deposed. The lesson of Guatemala made him more cautious, but propelled him further to the left.

Letter to Tita Infante from Mexico

Mexico 29–9–54

Dear Tita:

Today, from a distance – material and spiritual – that separates me from Guatemala, I reread your letter to reply to it and it seemed strange. I found in it a special warmth in your desperation not to be able to do anything that really moves me. I would like to think that a lot of it was because of me, but I imagine that it was mostly caused by Guatemala. Inside and out we felt the same; just like the Spanish Republic, betrayed by those inside as well as those outside, we did not fall (allow me a little analysis) with the same nobility. The moment was different as well, as all that the comrades I took the liberty of sending you may have explained, but there was something missing anyway. From here I look at things with a totally different perspective and I begin to realise that Mexico played the role in this sad farce of France in that other one. The climate one breathes is totally different from that of Guatemala. Here too you can say what you like, but on condition that you are able to pay for it somewhere, that is, we breathe the democracy of the dollar. Frankly, I prefer to immerse myself in the ruins rather than hear one of the best poets of Mexico say that it was folly for Guatemala to 'flirt with Russia'. The enemies of Guatemala were the Communists, they have already forgotten who paid for the aircraft and who placed the puppet they have now, and all the rest of it.

Argentina manages to have – with its enormous proportion of castrated people – a strength that enables it to maintain a far more coherent policy than that of this country, where individual courage is an axiomatic requirement.

My aspirations have not changed, and my immediate goal is Europe and then Asia; how, that is another story. About Mexico, beyond that general impression, I cannot tell you anything definitive, nor about myself. I hope that you have finished, or are about to finish, that shit of a career you got into and are preparing your wings to fly off somewhere, if that one or another one does not cut them off with the prosaic scissors of marriage.

Tita, my ever ready hug and my thanks for writing me such a lovely letter as the one about Guatemala.

Ernesto

Letter from Ernesto to his father, dated 30 September 1954

Viejo,

I have seen enough of Mexico to realise that matters will not be very easy, but I have arrived here with a bullet-proof spirit. Petit [Ulises Petit de Murat] has looked after me really well, he took me to visit some sites in Mexico and invited me permanently to his home, but I have preferred to keep a certain degree of independence, at least while the money you sent me lasts. Petit talks of a scholarship, which would solve my financial problem and would allow me to do whatever I wanted, apart from studying something, which would not do me any harm after such a long time. [. . .]

Eventually I will apply for a visa for the USA and will accept whatever is offered over there, but that would be in a few months' time.

Letter from Ernesto to his mother from Mexico

10 October 1954

Esteemed and venerated mother,

[. . .] As for the bitterness you see in my recent letters, it is possibly true, but I do not notice it, except in a certain scepticism when confronted with matters in which in the past I saw some good. My utmost disenchantment is with certain situations that are neither fish nor foul and out of which I thought I could get something; now I am totally convinced that the middle of the road cannot be anything but a first step towards treason. The bad thing is that, at the same time, I do not have the decisive attitude that I should have had a long time ago, because deep down (and on the surface too) I am a total slob and do not wish to see my career thwarted by iron discipline. My faith in the final triumph of what I believe in is total, but I will not even be an actor or a spectator who is interested in the action. Perhaps it is from this situation that the tinge of bitterness that others have also noted comes. The truth is that the Barabbases are always going against the current in everything and I have not taken the decision to stop being one.

The triumph in Guatemala of Castillo Armas over President Jacobo Arbenz, and the collapse of the government presided over by the latter, were a hard lesson for Ernesto, so he is examining his conscience in depth here. He had always been able to do this and could be ruthless when judging himself.

The letter ended with jokes for all the family.

Another letter from Ernesto to his mother from Mexico

This letter has no date or place, but it must be early November 1954. Once Ernesto left Guatemala and arrived in Mexico, he had to earn a living somehow and he became a street photographer. Many of those who knew him then remember him like that. He bought himself a rather good camera and went from being a doctor to being a street photographer. In some of his letters, with his trademark humour, he would tell how he used his charm to entertain the mothers who brought their children to have their picture taken.

Vieja, my vieja (I confused you with the date)
[. . .] Even Beatriz has decided to retaliate and the telegrams she used to send no longer come.

To tell you about my life is to repeat myself, since I am not doing anything new. Photography continues to give me enough to live on and there is no solid hope that I will leave it in the near future, in spite of the fact that I work mornings in research in two local hospitals. I think that the best thing that could happen to me would be to be smuggled in as a rural doctor very near the capital, which would enable me to devote more time to medicine more comfortably for a few months. I do this research because I realise that all that I learned about allergies from Pisani, including his methodology – now that I have the opportunity to compare myself with people who have studied in the USA and who know what they are doing as far as orthodox knowledge goes – is several leagues ahead of all this, and I want to practise all the tricks of his system so that I can land on my feet wherever I go. [. . .]

The scholarship is a dream that I have now abandoned and I believe that in that large country one should not ask, one should just do it and that's that. You know I've always been in favour of drastic decisions and here they pay really well because everybody is very lazy, but they do not mind others doing the work, so I have free rein, be it here or in the countryside, where I might yet go. Naturally, this does not make me lose sight of my true north, which is Europe, and where I intend to go no matter what. I have not lost even half a gram of anger and antipathy, but I want to see New York at least. I do not have the slightest fear of the result and I know that I shall leave as anti-American as I arrived (if I arrive).

Communists do not have the same idea of what friendship is as you have, but between them they do, and it is the same as yours or better. I saw that clearly in Guatemala after the coup, when it was every man for himself; the Communists preserved their faith and their camaraderie intact, and they were the only group that kept on functioning there.

This letter is in reply to a letter from Celia, in which she wrote about the Communists whom Ernesto sent to her in Argentina, with a recommendation asking her to look after them. It is possible that one of them may have behaved incorrectly. Ernesto says the following to his mother:

I believe that they deserve respect and that sooner or later I will join the Party. What prevents me from doing so is above all the fact that, at the moment, I have an enormous desire to travel around Europe and I could not do that while submitting to a rigid discipline.
     Vieja, see you in Paris.

As usual Ernesto ends the letter without a signature.

Letter to Tita Infante

Mexico, 29 November 1954

I did not reply immediately because I'm still in great financial straits and I have to do conjuring tricks, as well as fast, to get to the end of the month without debts. The information you offer me[1] is of interest and will also be very useful for the people here who have no news. Do send them in full detail and with no scruples – any strange nose that comes sniffing, where it should not, stops taking an interest when it finds out it is for

---

[1] 'The information you offer me': he is referring to information about the political situation in Argentina.

me because I have the reputation of being a first-class madman, and nobody attaches any importance to anything I say, think or do.

Talking about you, I can see that your small disaster is going to your head and preventing you from doing anything right. Although I am full of vitality by nature – unlike you – I have had my moments of abandonment or, better still, of pessimism. I imagine it must be something similar to that boredom without horizons that you find yourself in. When that happens as a passing thing that lasts a day, I cure it with some maté and a couple of poems; when it comes with a will to remain, I do like the Chinese in wartime,[2] until it leaves the way it arrived. Giving advice is something new for me, and to give advice to you who always felt like my mother is even more strange, but I will attempt it in general anyway: first, finish your degree as soon as possible, bluffing or any other way. Second: as soon as you have your degree, you must get the hell out of there, at least for a while.

I would really like to inject you with some of that materialistic love that I have for life, of which I con-scientiously enjoy every moment. But for that I would need more than a letter and my poor capacity to convince you. Besides, I would be a hypocrite if I put myself forward as an example, because all I did was run away from all that bothered me and even today, when I believe that I am about to face up to the struggle (above all in the social aspect), I carry on my pilgrimage wherever events take me, without even thinking of going back to Argentina to fight my war. I admit that this is my greatest headache, because I have this terrible

---

[2] 'Like the Chinese in wartime': an Argentine colloquialism meaning you put up with it.

struggle between chastity (there) and desire (above all to wander around Europe) and I can see shamefacedly that I prostitute myself at every opportunity. I started off trying to give you some advice and ended up telling you my problems. Going back to the uncomfortable subject of advice, I will give you my last: always throw fears overboard because they complicate matters. It is always better to have the bitter-sweet taste in your mouth of a frustrated yearning than an unfounded image of what might have been.

To conclude, that business of thanking me for the trust I place in you sounds hollow or like false modesty; you know full well that I trust you completely because this does not depend on some isolated fact, but on the full knowledge I have of your qualities, and playing the shrinking violet is not right. I do not thank you for that type of proof, I demand it, which is quite different.

This is now getting very dogmatic, so to put an end to it: let me tell you that I earn my living photographing kids in the park and doing interviews with 'ches'[3] who turn up here, for the Latin News Agency, that progeny of Perón's. As I was telling you at the beginning, it does not always yield enough to eat, above all to calm my hunger, which is that of a wolf, but there are signs that this will improve, and if it does not, it cannot get worse either, which in itself is some consolation. My financial misfortune becomes as immaterial as it is chronic while, on the other hand, the scientific accolade I have had in Mexico gave me medical optimism and I went to work like mad on allergies, for free, for a hospital. In any case the results will be good because Pisani is several leagues ahead of any other allergist of the Western

---

[3] 'Ches': people from Argentina.

world at least, although you have your doubts. This leads me to think that my financial situation will also change, since success in these happy lands of God turns into money if one is not a total idiot.

Well, I will now exercise some self-control, otherwise I will write an encyclopaedia in one sitting.

Ciao, Tita, I send you the always affectionate hug of your roving friend, together with the hope of material-ising it soon in some corner of the world, and from 'doctor to doctor', tell them to write if you see one.

Letter from Ernesto to his mother from Mexico
This has no date, but it was written towards the end of 1954.

Vieja, my vieja,

It is true that I am rather lazy when it comes to writing, but the guilty party was, as usual, Mr Money. It seems that the end of the unfortunate financial year of '54, which treated me like dirt, coincides with the end of my chronic hunger. I now have a job as a columnist with *Agencia Latina*, where I earn 700 Mexican pesos, which is the equivalent of 700 of yours and provides me with the financial means of subsistence. Besides, it has the advantage of requiring only three hours three times a week. This enables me to spend the mornings at the hospital, where I am stirring things up with Pisani's method.

My immediate plans are to spend six months in Mexico, which interests me and which I like a lot, and, during that time, casually ask for a visa to go and meet properly 'the sons of a big power',[4] as Arévalo calls

---

[4] Sons of a big power: sons of a bitch (in Spanish, *hijo de un gran poder*; the common expression is *hijo de una gran puta* – that is, son of a great whore). Arévalo was referring to the USA.

them. If I succeed I will go, and if not I shall decide what to do instead. All this without discounting the possibility of a direct trip behind the Cortisone[5] to see what is going on there. As you can see, nothing new since my previous letter.

In the scientific field I am very enthusiastic and take advantage of it because this will not last. I am doing two pieces of research and I might start on a third one, all about allergy, and although I do it very slowly, I continue to collect material for a little book that will see the light of day – if it does – in several years' time, and which carries the presumptuous title *The Function of the Doctor in Latin America*. I can speak with some authority on the subject because, although I do not know a lot about medicine, I have Latin America well sussed out. Of course, there is nothing yet beyond the general outline and some three or four chapters, but I have a lot of time.

Ernesto's mother had written him a letter in which she said the difference in the way she saw things and the way he saw them was growing. Ernesto replied as follows:

With reference to the differences between the way you and I see things, which you say is growing, I can assure you that it will not be for much longer. That which you so fear is reached by two paths: the positive one, where you are totally convinced, or the negative one, as a result of total disillusionment. I arrived via the second one, to be immediately convinced that one must continue by the former. The way in which the gringos

---

[5] Behind the Cortisone: the Soviet Union, which was behind the Iron Curtain. In Spanish, cortisone is *cortisona* and curtain is *cortina*. Ernesto was obsessed with the word *cortisona* because of his asthma.

treat Latin America (remember that 'gringos' means Americans) was causing me a growing indignation, but at the same time I was studying the theory behind the motives for their behaviour and found it to be scientific. Then there was Guatemala, and all that is difficult to describe, to see how the object of one's enthusiasm was being diluted by the will of those gentlemen and how the new tall story of Red culpability and criminality was forged, and how the same Guatemalan traitors lent themselves to the propagation of it in order to be in a position to beg something from the new order. At what point I left behind reason to have something akin to faith, I cannot tell you, not even approximately, because the road was long and full of setbacks. [. . .]

The year was 1955. Argentina was beginning to experience popular discontent due to the economic crisis that led to the devaluation of the currency. The opposition, allied to the clergy, were cornering the government of General Perón. Ernesto's letter goes on:

Please send me all the news you can from there, because we are totally confused here, since the newspapers only publish the mess Perón is in with the clergy and we know nothing about the upheaval. I would like you to send me, even by sea, several pages of *La Prensa* over the next few days; after all for twenty cents you can send a lot of newspapers.

Using that sense of humour and irony that is particular to Buenos Aires, and because he was really close to his mother, Ernesto says, referring to an aunt of hers who was ill and very wealthy:

In order to earn yourself a little inheritance, tell your Aunt Mecha that I lit a candle to the Virgin of Guadalupe[6] and prayed for her eternal return to health.

Referring to his brother Juan Martín, whom he adored, Ernesto says to his mother:

Tell Tudito[7] that I cannot send him any photos because they are so good that I sell them before they have dried, but I am sending him my noble likeness so that he can show off.

He then adds a few illegible words and says goodbye to his mother with a hug and a happy new year.

Letter from Ernesto to his father from Mexico
The date of this letter says 10th (possibly February or March); the year is 1955.

Dear Viejo,
  As usual I am writing late to congratulate you on your tififth[8], a memorable age when you will begin to settle down and all that. I imagine that you spent the ominous date trying to forget it as much as possible and that by now you will have accepted being a year older. I am always waiting for my financial situation to become sufficiently comfortable to be able to send a present to

[6] Virgin of Guadalupe. Roman Catholics have considered her the patron saint of Mexico since 1895.
[7] Tudito: Ernesto's youngest brother, Juan Martín. Tudito is a diminutive of *pelotudo* (a very vulgar expression in Argentina, which refers to male genitals).
[8] Tififth: an Argentine colloquialism used to avoid actually mentioning the correct age (that is, 'fifty-fifth'). The story goes that an old lady who was reluctant to admit her age would skip the first part of the word, so that it could stand for twenty-fifth, thirty-fifth, etc.

a member of the family, but there seems no way of reconciling the debits and the credits. For the moment I am just about managing. When I am able to do so, I will send you the missing present in the shape of a book, which may be: *The hidden truth of the Korean War* or *Guatemala, Democracy and the Empire* – you know, any little thing that will inform as well as delight you.

So that you stop whining about my phoney plans, I will tell you about one that is serious: to catch a fair wind and set sail towards Europe. This plan is a bit vague, but it is all I can tell you for now. My intentions are to get a scholarship from France, stay there for a year and then head for the Cortisone any way I can, with Comrade Mao* as the final goal, but India is also on the agenda. The scholarship is up in the air, but there are signs that it could yet happen. My weapons would be three or four scientific papers, which (with Guevarian modesty) are very good. One of them in particular I hope will open the doors of any European university so that I can improve myself at leisure.

Perhaps I had written to Ernesto that I was considering going to Mexico to work. He says about that country:

As to what you say about Mexico, it is ridiculous in every sense and I will not tire of repeating what I said to Ani [Ana María]: the upheaval is taking place throughout the world and now in giant steps with the change of government in Russia. Mexico is totally in the hands of the Americans, so much so that for Nixon's* arrival they threw all the Puerto Rican nationalists as well as dissidents of any other flavour into jail, and they are keeping them under lock and key, nobody knows where. The press does not say anything and they have been forbidden to print anything, under threat of closure. Far more dangerous than the Mexican police is the FBI. They move around here as if they were at home and arrest people without any justification. This is the political scene, the financial one is terrible; prices go up at an alarming rate, and the rot is such that all the trade-union leaders have been bought and betray their members by signing unfair contracts with various American companies, thus delaying the possibility of strikes for one or two years. In Mexico there are practically no independent industries and even less free trade. This country is heading for total disintegration and I am not exaggerating; the only way you could make any money here would be by being a pimp for the Americans, something that I advise you against for a variety of reasons. Argentina is an oasis in our America, we should give Perón all the support possible to avoid going into a war that promises to be terrible; whether you like it or not, that is how it is. Nixon is already touring all those countries, apparently to set the quotas of men and cheap raw materials (paid for with very old and very expensive machinery), which each of the poor countries of America will contribute to the new Koreas.

You may find all this rather a wild rant and maybe false, but not for very long, I believe. Beyond this subject I have little to tell you, having informed you about the main topics concerning my livelihood and projects.

I have grown tired of talking nonsense and you of reading it, more so now that our letters have crossed, so that I leave you wishing you all the things that one wishes when one's old man has a birthday, and sending you a big hug for you and all the gang. I am not sending you stamps because I am writing and sending it without

going home, but I will put them in my next.
   Ciao

Letter from Ernesto to his Aunt Beatriz

9 April 1955

Little Auntie,
   I know, I am ungrateful, a bad nephew, a hypocrite, a
Red, etc. The following happened: when I was full of
enthusiasm and about to tackle the pile of all my
unanswered mail, the hurricane of the 2nd Pan-
American Games fell upon me and I surrendered to the
worthy task of informing the Latin American public in
great detail about the development of events, besides
supplying them with beautiful photographs which
brought together immediacy and beauty. Once the great
event came to a close, I proceeded to carry out the last
interviews with those who had harvested their sporting
laurels. Once the operation was finalised, and having
conveniently congratulated the staff covering the
Games, a laconic telegram arrived from the *Agencia
Latina*, in which it informed us that it was bringing to a
close all transmissions and that each correspondent
could do what he thought best with the personnel in his
charge (not a word about salaries). To learn this news
and to devote myself body and soul to biting my bottom
were one and the same. I succeeded yesterday, belonging from that day on to the race of the single-cheeked.

His Aunt Beatriz probably offered to ask someone for a job
for Ernesto in some pharmaceutical company, to which he
replies:

Of the famous position you offered me in several letters,
I can only tell you – to introduce a pinch of seriousness
– that in spite of all my roaming around, my repeated
fecklessness and other defects, I have deep and well-
defined convictions, and these convictions prevent me
from taking over a position of the type you describe,
because those companies are dens of thieves of the
worst species, since they traffic in human health, of
which I consider myself a protector. I did not reply
earlier because of the assignment at the Games, but in
any case the reply is the same; I am poor but honest, as
the thieves say.

A large hug for you, for the timid newly wed, for her
bald groom and Hercilita.[9]

Always lovingly
Stalin II

Letter to Tita Infante

Mexico, 10 April 1955

Dear Tita,

As always, I received your letter with great joy and as
usual I have taken a long time to reply. Apologies are
unimportant, but I have had to give them lavishly
because my silence was almost total during this period,
so that with you I omit them. I will only tell you that I
had the coveted post of sports commentator for *Agencia
Latina*, which operates with capital related at the very
least to Our Daddy in the Pink House.[10] My work

---

[9] The timid newly wed: the newly weds were Ernesto's aunt Hercilia (a
widow with a daughter called Hercilita) and her second husband.
[10] Our Daddy in the Pink House: the President. The Argentine presidential
palace is called La Casa Rosada – that is, pink house.

during the Pan-American Games was exhausting in all sense of the word, since I had to compile the news, take the photos and be a guide to the journalists who arrived from South America. The average hours of sleep did not exceed four during the games, owing to the fact that I was the one who also developed and printed the photographs. All this work was supposed to have its financial compensation in the shape of some $4,000, which would be mine after so much coming and going, but the unexpected happened when the *Agencia Latina* went bust without any warning, from one day to the next and without paying out a quinto (a Mexican expression). I suspect that it is due to a secret negotiation between the two Daddies (the one in the Pink House and the one in the White House). Or maybe the one in the Pink House got stuffed without further ado. You probably know all this better than I do, because here everything arrives distorted by distance and one never knows what to believe. [. . .]

My projects are fluid and conditional, for a change. If they give me the money they owe me (improbable, but not impossible), I will go on a trip across Mexico in order to see this country well, and then I will go to visit Cuba to complete my Latin American map. Maybe at the end of the year I will be in Caracas again, with my great friend Granado, who constantly insists that I join him 'so that we can carry on together'. What stops me is that Alberto is earning a lot of money, and that is always a deterrent that deprives the subject in question of the energy to roam. In any case, he and I went on that lengthy trip together all over Latin America (the first one) and I have never found a companion like him, in every sense. During our lengthy materialistic debates we looked for the place to set up our stall together, and

not long ago he wrote to me from Italy where he is on a
course (not really, a phoney one), suggesting we renew
our association, around 19—.

Scientifically speaking, I am a first-class failure. All
my great research projects went with the same wind
that swept the *Agencia*, and I find myself limited to
submitting a modest paper in which I repeat the
research done by Pisani about semi-digested foodstuffs.
This paper will be read at the Mexican Conference on
Allergy on the 23rd of this month and I will send it to
you if it is published anywhere, simply for its curiosity
value, as there is nothing new in it, since it is a
repetition of theories.

As for my other problem, it seems that I prostituted
myself completely and my last crisis of conscience
went with the wind. Maybe your letter had an influence
on this, but if so, it was because the seed was already
there. I sent a brainy study about the fall of Uncle
Jacobo[11] (in the claws of the 'Lineage of Blond Octopus
Centaurs'[12]) to the capital behind the Cortisone and, on
the basis of this, I asked for an invitation to travel there,
but the operation failed so I go on my cheeky way,
abandoned and ignored.

I hope, Tita, that we will meet soon when turning any
corner of any old European city, I with a passably full
stomach and you with your degree in your hand. For the
moment this is all we can aspire to, but the future

---

[11] Uncle Jacobo: Jacobo Arbenz, left-leaning President of Guatemala, who
was ousted during Guevara's stay in that country.
[12] Lineage of Blond Octopus Centaurs: a phrase concocted by Che to refer
to the US Marines sent to support the coup led by Colonel Castillo Armas
that toppled the legitimate government of President Arbenz of Guatemala
in 1954. The word *pulpo* in Spanish (octopus) has the connotation of
someone who grabs with his tentacles something that does not belong to
him – as the USA was doing at the time in Latin America.

belongs to the people, so let us await it with confidence. Until the distant future – or the less-distant one of our European meeting – arrives, receive a warm and tight embrace from your friend, as always.

Letter from Ernesto to his mother from Mexico

9 May 1955

Oldest Vieja,

Your first-born has already joined the annals of history as a distinguished doctor in allergies and would soon have gone into the police records as dead from starvation, had it not been for the charity of friendly hands first, and then due to my great scientific merits. The latter enabled me to obtain a scholarship at the General Hospital of Mexico. The scholarship includes lodgings, food, laundry, but no monies, said monies will be given to me by means of subterfuge beyond the budget, according to those who promise these things. I don't necessarily believe this, but it makes no difference: money is an interesting luxury, but nothing else. The work I read before an audience did not have the success that it would seem from the small article I include, but it was well received and resulted in congratulations from the chief of Mexican Allergy, as well as that poxy scholarship I have told you about. As you already know, the *Agencia Latina* went bust and left no trace of it ever having set foot on Mexican soil, owing me some four thousand pesos, which I do not envisage ever receiving. I was about to go to the United States or at least to Nueva Laredo on the frontier to work on allergies, but I decided to accept this position, which gives me the facilities and the opportunity to compile – during the period of the assignment (four to six months) – some three or four articles on the specialisation, which would be published in a magazine there is here. [. . .]

During a break I took while writing this letter, I received another one from you in which you tell me that there is another doctor in the family, as well as all the other stupidities[13] done by said new doctor. Well, the family is disintegrating in accordance with natural law, but at least you have them next to you so that you can have those juicy and 'low-key' discussions that are usual at home.

With reference to the ten years, two have already lapsed, but I do not think that this total separation will last more than two more years, at most, since my medical shares are going up and I think that at my next stop I will be able to live more in accordance with my status. The next step could be the USA (very difficult), Venezuela (feasible) or Cuba (probable). But my firm goal continues to be Paris, and I will get there even if I have to swim the Atlantic.

Large stocks of kisses for everyone and until the next one.

As usual he does not sign his name.

Letter from Ernesto to his father from Mexico

27 May 1955

Dear Viejo,
     The decreasing order of replies – note what an

---

[13] 'Another doctor in the family, as well as all the other stupidities': Ernesto's brother Roberto had graduated in law and become engaged to Matilde Lezica, whom he later married.

important person I am – means that it is now your turn. I have the problem again of what to say, since almost everything has been said to some other member of the family who so lovingly concern themselves over my health. I, with my post in the hospital, seem to be a copy of you and your aspirations, because I spend twenty-four hours a day discussing illnesses and how to cure them (I don't cure anything, of course). After submitting my paper, and when they finally approved my internship, I launched myself into the attempt to prove *in vitro* the presence of antibodies in allergic subjects (I believe that I will fail); to try to manufacture the so-called propectanes, a little bit of nourishment digested in such a way that if the patient then eats the complete food it does not harm him (I think I will fail); an attempt to prove that hyaluronidase – let us see if you know as much as you say you do – is an important factor in the mechanism that produces the allergy (my dearest hope); and two projects in collaboration, one is rather imposing, with the top man of allergy in Mexico, M. Salazar Mallen, and another project with one of the good doctors in chemistry that Mexico has, about a problem of which I only have an intuition, but I think something worthwhile will come of it. These are my scientific prospects. These same prospects enable me to suggest the possibility of a change in my aspiration to roam aimlessly. [. . .]

I am waiting for some recommendation to march on to the fields where dawn is maturing, as they say. In any case, although everything is green and although my convictions grow firmer by the day, I will not let slip the opportunity of embarking on some extra little trip: Havana in particular attracts my attention to fill my heart with landscapes well interspersed with quotes from Lenin*. All this that I'm saying is not to make you angry, it is the whole truth. I had for a moment the idea of going to the Conference on Allergy in Brazil and from there to drop in on you, but I discarded it because I would have had to start now to arrive on time, since it is difficult to travel that far without any means and I did not want to do that.

Ernesto writes about what he does and what he intends to do in the scientific field, but he cannot stop himself mentioning ideas and projects related to what he was really already doing. He talks of the landscapes he would see in Havana, but also of the quotes from Lenin. What did one thing have to do with the other? It was clear that Ernesto already knew where he was going, and what he was going for, and also that the expedition would end in a Socialist revolution. Although he had not yet met Fidel Castro, Ernesto was aware of the revolution he was preparing through the Cubans he knew in Mexico.

He tells me also not to get angry, that everything is true. He was referring to my frustrated hope that he would become a true scientist.

I think that I told you that the *Agencia Latina* has promised me a trip to Melbourne for next year, something that I have now totally forgotten, since they are not paying me, but I liked the idea and I would have loved to see some kangaroos.

Of my present daily life I cannot tell you anything because everything is a succession of ward, lab and library, enlivened by some translations from English.

Viejo, until the candles stop burning, and a hug.

As usual he does not sign.

June 1955 letter from Ernesto to his mother from Mexico

17 June 1955

Dear Vieja,

I am writing you this letter of congratulations in the midst of the uncertainties caused by the events and contradictory news that arrives from there.

Ernesto was referring to the events in 1955 when the Argentine navy launched its attack on the government of General Juan Domingo Perón. The political situation in our country had grown more explosive by the day. Perón was unable to govern even when he had the majority of the people on his side, and a coup was rumoured in the military circles opposed to Perónism. The Church had joined the protests, which came from all sides, and this was serious for the government.

I hope that matters are not as serious as we are told, and I hope none of our relatives are involved in a mess that cannot be resolved.

According to the news that arrived here, the figures for the dead are high, almost frighteningly so for Argentina. And the impression that the majority of the dead are civilians who got it without asking for it increases the feeling of discomfort and bewilderment that I get from reading the news, in spite of the fact that I do not believe most of what I read because it has been censored, twisted or simply made up in order to have something to publish, since people read the news from Buenos Aires avidly. I hope your day dawns without bombs or anything of that sort, since it is fitting that you start this new year of your life in peace after all the

upheaval you have had since I left. Please write to me
quickly giving me everybody's news and tell me what
the doctor is up to and when he is getting married.

Today, remembering you, I fell prey, like in tango
lyrics, to a melancholic need to miss those days when I
had no work or words to that effect; the main thing is
that I am in a tango mood, or feeling like an Argentine,
a condition I always ignored. I think that is an indication of approaching old age (which after all is
tiredness) or maybe that I miss my sweet and peaceful
home where, lulled by the soft rhythms of family
arguments, my childhood and my youth were spent.
However, you must get your aunt's inheritance, even if
you have to kill for it, and then you must go to Paris,
where we will meet. I think you would like it – for me
it is a biological need, which I feel is feasible and is
maturing continually. I don't know if it's the right
word, but I think it is an entelechy. My non-medical life
goes on with a monotonous Sunday rhythm, marked by
a prowess such as climbing the Popocatepetl (at last I
have seen the tonsils of Pacha Mama[14]), Mexico's most
important volcano, at 5,400 metres high. Honestly, for
me it was both easy and thrilling and as I see that I have
the minimal conditions required, I intend to repeat the
exploit on the highest peak of Mexico and the second-
highest in North America, the Orizaba, but I will have
to wait a little because it is expensive.

July 1955 letter from Ernesto to his mother from Mexico
This reads 'Buenos Aires, 20 July 1955'. Ernesto wrote
Buenos Aires instead of Mexico by mistake. Or because he
was thinking about his country.

[14] Pacha Mama: mythical goddess of the Incas who represented Mother
Earth.

With no excuse whatsoever I did not write for several days without really knowing why, because even in my work I am better organised and have a little time for myself. One of the reasons that made me wait a little before writing was your analysis of what happened in Argentina. I am in total disagreement with all your analysis, a little *a posteriori* and a little *a priori* with reference to the dates that you mentioned. Things from here look as dark as from there, but there are some things we are able to know because of the present news and because of previous experience. The 'monstrous' demos of Catholics is something that I cannot get into my head; I remember the monstrous demonstrations of the Unión Democrática,[15] which then turned into a mere trickle when there were clean elections.

Others, for whom there is no possible escape from the judgement of history, are those pilot-shits who, after killing people indiscriminately, fly on to Montevideo to say that they did their duty with their faith in God. It is astonishing that people cry because their Sunday churches were burned, but think it the most natural thing in the world that large numbers of 'black-heads'[16] were killed. Do not forget that many of them went to die for an ideal, because that bit about being forced can only be true in part, in any case, and that each 'black-head' had a family to support and that the people who leave the families of the 'black-heads' homeless are the same who depart for Uruguay to beat their breasts about

---

[15] Unión Democrática: a coalition of political parties in Argentina that opposed President Juan Perón.
[16] 'Black-heads': *cabecitas negras*, an expression used affectionately by President Perón to refer to his followers, who were mainly dark-haired, being primarily of Indian stock (as the aboriginal population of Argentina) or of mixed blood. The landed gentry used the phrase pejoratively; Guevara uses it ironically.

their macho prowess. Another important thing is the
number of 'people of good birth' who died, beyond the
fortuitous cases, which in itself is an indication of the
character of the people who were going to oust Perón
and the future of an Argentina governed by an Olivieri*
or by a Pastor*, which are the same thing in this case;
the army only stays in barracks when the government
of the day serves the interests of their class, and the only
thing that would be different is a certain democratic
façade, as you see in Mexico, where the deepest rot is
covered over by pseudo-democratic ways of cohabita-
tion. Olivieri or Pastor, or any other one of them, would
or will shoot – since not everything is clear yet – against
the people with the first big strike, and then there will
not be any Inchauspi[17] kids to die, but they will kill
hundreds of 'black-heads' for the crime of defending
their social status, and La Prensa will say with great
dignity that it is dangerous that the workers from one
vital section of the country declare a strike and,
moreover, resort to violence to win – as happened in the
case in point – when they fired against the police, for
good or bad; this only happened sporadically with
Perón, and for me this counts more than the people
from our social class who had the misfortune to be hit
by a bomb or by a machine gun. Also, I do not understand how you can believe that the navy is made up of
pure little angels and that the army is a pack of devils;
the only appreciable difference between them is that in
the navy there are more upper-class people full of
resentment because they have lost many class
privileges – a loss for which Perón is not responsible,

---

[17] Inchauspi: a young man who fell during the coup d'état against Perón, and
who came from one of the upper-class families of Buenos Aires.

since he is only an interpreter of the situation that was already created because of Argentina's make-up and, over and above that, no matter how many rumours to the contrary are circulated, the Church had a lot to do with the coup of the sixteenth, and our 'dear friends'[18] also had a lot to do with it. I was able to appreciate their methods closely in Guatemala. Don't forget that Olivieri was in the United States not long ago, on the one hand; and on the other, that the Papacy owns some of the main capitals of Europe and that, when it comes to international politics, they march hand-in-hand with the USA. The manner in which the Mexican press dealt with the subject leaves us in no doubt, beyond the fact that some commentator linked to the White House suggested that Perón was a dissolving influence (for the cohesiveness of the free world) because of his tendency towards neutrality and his propensity to trade with countries behind the Iron Curtain. Enough of politics.

Celia had suggested that Ernesto would have been thwarted in his ambitions, had he stayed with Dr Pisani.

Quite the opposite; for my scientific development, there was no better school, nor will there be for some years. All that my capacity for invention is developing here, in fits and starts and with no help, I would have been perfectly able to do with him, even if he had not had the perfect laboratory that he has. Here I work in a bacteriology lab that is one of the best in Mexico and it is far inferior to that one, as well as a physiology lab that is not worth mentioning, beyond the one specifically for

[18] 'Dear friends' – the US, said with irony as his father had supported the Allies during the Second World War.

allergies where everything has to be done by sheer effort, since sadly there is not even a gas burner.

My article was published in the allergy magazine, very smart. I will send you a copy as soon as I am given one. [. . .]

News of myself there is little to tell, except that I attacked the Popo – that's how they call it colloquially – and we were truly heroic without being able to reach the top. I was prepared to leave my bones there to reach the top, but a Cuban friend who climbs with me scared me because his feet were frozen, so the five of us had to come down. When we had come down some hundred metres (which at that height is a lot) the tempest stopped a little and the fog lifted and then we realised that we had been almost on the rim of the crater, but by then we could not go back. We had struggled for six hours with a blizzard that buried us to the groin with each step we took, and with our feet drenched due to the carelessness of not taking adequate equipment (I still have Roberto's boots).[19]

The guide had got lost in the fog when avoiding crevices – which are somewhat dangerous – and we were all exhausted from struggling against the snow, which was soft and deep. We came down tobogganing by throwing ourselves down the slope, just like in the swimming pool of the Sierras and with the same result, since I reached the bottom without my trousers. My Cuban friend won't go up again. As soon as I've saved up the few pesos required to do it again, I'll go back to the Popo, not forgetting that in September I have the Orizaba to tackle.

[19] 'I still have Roberto's boots': Ernesto left Argentina wearing his brother Roberto's fatigues and boots, part of his uniform as a conscript in the Argentine navy.

This was the first time that Ernesto mentioned a Cuban in his letters from Mexico. It is evident that this Cuban was one of the ones who was already committed to go to Cuba for the revolution, and that these climbs were no mere sport, but the physical exercise required to stay agile and strong. During that July Ernesto had already struck up a relationship with Fidel Castro and he was by now a member of the army of the 26 July Movement.

Ernesto's letter continues:

My trotters thawed when we came down, but my face and neck are burned as if I had spent an entire day in the sun in Mar del Plata. At the moment my face seems a copy of Frankenstein's, what with the Vaseline I apply and the liquid that oozes from the blisters that have formed. My tongue is also in the same condition because I swallowed a lot of snow. Climbing is marvellous and the only thing that gives me an inferiority complex is that, last time, an old man of fifty-nine climbed with us. He looked just like Angel Face[20] and he started by saying that his mummy had told him that he was mad to join us, and he began to climb and our spirits sank because he climbed like a goat.

In his letters Ernesto always mentioned the possibility of obtaining a position as a professor of physiology, but later on we discovered that said position was only a smoke-screen so that we did not suspect what he was really doing. He wrote again to his mother from Mexico:

. . . there is a shortage of physiologists and I am being

[20] Angel Face: Cara de Ángel, a character in The President, a novel by Guatemalan writer Miguel Ángel Asturias (1899–1974), winner of the Nobel Prize for Literature in 1967.

asked to devote myself full-time to it so that I can be given a position in the provinces. It would, of course, be temporary, to find me subsequently a position in a more important place, but I do not see myself even as a teacher in a primary school.

September 1955 letter to his mother from Mexico

24 September 1955

Dear Vieja,

This time my fears have come true, it seems, and your hated enemy of so many years has fallen. We did not have to wait for the reaction here – all the newspapers of the country and the foreign press announced, full of joy, the fall of the sinister dictator; the Americans sighed with relief over the safety of 425 million dollars that they will now be able to take out of Argentina; the Bishop of Mexico showed himself to be satisfied with the fall of Perón; and all the right-wing and Catholic people I met in this country also showed their happiness; my friends and I, not. We all followed with natural anguish the fate of the Perónist government and the threats of the fleet that they would shell Buenos Aires. Perón fell as the people of his type fall, without the posthumous dignity of Vargas, or the energetic denunciation of Arbenz, who named in great detail those responsible for the aggression.

Here, progressive people have defined the Argentine process as 'another triumph for the dollar, the sword and the cross'.

I know that today you will be very happy, that you will breathe the air of freedom. [. . .]

Not long ago I pointed out to you in a previous letter

that the military do not surrender power to civilians if they do not guarantee them the dominance of their caste; these days they will only surrender it to a government that comes from the democratic party – that is, one of those recently created Social-Christian parties in which I imagine ——[21] will be acting, a future deputy of the honourable Chamber of Deputies, where maybe with the passage of time —— will sit, a leader of the Argentinist party, yet to be founded. You will be able to say whatever you like everywhere with the absolute impunity guaranteed to you because you are a member of the ruling class, although I expect you to be the black sheep of that flock. I confess, in all sincerity, that the fall of Perón made me very bitter – not for him, but for what it means to the whole of America, because whether you like it or not and in spite of the forced backing down of recent times, Argentina was the champion of those of us who believe that the enemy is in the north. For me, who lived through the bitterness of Guatemala, this is a far-away carbon copy and when I saw next to the loyal news (it feels strange to call it that) the voice of Córdoba was heard, it being theoretically under occupation, I began to see the situation getting worse, then it all happened exactly the same way: the President resigned, a junta began to negotiate, but from a position of resistance, then it came to an end; a military man, with his little sailor by his side, took over, the only difference with Guatemala; then Cardinal Copello* spoke to the people full of pride and making a calculation as to how his business would fare under the new junta; the newspapers of the entire world – from this side of the world – launched their

---

[21] 'In which I imagine ——': this name and the following one were deleted from the original letter.

well-known shouts; the junta refused to give Perón a
passport, but announced freedom for all. People like you
may see the dawn of a new day; I assure you that
Frondizi* does not see it like that, because assuming
that the Radicals take power, it will not be he who does,
but Yadarola*, Santander* or some other who serves the
interests of the Yankees and the clergy, let alone the
military. Maybe in the beginning you will not see the
violence because it will take place in a circle far from
yours. [. . .]

The Communist Party, with the passage of time, will
be removed from circulation and the day may even
come when Father feels that he was mistaken. Who
knows what will have happened in the meantime to
your wandering son. Maybe he will decide to settle in
his native land (only possible decision) or to start up a
true struggle. [. . .]

Maybe a bullet, of those that are so frequent in the
Caribbean, puts an end to my existence (this is not a
boast, but neither is it a concrete possibility, but bullets
travel a lot in this area); maybe I simply continue to be
a vagabond long enough to complete a solid education
and give myself the pleasures that I allotted to myself
within my programme for life, prior to devoting it
seriously to pursuing my ideal. Things move with great
speed and nobody can predict where or for what reason
he will be next year.

I do not know if you have received the formal news of
my marriage and the arrival of the heir. From Beatriz's
letter it would seem not. If this is the case, I give you the
news officially so that you tell the others: I married
Hilda Gadea and we will have a son some time from
now. I received the newspapers from Beatriz, I am really
interested in them; I would like some recent ones and

above all *Nuestra Palabra*[22] every week. Ciao. A kiss for all the family. Hilda sends you her regards.

This letter from Ernesto to his mother was one of the most important ones we received. The analysis that Ernesto makes of the political situation in our country in 1955 is really accurate. He saw the phenomenon of Perón far better than any of us in the family – most of whom had been against Perón. He saw General Perón in perspective, and from other countries in the Americas that felt in depth the Yankee exploitation. In those countries Perón was seen as the future liberator of our America, which was oppressed by the imperialism that originated from the USA.

But I must say that Perón did not pronounce himself clearly on this point, neither at the time nor during the eighteen years that his exile in countries dominated by Fascist regimes lasted. Those of us who had been at the receiving end of the repression by the government of Perón could not accept that said repression had been for the sake of a possible liberation of the oppressed peoples.

Perhaps that was where our mistake lay. While we felt personally aggrieved, Ernesto could draw social conclusions from Perón's government. In my personal case, I could not see the wood for the trees.

His letter was very bitter, and this is understandable, and he vented his anger against his family. In the case of Celia, his mother, it was unfair. She was not only not deceived by the Revolución Libertadora, which she sussed out immediately, but she also enrolled politically on the opposite side, where she acted with great energy, which cost her three months in prison when she was well into her fifties.

As for me, when he refers to me personally, he says even

[22] *Nuestra Palabra*: the official newspaper of the Communist Party.

the day may come when Father thinks he was mistaken; I confess that the day did come when I understood my mistake, which consisted of supporting a military junta against the government of Perón; but my mistake did not last long, because I turned against the military junta as soon as it was formed.

Also, President Perón returned to the presidency in 1973 and proved to be placed politically to the right when he repressed his followers who were left-wing, as well as all parties of that tendency.

As Ernesto in his letters to our family criticises the position of the military of the so-called Revolución Libertadora, which brought about the advance of the right in our country, that criticism may give the impression that Che supported Perón. As I have the expectation that this book will help to clarify the matter, I would like to say the following: in Punta del Este, in Uruguay, in 1961, Che and I had a long conversation about the political and social position of Perón and his party. Che said these categorical words: 'Of Perón's party there is only one redeemable person, and that is John William Cooke*.' This leader had stayed in touch with Che for almost a year then.

October 1955 letter from Ernesto to his Aunt Beatriz from Mexico

Mexico, 7 October 1955

My very dear auntie:

After thousands of years I approach my typewriter to despatch some of my correspondence and this time it is your turn. The most important news in the area of affection you must already know from Mother: I got married and I expect a Vladimir Ernesto; obviously I expect him, but it is my wife who will give birth.

I did not climb the Orizaba peak, but tomorrow I leave for the Popocatepetl, where I will climb with the flag of the flaming sun.[23] It is a great ceremony held on the summit of the volcano, and will be attended by climbers from all over, the figure reaching 5,000. If there is a good photo of the ascent I will send it to you.

Talking about something else, I would like to have as much news as possible of Argentina. The newspapers you send me arrive well and I have thanked you seventy or sixty times, as Cesar Bruto says.[24] As you can imagine, the pleasure you feel due to the fall of the tyrant is the opposite of what I feel; this may be due to the fact that I have an innate desire to be firmly muzzled and get a little wallop every now and then because I have been poisoned by Red propaganda. I do not know why, but I felt something about the fall of Perón. Argentina was a little pale-grey sheep, but she was different from the others; now it will probably be the same shade of white as its exquisite sisters, mass will be said in the presence of many grateful believers, people will be able to put the riffraff in their place, the Americans will invest large and beneficial capitals throughout the country – in brief, a paradise. I frankly do not know why I pine for the grey sheep. On to another subject.

These last few days it rained enough to go through my raincoat, which is of weather-beaten cloth from Córdoba (by adoption); an area of the city was flooded and people were left homeless, but it is not important because there were no members of the bourgeoisie and

---

[23] Flag of the flaming sun: the Argentine flag has a bright yellow sun in the middle.
[24] As Cesar Bruto says: an Argentine humorist who was very famous at the time.

they were all Indians. I live in a really good area in the company of my respectable other half, who is an officer of the United Nations. Hurricane Hilda – look at the symbolism and precision of the name – took over the city of Tampico, a port on the gulf, and left it in ruins; then came the Panuco, it overflowed and almost swamped it, and now ruffians of every type have fallen on it. I offered to go and help, but the government disdained my services and I was unable to see the disaster at close quarters. At the end of the month I will take a holiday and go with Hilda to tour the devastated area and the ruins of the Mayas, which are a little older.

I am tired of writing and it is very late. Huge kisses for you and the Hercilias from your adored nephew.

December 1955 letter from Ernesto to his Aunt Beatriz from Mexico

Mexico, 15 December 1955

My very adored auntie,

[. . .] I carry on with my life, once again the boring life of a student, brightened up only by sporadic trips to the volcanoes, one of which, the Ixtaciuatl (sleeping woman in the vernacular), was a witness to my defeat because the snow, the hurricane force wind, the terrible avalanches that went by heralding the possibility of a terrible death and a small dose of shitting ourselves with fear (just a pinch for the flavour only) prevented the valiant column from reaching the bosom of the sleeping beauty. We returned after two days of struggling without being able to recognise the road, since what had been rock was now snow.

My laboratory work continues slowly on its way to a

better future and I am preparing for the new conference on allergies, which will take place in Veracruz in March 1956 [. . .]

Write me letters, send me newspapers (I have a good provision of maté).

I have spoken.

Another letter from Ernesto to his Aunt Beatriz from Mexico

This letter, which I reread after many years, moves me. In it he tells Beatriz that when he is rich he will buy her a house made of gold. I remember that when I was a four-year-old and was my mother's favourite, I always used to say to her that when I became rich I would buy her a house made of gold. Ernesto had heard that story and he appropriated it when he wrote to the aunt he loved most. He then says:

Life goes on with bourgeois sloth, without anything to cloud my daily work, not even the proximity of the baby, which will apparently arrive between the last week of February and the first of March.

He then comments that his friend Granado is in Venezuela and asking him to go there. Ernesto adds:

But I am thinking of leaps to places further away, thanks to the fact that Hilda works for the United Nations and any transfer includes her family, so I would be eligible as Prince Consuerte,[25] and we might get Indonesia or another place like it, with redemption, bullets, turbans and mosquitoes.

[25] Prince Consuerte: for Prince Consort, a play on words as *suerte* means luck.

I also still hope that during this year I will be able to complete a couple of pieces of scientific work, or at least pseudo-scientific. I am strong, optimistic, I climb volcanoes frequently, I frequently visit ruins, I read St Charles[26] and his disciples frequently, I dream of studying Cortisone with one of those French young ladies who know about everything (for amusement only) and dream of you all, my family that I so love. Arrivederci, my love.

Strong hugs and assorted seasonings.

This letter shows us Ernesto in full. His good humour, his mockery and, between one joke and the next, the important announcements. The last paragraphs summarise his life at that time, his thoughts and his actions. He reads Marx, says that he dreams of studying Cortisone with a French young lady to shock his aunt, and then adds 'dream of you all, my family that I so love' in order to put her mind at rest. And he goes on to mention that he climbs volcanoes quite casually, which we now know was part of his training to enter Cuba as a guerrilla.

Letter from Ernesto to his mother from Mexico

Mexico, January 1956

Mummy of my heart,

Here I am again in front of this machine invented for typing, but struggling more energetically in front of the artefact and almost without looking at the keyboard (when I conquer it, I will learn embroidery). The pur-

---

[26] St Charles: Guevara's way of referring to Karl Marx without actually naming him.

pose of this letter is to send you greetings in the hope that you have started the new year very happy in the company of my gentleman father and my gentlemen brothers and lady sisters and, after greeting you, to inform that no letters from you arrive in these lands of God, a matter that greatly concerns me, in view of the developments in that good land that was a witness to my birth where days are now turbulent. I fear that you might be with Monsignor Copello preparing a new attempt against the Freemasons of the government. From here I watch and do not speak, because if I spoke I would have to ask what they'll do to obtain that very substantial loan that the gringos will give them? Will it be a present? I would ask if I spoke.

I have to go back to work (oh! the tough demands of daily bread – actually this is not true) and I have run out of steam. It was really cold here. The baby will be born the last week of February. After March (allergy conference) I will decide my life for the financial year '56–7.

I send you a big strong hug and kisses and all the rest. Hand some over to the other members. Ciao. Write to me.

Letter from Ernesto to his father from Mexico

February 9 1956

Dear Viejo

As usual, I am writing this letter of congratulations so that it arrives when the illustrious date is almost forgotten. I imagine that you will spend the day surrounded by old friends [. . .] and that you have had a happy birthday.

All the newspapers and magazines that you may wish to send will be very well received here, where news is rather scarce and only sporadic rumours of some failed conspiracy reach us. Here they are about to show a film called *Perón Laid Bare*, in which they endeavour (to judge by the book of the same name that I read) more than laying bare Perón, to show his terrible connections with Red imperialism. Because you should know that burning the churches was not an act of the Fascist Perón, but of the Communists. Another terrible proof against him is the commercial agreement with the USSR, which shows the degree of subservience of a country that disdains (the greatest ingratitude) the generous trade with the Yankees.

... life is more expensive every day and when a Yankee admiral arrives (like now), all the representatives of the really democratic sectors or simply anti-imperialists, such as the Puerto Rican nationalists, are thrown in jail.

Talking about Dr Guevara, let me tell you that after many doubts and much consultation with the pillow, etc., he took advantage of the opportunity and became a Professor of Physiology. Did you hear me? Of Physiology.

It would be wonderful if the Vieja could get it over with and come and meet her grandson, together with her daughter-in-law and everything, and it would be better still if she did it quickly so that it can be in Mexico, a country that is worth seeing, because it is highly probable that next year we will not be here.

Many hugs from Siddharta Guevara*.

Letter from Ernesto to his mother from Mexico

Mexico, twenty-fifth day of the new era

Granny,

Both of us are a little older, and if you think of yourself as a fruit, a little more ripe. The baby is rather ugly, but you only have to look at her to realise that she is different from all the other children of her age, she cries when she is hungry, she pees frequently . . . the light bothers her and she sleeps most of the time; however, there is something that makes her different from any other baby: her father is called Ernesto Guevara.

Old girl, I hope to see you in some place on this little turd of God called Earth within the next millennium.

Kisses from Hilda Beatriz and me; old Hilda we leave aside, she has nothing to do with these matters of the young.

Arrivederci, vieja.

April 1956 letter from Ernesto to his mother from Mexico

13 April 1956

Dear Vieja,

[. . .] I had even lost the habit of writing, but I am now convinced that it is the only way to get news from the high spheres of Buenos Aires. [. . .]

I will now go on to speak of the *chamaca*;[27] I am very happy with her, my Communist soul swells with pride as she is identical to Mao Tse-Tung. Even now the bald patch in the middle of her head can be seen, the kind eyes of the leader and his protruding double chin; for the time being she weighs less than the leader, since she barely surpasses five kilos, but with time she will catch up. She is more spoilt than the majority of children and she eats like I used to eat, according to tales told by the grandmother (her grand-

[27] *Chamaca*: a Mexican colloquialism meaning girl.

mother) – that is, sucking in without breathing until milk comes out of her nose.

And he goes back to the subject of the professorship in physiology, as he does in other letters:

> I will be a professor of physiology at the National University of Mexico, with a meagre salary of the type customary in universities here, but with all the status that comes with such a post. [. . .] I work ceaselessly in order to finish some work that I am really fed up with, so that I am able to devote myself to my new speciality, which is conditioned reflexes. The idea has got into my head of producing a painkiller against asthma based on those reflexes, but I don't know where it will all end, because I am given whatever I need for an allowance, but no staff in spite of the fact that the poor patients of this hospital, as long as you take care of them, do not mind whether they are hanged or shot.

And he takes his leave always joking, as follows:

> I send you a hug the size of the monument to the *descamisados*,[28] not the one they were about to build, but the one that is in the heart of the Argentine people,

[28] *Descamisados*: literally, 'shirtless' – Perón's followers in Argentina. The nickname originated after an incident at the Argentine Chamber of Deputies, when a deputy who was an opponent of Perón referred to a supporter of Perón as shirtless, to imply that he did not even own a shirt. The following day Perón took off his jacket at a public gathering as a gesture of solidarity with his people. The top echelons of his government did the same. From that day on, Perón attended official functions not wearing a jacket. Not long before he was ousted from government, Perón decided to build a gigantic monument to his 'shirtless' followers, which would represent the poor *peronista* people; the monument was never actually built.

next to the image of our beloved presidential couple, whom God preserve, amen.

Joint embrace to all other members of the family.

Ernesto finished his letter in this way to tease the family, who were not in agreement with the government of Juan and Eva Perón*.

Part Eight:

Mexico en route to Cuba, 1956

Ernesto now defines himself politically; in plain language he tells us that at this point of his life it is much more important for him to learn about Communism (St Charles) than devote himself to the professorship of physiology.

Letter from Ernesto to his father from Mexico

15 April 1956

Dear Viejo,

Now fully recovered from the long bout of lazybonitis that afflicted me, I pick up this gadget. I do not know what to add to the letter I am sending the old lady, since these are almost simultaneous, but I wanted to send you a personal letter typed in my own hand as a testimonial of my filial love and all that.

Hilda is also in excellent health and carries out her maternal duties with ease, considering that she also has a job and, to make matters worse, has to put up with me as I become more difficult and grumpy than you at my age – a chip off the old block.

Within a short time I will become famous in the sphere of medical sciences, if not as a scientist or professor, as a divulger of the doctrine of St Charles from the high benches of the University. Because I've realised that physiology is not my forte, but the other subject is.

The expedition on board the *Granma* was to leave Mexico for Cuba only a few months later, and in his letters Ernesto could no longer conceal the tension that he was being subjected to on the eve of the invasion of Cuba, but he had to keep this from his family and, when I reread these letters today, I can see clearly the subterfuge. If one reads them carefully one realises that Ernesto was almost saying goodbye to each one of us. His letters had become less frequent and more laconic. You can tell that something strange was happening.

This is how he says farewell:

A big hug for everyone and especially for you, the authorised recipient, from this misunderstood champion of freedom.

It was July 1956. The previous letters had not said anything important. We later knew that Ernesto was very busy and couldn't write much. We were rather off the scent and still believed that he was involved in the activities with which he fooled us.

Almost at the same time as this letter arrived, the international telegraph went mad: Fidel Castro had been taken prisoner with a group of Cuban revolutionaries and some foreign ones, amongst whom was Dr Ernesto Guevara de la Serna. The news went through the family like wildfire. In view of the impossibility of communicating directly with him, I decided to do so by indirect means. Colonel Fernando Lezica was posted to the Argentine Embassy in Mexico. My son Roberto was married to his niece, so I tried to obtain news through this channel. Also, the then-retired Rear Admiral Raúl Lynch of the Argentine navy, a first cousin of mine, was the Argentine Ambassador in Cuba and through him I obtained much information. Press cuttings arrived from the main Cuban and Mexican newspapers. My friend Ulises Petit de Murat was also bombarded with letters, telegrams and phone calls. All this only served to soothe our nerves and keep us a little calmer, because the truth was crude: Ernesto had been taken into custody and was accused of being committed to an armed revolution against the government of Cuba. There was nothing we could do to get him out of that situation.

Dr Fidel Castro Ruz, the leader of the 26 July Movement, had been taken prisoner with Ernesto and had been in charge of the legal defence of the whole group. Not long after, he was put on probation with the majority of his group, but Ernesto and another comrade remained in jail at Miguel Schultz Street in the city of Mexico.

News from Ulises Petit de Murat said that Ernesto and some comrades decided to go on hunger strike as soon as they were taken into custody. All this worried us. We had just learned of his decision to join the Cuban Revolution and we began to realise that all that news about possible professorships or assignments was simply a smoke-screen to deceive us, as well as the Mexican and American Information Services, which were on the lookout for any clues that could enable them to frustrate the invasion of Cuba.

Now we knew that all that volcano-climbing was no tourist activity, but part of the physical training required to acquire the strength and agility to become a guerrilla.

In view of this, I wrote a very serious letter to Ernesto asking him to explain to me, without beating about the bush, his position within the 26 July Movement (a movement that until then I was not aware of). I asked him to write to me without any reservations. On or around 10 July we received a letter from him, which I transcribe here in its entirety. It needs no comment: it is explicit and in it he admits that he has lied to us about his work as a professor of physiology and tells us the purpose of his prolonged stay in Mexico, as well as expressing clearly his faith in the revolutionary movement.

As was to be expected, that letter fell like a bomb on our family. Our hopes that Ernesto would one day become a scientist, following his medical career, melted like snow in the sun.

Now the truth was out in the open. We could no longer harbour any doubt. He had just exchanged all his studies and his medical career, all his intellectual and archaeological baggage, all his political, social and economic studies for something much more dangerous and difficult in which he had placed all his faith: armed struggle against the American imperialists who were exploiting the underdeveloped peoples of Latin America.

Letter from Ernesto to his parents from prison

Mexico, 6 July 1956. Municipal Prison

Dear Viejos,

I got your letter (Father) here at my new and luxurious residence at Miguel Schultz Street, as well as the visit of Petit, who informed me of the fears you both have. I will give you the background to the story so that you can get an idea of how events have unfolded so far.

Some time ago, quite a long time actually, a young Cuban leader invited me to join his movement, a movement for the armed liberation of his land, and I, of

course, accepted. I spent the last few months keeping up
the lie to you that I had a job as a teacher, when I was in
fact devoted to the task of giving physical instruction to
the boys who must one day set foot again in Cuba. On
21 June, when I had been away from home in Mexico
City for a month, as I was at a ranch in the suburbs, our
leader Fidel and a group of *compañeros* were taken into
custody. Our address in the suburbs was found in their
house, so we were all picked up by the police. I had with
me my papers, which describe me as a student of
Russian, and this was enough for me to be considered an
important link in the organisation, and the news
agencies that are the friends of Daddy's began to screech
across the world.

This is a summary of past events; the future can be
divided into two: medium-term and immediate. Of the
medium-term, I must tell you that my future is linked
to the Cuban Revolution. Either I succeed with it or I
die there. Of the immediate future I have little to say,
since I do not know what will happen to me. I am at the
disposal of the judge and I could be deported to
Argentina unless I find asylum in a third country, something that I believe would be beneficial to my political
well-being.

In any case I have to leave for somewhere, whether
deported straight from this jail or whether I am set free.
Hilda will return to Peru, since they have a new government that has issued a political amnesty.

For obvious reasons my letters will be less frequent,
also the Mexican police has the pleasant habit of
confiscating letters, so please write only about family
matters or mundane things. Nobody likes these sons of
bitches to know about their intimate problems, however insignificant. Give Beatriz my love, explain to her

why I am not writing, and tell her not to bother to send me the newspapers for the moment.

We are about to go on an indefinite hunger strike in protest at the unjustified detentions and the torture to which some of my *campañeros* were subjected. The morale of the group is high.

For the moment please continue to write to my home address.

If for any reason, although I do not believe it will happen, I cannot write any more and it is my turn to lose out, consider these lines a farewell, not very grand, but sincere. I've gone through life in fits and starts looking for my truth and, now that I am on the right path and I have a daughter to perpetuate me, I have closed the cycle. From now on I will not consider my death as a frustration, but simply, in the words of Hikmet[1]*, 'I will only take with me to the grave the sorrow of an unfinished song.'

Love to you all,

Ernesto

Seeking contacts

When we received the news that Ernesto was in jail in Mexico – news that was published in Argentina by the main newspapers of the capital and the provinces – our family was disconcerted. Although his letters to his relatives were not totally candid, we thought this was his style; he wrote untidily and as if talking to himself, but none of us had ever arrived at the conclusion that Ernesto had enrolled in a revolution to topple a Latin American government. But now, confronted by the facts transmitted by the news agencies, we had of necessity to resort to reading his last

[1] A poem by Turkish revolutionary poet Nazim Hikmet.

letters to try and find out the motives that led Ernesto
to abandon his medical career, his archaeological and
anthropological studies. We thought his decision was madness. I personally was disheartened; I couldn't understand
why my son had enrolled in a dangerous adventure far from
his own country.

But the fact is that our family was not aware of the
political and social situation of those countries of Central
America in which Ernesto had now been living for years. In
order to be able to do something for him, we now had to find
out the truth from third parties.

I wrote, after having telephoned him, to my friend Ulises
Petit de Murat, and it was he who gave us the first concrete
news of Ernesto's imprisonment. I transcribe below some
paragraphs of the long letter that Petit wrote to me dated 30
June 1956.

My dear Ernesto:

I postponed this letter until I was able to see your son.
I went to the immigration jail. He lives there in the
company of his Cuban friends from the failed adventure
against Batista. Of course, that son of a bitch Batista
(like all military men) has enormous resources at his
disposal. In his capacity as a small-time military tyrant
he uses public funds for his personal aims. This is the
sordid drama of all Latin American countries, especially
of our convulsed Latin America, with the exception of
Mexico and Uruguay, army and navy are two dreadful
plagues that do not allow us to live in peace. Batista has
used the golden key of his corruption here and
consequently there has been quite a fuss. But Mexico
will not send the Cuban conspirators to Cuba. This is
more than a certainty. As for Ernesto, the thing that
causes him more concern is the fact that his Mexican

papers were not in order. His original tourist visa had expired a long time ago. Consequently, it's almost certain that the strongest punishment for him will be deportation. [. . .]

I will refer to Ernesto personally. He is in fine health, his wife and child are very charming and his wife is very courageous. Ernesto greeted me with laughter, he reads a lot and sunbathes a lot in the courtyard of the jail. He does not want anything special done for him. His moral attitude – whether one is in agreement with his ideals or not – is great. He rejects any attempt for anyone to do anything on his behalf before the Cubans are cleared. As you can imagine, I didn't pay any attention to this.

I make enquiries about him at the Argentine Embassy. This, of course, prevents the police from committing any atrocities. [. . .]

Batista has given a lot of money to lowly police elements who are not very different from thugs. That's why the police exaggerated their attitude. And besides, Batista used the influence of the United States, associating the young men – falsely, of course – with Russia. These reports must by now be in the hands of the Police in Buenos Aires, and this is why I believe that Ernesto would be better off if he were able to stay in any country of this area. But you and Celia and the rest of your family can be perfectly reassured. Ernesto has been treated well, and he will be treated even better in future. [. . .]

I send you a big hug and I repeat that you must not fear for Ernesto.

Petit

Now reassured by the letter of our old friend, I got in

touch by phone with the Argentine Ambassador in Cuba, retired Rear Admiral Raúl Lynch (my first cousin), who was a close family friend. As was to be expected, Raúl's political position was not remotely similar to that of Ernesto, but – attending to my request – he sent me a good number of Cuban papers (which were a good example of the total political and social corruption that reigned in Cuba). All that servile journalistic literature could not give us an idea of Ernesto's real situation while he was in jail in Mexico. The information sent by Raúl was practically useless. On a personal note, he advised me to impose my authority to keep Ernesto away from those 'warlike adventures'.

On the other hand, many letters arrived at my house in Aráoz Street from all over Argentina as well as the rest of the world: old acquaintances of mine, personal friends of Ernesto, relatives, fellow students of Ernesto and people who shared our political views. They were all interested in learning something more than what the newspapers said about our son.

July 1956 letter from Ernesto to his mother from Mexico
A few days after receiving that significant letter written in prison in Mexico, Celia received another letter, also written in jail. My wife had probably given Ernesto a fillip rather like a sermon, trying to make him see the error of his ways in relation to the hunger strike, and he replies:

Mexico, 15 July 1956

I am neither Christ nor a philanthropist, I am exactly the opposite of a Christ and I think philanthropy is [illegible word], but for the things I believe in I fight with all the weapons within my reach and I try to leave my opponent flat on the floor, instead of letting me be nailed to a cross or to any other place. With reference to the hunger strike, you are totally wrong: we went on strike twice. The first time they released twenty-one of the twenty-four detained, the second they announced that they would release Fidel Castro, the leader of the Movement, and that would be tomorrow. If it happens, there will only be two of us left in jail. I do not want you to think, as Hilda is suggesting, that the two of us who remain are being sacrificed; we are simply those who do not have their papers in order, and that's why we have not been able to resort to the resources that our comrades used.

My project is to leave for the nearest country that gives me asylum, something that is difficult in view of the inter-American notoriety that has been attached to me, and there I will be at the ready for when my services are needed. I repeat that it is possible that I will not be able to write for a more-or-less lengthy period.

What really horrifies me is your lack of understanding of all this and your advice on moderation, selfishness, etc. that are the most execrable qualities that a man can have. Not only am I not moderate, I will try never to be so, and when I recognise that in me the sacred flame has given place to a timid little votive light, the least I should do is puke over my own shit. As for what you refer to as moderate selfishness – that is, crass and fearful individualism, to the virtues of you know who – I must tell you that I have done all I could to purge myself not only of that unknown, moderate being, but of the other one, the bohemian, unconcerned about his neighbour, with a feeling of self-sufficiency due to the knowledge, misguided or otherwise, of his own strength. During these days in jail, and during the previous ones in training, I totally identified with my comrades and our cause. I remember a phrase that one day seemed stupid or at least strange, which referred to an identification so complete between all members of a combating unit that the concept of 'I' had totally disappeared to give way to the concept of 'us'. It is a Communist moral and naturally it can seem a doctrinaire exaggeration, but it really was (and is) good to be able to feel that removed from the self.

Always prepared to see the humorous side even when he was being very serious, Ernesto says in his letter:

(The red stains are not tears of blood, but tomato juice.)
    A deep mistake of yours is to believe that 'moderate selfishness' is where capital inventions or masterpieces of art come from. For any large undertaking one needs passion, and for the Revolution we need passion and courage in large doses, something that we have as a human group.

Further down he says to his mother:

Besides, it's true that after dealing with the injustices in Cuba, I shall go to any other place and it's also true that, cooped up in a bureaucratic office or in a clinic for allergenic illnesses, I'd be so fed up. In spite of all this I believe that your pain, the pain of a mother reaching old age and who wants her son alive, is worthy of respect and something that I am under the obligation of paying attention to, and also that I want to attend to, and I would like to see you not just to console you, but also to console myself of my sporadic and unmentionable longings.

Vieja, your son kisses you and promises his presence if there are no further developments.

Che

I am certain that jail brought about the total definition of Ernesto.

In this crucial letter he describes himself with complete accuracy: he is a revolutionary with a sacred flame. In the letter he is also deeply self-critical when he admits that there was a time when he was careless, bohemian and self-centred.

Undated letter from Ernesto to his mother from Mexico

Ernesto often started his letters without saying where he was posting them from and without a date. We used to add the date when we remembered to do so, but many of them remained undated so that they were difficult to classify. This letter is one of the ones that remained undated and we have placed it according to the possible date of its arrival and in accordance with its contents (probably August or September 1956).

Dear Vieja,

I am writing from any place in Mexico, where I am waiting for matters to be resolved. The air of freedom is in actual fact the air of the underground, but it does not matter, it provides an interesting nuance like that of a mystery film.

My health is very good and my optimism even better. With reference to the 'liberators',[2] I notice that little by little, almost without realising it, you are losing your trust in them.

[2] Liberators: the de facto junta of Argentine military men who had ousted President Juan Domingo Perón.

Well, I do not have a lot of time to write and I do not wish to spend it on those subjects. Although about my own life I have very little to tell, since I spend all my time in physical exercise or reading. I think that after this I will be well versed in the economy, although I may have forgotten how to take a pulse and use a stethoscope (I never did this well). My path seems to divert slowly but firmly from clinical medicine, but it is never sufficiently far away for me not to be nostalgic for a hospital. That story I told you about a professorship in physiology was a lie, but not a total one. It was a lie because I never had the intention of accepting it, but the proposal did exist, as well as a strong probability that I would be called, because my appointment had been approved. In any case, it now definitely belongs to the past. St Charles has acquired a devoted convert.

I cannot say anything about the future. Please write quickly and give me news of the family, which in these latitudes is very refreshing.

Vieja, a big hug from your
clandestine son

Letter to Tita Infante
Approximately October 1956.

Dear Tita,

It has been so long since I wrote that I've lost that familiarity of regular communications (I am sure that you will not understand my handwriting, I will explain everything little by little).

First: my little Indian girl[3] is already nine months old. She is rather cute and is very lively, etc.

[3] 'My little Indian girl': Hilda Gadea was of mixed Indian and Chinese blood.

Second and most important: some time ago some Cuban chaps, revolutionaries, invited me to help their movement with my medical 'knowledge' and I accepted because, as you probably know, it's the type of job that I like. I went to a ranch in the mountains to direct physical training, inoculate the troops, etc., but I became so *salado* (a Cuban expression meaning unlucky) that the police took us all into custody and as I was *chueco* (Mexican for illegal) with my papers, I spent two months in the nick, apart from the fact that they stole my typewriter, amongst other fripperies, which is why I am writing by hand. Then the authorities made the serious mistake of believing the word I gave them as a gentleman and they set me free so that I could leave the country within ten days. This was three months ago and I am still here, although in hiding and without any prospects in Mexico. I am waiting to see what happens with the Revolution. If all goes well I will leave for Cuba; if all goes badly I will start to look for a country in which to settle. This year could be the turning point of my life, although I have had so many that nothing surprises me or moves me very much.

Of course, all scientific work went to hell and now I am only an assiduous reader of Charlie and Freddie[4]* and other diminutives. I forgot to tell you that when they detained me they found several little books in Russian as well as a card of the Mexican-Russian Exchange Institute, where I was studying the language because of the problem of conditioned reflexes.

You might be interested to know that my married life is almost totally at an end and that this situation will become final next month when my wife leaves for Peru

[4] Charlie and Freddie: Karl Marx and Friedrich Engels.

to visit her family, whom she has been away from for eight years. There is a certain bitter taste in this break-up because she was a loyal *compañera* and her revolutionary behaviour was beyond reproach during my enforced holiday, but our spiritual discord was great and I live with this anarchic spirit that leads me to dream of other horizons when I have 'the cross of your arms and the land of your soul',[5] as Pablito* used to say.

I leave you now. Do not write to me until I write again with more news, and at least with a fixed address.

With the always affectionate hug of your friend

Ernesto

Letter from Ernesto to his mother from Mexico
Approximately October 1956.

Dear Mother,

Your filthy son, son of a bad mother to boot, is not semi-anything, he is like Paul Muni* was when he said what he said with a dramatic tone of voice and began to disappear into the enveloping shadows to the sound of music for that particular purpose. My present pro-fession is that of a grasshopper – here today, there tomorrow, etc. – and as to our relatives, I didn't go to see them for that reason (also, I must admit that I would have more affinity in my tastes with a whale than with a bourgeois couple, worthy employees of distinguished institutions that I would wipe off the face of the earth if I had the power to do so. I don't want you to think that I have a direct aversion for them, it is distrust, rather;

---

[5] From 'A Song of Despair' by Pablo Neruda. In English: 'Ah! Woman I do not know how you could contain me in the earth of your soul, in the cross of your arms.' Pablo Neruda, *Twenty Love Poems and a Song of Despair*, translated by W. S. Merwin, published by Jonathan Cape, 2004.

Lezica already showed that we speak different languages and have no points of contact). All this lengthy explanation inside the parenthesis was because I had the impression that you imagined that I am in devouring-bourgeois mode and, out of laziness to remove the paragraph and start again, I got into all this interminable explanation, which I feel is not very convincing. Full stop, new paragraph.

Hilda will go to visit her family in Peru in a few days' time, taking advantage of the fact that she no longer is a political delinquent, but a rather wayward representative of the very dignified and anti-Communist Aprista Party. I am about to change the direction of my studies. So far I used to spend my time, off and on, studying medicine and devoting my free time to the study of St Charles in an informal manner. This new stage of my life demands a rearrangement of my time: now St Charles is paramount, he is the axis, and will be so for the years that the spheroid accepts my presence on its external layer. Medicine is a game, amusing sometimes, but of no consequence, except for a small parenthesis that I intend to devote to a core study, one of those studies that make the basements of bookshops tremble under its weight. As you may remember – and if you don't remember, I remind you now – I was involved in drafting a book about the function of the doctor, etc., of which I only finished a couple of chapters, which reek of pamphleteering in the style of Maxence Van der Meersch's* novel *Bodies and Souls*, except that it was badly written and showed at every step of the way my total ignorance of the depth of the subject, so I decided to study instead. Besides, I had to arrive at a series of conclusions that were at loggerheads with my essentially adventurous way of life, so I decided to comply first with the main functions, to rush forth against the order of things, protected by my shield, pure fantasy, and then, if the windmills did not break my head, to write.

I owe Celia a laudatory letter that I will write after this one if I have enough time. The rest are in debt to me because I have the last word with all of them, even Beatriz. Please tell her that the newspapers arrive splendidly well and give me a good overview of all the 'wonderful' things that the government is doing. I cut them up with care following the example of Pater, since Hilda has undertaken to follow the example of Mater.[6] A kiss for all of you, accompanied by all the suitable accessories plus a reply, whether negative or affirmative, but categorical, with reference to the Guatemalan guy.[7]

Now all there is left is the final part of the speech with reference to the little man himself and which could be titled: 'And now what?' Now comes the difficult thing, that which I've never avoided and which I've always liked. The sky has not turned black, the constellations have not been affected, nor have there been any nasty floods or hurricanes. The signs are good. They augur victory. But if they were mistaken, since even the gods make mistakes, I believe that I will be able to say like a poet you do not know, 'I will only take with me to the grave the sorrow of an unfinished song.' In order to avoid being pathetic 'pre mortem', this letter will only leave when the time has come and then you will know that your son, in a sunny country of Latin America, will be cursing himself for not having studied a little surgery to be able to help the injured and will

[6] Pater and Mater: Guevara Senior used to cut out newspaper articles and keep them, and his wife would do a clean-out every now and then and throw them out.
[7] The Guatemalan guy: one of Ernesto's friends who arrived in Argentina as a political exile.

curse the Mexican government for not letting him practise his already respectable aim to topple targets with greater ease. And the struggle will be with our backs to the wall, like in the hymns, until we win or die.

I kiss you again with all the affection of a parting that refuses to be the final one.

Your son

It's easy to imagine the state of mind of our entire family when we received this letter, which reached us a few days after we had received the terrible news that Ernesto had fallen next to Fidel Castro and his main comrades when landing in Cuba.

I remember that Celia read the letter out loud in front of the whole family, with a serene and firm voice. I could not understand Ernesto's attitude. I still refused to believe that he had changed his direction, which would have led him to become a scientist, and was throwing overboard all his work and knowledge to embark on what seemed to me an uncertain adventure in a strange country.

The letter, which initially confused us, clarified all our doubts when analysed in detail.

What Ernesto was doing with his life was no simple whim. He said, 'This new stage of my life demands a rearrangement of my time: now St Charles is paramount, he is the axis, and will be so for the years that the spheroid accepts my presence on its external layer . . .'

His studies of Marxism had convinced him that first one has to attack the order of things. He states his complete conviction that, while the social structure of a people has not been uprooted, bringing about their total liberation, the rest (writing or anything else) is but an excuse of little consequence. I have transcribed this letter in its entirety. To edit it would be improper.

Now that we knew the path that Ernesto had embarked on, we understood clearly what he meant when his train left for Bolivia and he shouted: 'Here goes a soldier of the Americas!'

It was a fact. There went a soldier of the Americas, whom fate decided would be one of the comrades-at-arms of Fidel Castro.

When we received the news that Ernesto had enrolled in the expedition that Dr Fidel Castro Ruz was preparing in order to invade Cuba, with the intention of ousting the government of the dictator Batista, we were deeply dis-enchanted. Nobody in our family agreed with that decision. We were all aware of Ernesto's scientific capacity, he had given ample proof of it on various occasions, and now we found him enrolling in an expedition the details of which we did not know and the final purpose of which we ignored. Our family found out exactly who Fidel Castro was and what the purpose of his expedition was – which in the beginning seemed to us a mad adventure – only some time after Castro had left with his contingent for Cuba.

We knew little of Fidel Castro's revolutionary past. We knew something about the assault on the Moncada Barracks and his later imprisonment on the Isla de los Pinos, but then events began to clarify when reading what had been published, and only then did the picture of the future Cuban leader become clear to us. We learned from his writings, his speeches and his statements that he was sufficiently talented, courageous and prepared to start a revolution. And when we read his own defence after his incarceration, which he himself entitled *History Will Absolve Me*, we had a more precise idea of who Fidel was, and only then did we fully understand that Ernesto was not following an adventurer. Fidel had acquired his prestige through his actions and had consolidated it with his own defence before the tribunal that had judged him.

November 1956 letter from Ernesto to his mother from Mexico

Mexico 15

Dear Vieja,

Still on Mexican soil, I reply to your earlier letters. I can give you some news of my present life because these days all I do is gymnastics, I read a lot, particularly about what you can imagine, and I see Hilda some weekends.

I've given up resolving my situation through legal means so that my stay in Mexico will be transitory. In any case Hilda will leave with the baby to spend the end of the year with her family. She will be there for a month and then we will see what happens. My long-term ambition is to see Europe and, if possible, live there, but it's extremely unlikely this could happen. When one is taken over by the illness I suffer, it seems that it is exacerbated and does not let go of one until one is in the grave.

I had prepared a life plan that included ten years of wandering, later years studying medicine and later, if there was any time left, I would take up the great adventure of physics.

All that's in the past, the only thing that's clear is that the ten years of wandering might grow longer (except if, due to unforeseen circumstances, all wandering is forbidden), but it will now be of an entirely different type from the one I dreamed of, and when I arrive in a new country it will not be to go to museums and look at ruins, because that still interests me, but also to join the struggle of the people.

If I tell you things that you might find harsh it's

because I love you. I am now sending you a hug, one of the last ones from Mexican soil and, as an admonition, one final one: the mother of the Maceo brothers[8] regretted not having had more sons to offer Cuba. I do not ask for so much, simply that my price or the price of seeing me is not something that goes against your convictions or something that you might regret one day.

Ciao.

An interview with Dr Alfonso Bauer Paiz about his relationship with Che in Mexico, for the newspaper Granma

In Mexico City Ernesto met up again with Dr Alfonso Bauer [Paiz], who arrived from Guatemala where he had been in prison for several months. Their friendship continued there, and at a certain point Ernesto was forced to go into hiding, when he left the prison at Miguel Schultz Street, so he lived with Dr Bauer and his family for several days.

In the interview he granted *Granma*, Dr Bauer states:

I met him at Chapultepec Park. We were both exiles after the events of June 1954 in my country. Ernesto, camera at the ready, was with my fellow countryman Julio Cáceres, known as El Patojo. 'What are you doing with a tourist camera?' I asked him. 'It's not a tourist camera,' he replied. 'With it we earn the pesos we need for our livelihood.'

I knew there an Ernesto whom I did not recognise: the father who was pleased and happy with the birth of Hildita, his first child. However, he was to enjoy such deep and tender affection for a very short time. He had already been introduced to the Cuban leader Fidel

---

[8] The mother of the Maceo brothers: Mariana Grajales, mother of three heroes of the war of Cuban independence from Spain.

Castro and a deep friendship was born between them, based on mutual trust, the purity of their ideals and the unconquerable will to make them a reality.

In Guatemala, Ernesto met several combatants from the assault on the Moncada Barracks: Ñico López, Mario Dalmau*, Darío López*. In Mexico, Ernesto developed a deep friendship with Raúl Castro and at a later date he had a meeting with Fidel Castro. It was in July or August 1955 and that evening he became a member of the future expedition of the *Granma*.

One evening several members of the Patriotic Union of Guatemala (UPG) were meeting in the living room of my apartment, when someone rang the bell to the main entrance of the building. From our meeting place on the ground floor we saw through the frosted glass the figure of a large man wearing a rolled-up hat that was fashionable with the diplomatic community. We thought it might be Guillermo Torriello, an ex-Foreign Minister of the Arbenz government. I asked my wife to attend to the visitor and we continued our session behind closed doors.

Not long afterwards Ernesto sent word to me through my wife that he needed a box of medicines that had arrived for him a few days earlier, and which had been left in a corner next to the patio. Four people could hardly pick it up. These medicines will be some remedy, I thought to myself.

Later, when we were alone, my wife told me that when she had gone to open the door, instead of Torriello, there was a man she did not know and who had a Caribbean accent, who asked directly, 'Is Ernesto in?' Nobody by the name of Ernesto lives here, she replied, but he insisted, saying, 'I know he is here and I am coming in' and as he spoke he put his foot delicately against the door to prevent it being shut; he pushed and then ran up the stairs until he reached Ernesto's room. That's how my home, once again, over a very brief period of time, was touched by history: the unexpected visitor was Fidel Castro.

A few days after these events I received the worrying news that Ernesto was missing. He had not come down to breakfast, lunch or dinner. I went upstairs to his little flat to find that the door had been padlocked from the outside. We forced it open.

His room was in total chaos, the bed unmade, the maté straw here, the small spirit stove there, his clothes all over the place and half a dozen books opened as if he had been reading them all at the same time. Among these books were Lenin's *The Estate and the Revolution*, Marx's *Das Kapital*, a manual of field surgery and a book written by me: *How American Capital Operates in Central America*.

We realised that he had left in a hurry and, as he didn't return, I informed Hilda of his disappearance and handed over his scarce and modest belongings.

His total discretion in every sense, and in particular the rigour with which he kept a secret, were qualities that made Ernesto Guevara one of the great revolutionaries of America.

He had spent a couple of weeks in the intimacy of our home and never had he allowed any of the plans in which he was engaged to be revealed, nor did he ever mention anyone by name or otherwise. If I, or any member of my family, had been taken into custody by the police, interrogated and intimidated, we would not have been able to give anything away, because we knew nothing. How could the revolution fail with combatants of such qualities? [. . .]

That day we also discussed the experience of the Cuban guerrilla force, and he stated that one of the main causes of their success was the excellent leadership of Fidel. 'You cannot imagine how Fidel is,' he said and then added, 'You have to be close to him to realise what his personality is like, his greatness, the discipline he imposes on the guerrilla force through his strength of character. When we were all weak with fatigue, he raised our spirits. He is a tireless man, he is studious and reflective, enterprising, his moral values are invaluable, he is a great friend and is incapable of abandoning a comrade even in the most adverse circumstances. Fidel's constant thoughts are for his people, for the revolution, he is an extraordinary leader.'

Letter from Tita Infante to Ernesto Guevara de la Serna

Buenos Aires, 9 December 1956

My dear Ernesto,

I do not have the peace of mind required to analyse and understand the meaning of these lines I am writing to you: that is, I do not know if I am writing to you or only to myself.

I am spending a couple of days in Beccar, in the home of some friends. This morning when I woke up I picked up yesterday's *La Prensa*, which I had not yet read, and of course what I look for immediately is Egypt, Hungary and, for the past ten days, Cuba before all else. From the first news of the landing and of Fidel Castro's movement, apart from the interest it has for me, just like the attempts of all peoples to set themselves free, I have thought of you constantly with a pitiful fear of anything that might befall you.

I received your last letter some fifteen to twenty days ago. Believe me, it was a great joy, greater still because I didn't expect it, since it was I who was in your debt letter-wise, but also because I had learned from the newspapers of your difficulties in Mexico.

I have not written to you throughout the current year, my friend, but I do not forget you. My affection and my friendship for you, Ernesto, have never wavered; on the contrary, time and even distance, with the maturity that comes from the years that have gone by, have made my friendship for you more firm and indestructible, and I will never cease to think about Ernesto as the great friend of yesterday, today, always, whatever may come.

I feel the need to tell you why there has been such a long and unusual silence from me. I do not want to give you useless details. I only want to tell you that for the past year my intimate difficulties became greater and greater, until in February I fell into a state of serious illness that reached its climax in July. I could not tell when and where I have been, I was like a dead person among the living, in a world of madness and lack of hope that enveloped me in its web, threatening my physical, moral and even mental health.

Now, more at peace, and in the light of what I've gone through, I finished my studies three weeks ago. I ended my absurd betrothal, or whatever you would like to call it, and here I am in search of my future path. I didn't want to write to you when I was in such a deplorable state, and when I learned through the press in June or July of your first troubles in Mexico, I was sick in a sanatorium. I couldn't write to you because I didn't know where you were. Recently I was looking for a way to communicate with you and I thought of your home. Then the revolution started and then the landing, and I had no doubt that was where you were. A few days earlier I had received your letter. I tell you again about my infinite joy, I realised that in spite of my silence I still had your friendship and I thanked you for it from the bottom of my heart, that sad heart that you have perceived over the years of correspondence between us.

Today, my dear friend, I read in the papers the statement of a revolutionary Cuban made prisoner. You were with the revolutionaries, according to the statements of José Díaz and Mario Fuentes Alonso, and further down the page it said that you had died during an attack by government forces.

I do not know why I am writing to you in the certainty that you have not died, that it's a lie, that it's not possible, that it is false, that many of the statements show that they have been distorted by the Cuban press or the Cuban government.

Am I writing to you? Yes, Ernesto, I know that you are still among us, I know that one day in some place or other I will see you again, or at least that I will be able to send you these lines somewhere in the world.

That's why I am leaving these lines here with me, in the certainty that they will be sent one day, happily seeking you out. Meanwhile, Ernesto, I feel very close to you, I accompany you from here with all the energy that I have left, by which I mean, with the necessary capacity for affection, and I hope . . . I know that I will soon hear from you.

You will find this letter, addressed to you, which I cannot send yet, some day. Forgive me if it is absurd because in it I place all my affection and my faith in you.

Farewell, see you soon, goodbye my friend. We will meet one day.

Tita

Epilogue: Tita Infante remembers
Che a year after his death

When I was asked to contribute to this 'Argentine Testimonial' I knew – and I said so at the time – that the task was beyond my capabilities. But how could I refuse such an honour! How could I shirk such a duty!

Today, facing these blank pages, I feel unable to complete the task. To bring back the memory of a great man is always a difficult undertaking. If that man today in 1968 is Ernesto Guevara, the task seems unattainable.

It was precisely one year ago, when I was returning to my country after a long absence, that the first newspapers I read with unbelieving eyes, trembling hands and bated breath brought the news, confirmed little by little, of his tragic death, of that unmentionable assassination for which our America will one day demand amends. One year. So far away already. And yet so fresh, like the blood soaked up by the Bolivian soil, like the gaze of his large eyes that transcend death and go beyond time and space. His valiant body on a miserable canvas, his beautiful head with the beard and long hair of a guerrilla, his Christ-like face without any expression of pain . . . Earth and wood, water from a spring, wild sap . . . Ernesto has died, but he had already been born to eternity. He always lived cheerfully on the road to tragedy. Death closed his path, but opened up so many new doors towards the life that he so loved. The

memory of his person, of his life, of his struggle, will live for
ever in the heart of the people of this world because Ernesto
Guevara is one of those men whom Destiny occasionally
bestows on humanity.

A year from his death and a lot has been written about
him. Books, articles, studies, essays, biographies. What can
I say about him?

A close friendship united us over many years; almost six
of personal communication and then many more of
correspondence.

It was early 1947. In the Anatomy Theatre at the Faculty
of Medicine I kept hearing the deep, warm voice of a man
who, with his irony, gave himself and the others the courage
needed to face up to a spectacle that could shake even the
most insensitive of those future doctors. Because of his
accent I could tell we came from the same province. He was
a beautiful and confident young man . . . The fire that would
one day consume him was latent inside his young body, but
it was already present in his eyes. There was a mixture of
timidity and haughtiness, maybe of courage, which masked
a deep intelligence and an insatiable desire to understand
and, deep inside, an infinite capacity for love.

We never belonged to a cultural or political group, nor did
we have a single group of friends. Both, for different reasons,
were somewhat foreign to that Faculty. He, because he
probably found there very little of what he sought . . . Our
contact therefore was always at an individual level. At the
Faculty, in the cafés, in my home, occasionally in his . . .
Also at the Museum of Natural Sciences, where we met on
Wednesdays to study the origins and development of the
nervous system. At the time we were devoting our studies
to fish, and so we alternated between dissections, prepara-
tions, paraffin, microtomes, microscopes, etc., sometimes
under the guidance of an old German professor. But

Ernesto's entertaining conversation always shortened the hours, which otherwise would have seemed interminable. He never missed an appointment and he always arrived punctually. He never forgot to return a call. What unusual behaviour for a bohemian!

Each time we were surprised by a discovery, we would repeat the verses of Gutiérrez* that we both loved:

> Do not raise hymns of victory
> on the sunless day of the battle.

I often thought how many times he must have repeated these words in the Sierra Maestra, in the Congo, in Bolivia . . . His whole life was a struggle, maybe that is why those lines were so much a part of him.

I often saw him worried, grave or deep in thought. Never really sad or bitter. I cannot remember a single meeting in which he didn't smile or behave with that warm tenderness that those close to him so appreciated. In his conversation there was never any room for that which should be despised; with a short sentence he made a profound criticism, then went on to something positive, to a constructive future. You perceived him to be for something, more than against anything. Maybe this is why he never felt the slightest rancour.

As he never wasted a moment, not even when he was travelling, he always appeared with a book in his hand. Sometimes it was a volume of Freud*: 'I want to review the clinical history of a case that I am interested in.' At other times it was a textbook. Or a classic.

He never had money to spare. On the contrary. At that time he earned a living working with Dr Pisani, investigating allergies. But his lack of funds never represented a serious concern, nor did it ever prevent him from complying with what he considered an obligation. Neither his apparent free and easy manner nor the carelessness reflected in his attire was ever able to disguise what a distinguished person he was.

A trivial story comes to my mind. We frequently lent each other books. Once I lent him *The Sponge-Fisher* by Panait Istrati*; he enjoyed it very much and we discussed it. Not long after that he turned up with a new copy of the book: he had been rereading it and had lost my copy, so he waited until he was able to buy another one to return it to me – even when it was a poor edition, badly bound, which I had bought from a second-hand bookshop in Corrientes Avenue.

We had mutual trust and a great intimacy, which enabled us to confide in each other the incidents – whether happy or unfortunate ones – of our personal lives. However, because of that innermost sense of decency that was one of his traits, we were able to tell each other a lot without the need to talk too much.

As a student he didn't work very hard, but he worked well. Deep down, that young man who was always ready for an adventure, who 'felt under his heels the ribs of Rocinante'[1] ready to set forth, had a profound thirst for knowledge. Not in order to store treasures like some overly complex spirit, but rather as an indefatigable search for truth, and for his own destiny. Everything in him was coherent, and each experience or knowledge, of whatever type, became integral to his person.

He graduated in fewer than six years in spite of his travels, of having a job, of sports (rugby and golf at the time) and of the large part of his life that he devoted to reading and to cultivating friendships. He knew how to study. He would go to the core of the problem and from there he would go as far

[1] Rocinante: Don Quixote's horse.

as his plans allowed. He could stop and go deeper, a lot deeper, when he was passionate about the topic: leprosy, allergy, neuro-physiology, psychology . . . But he might also ask over the phone, the day before the exam, about the classification of the vegetable kingdom in A, B and C, according to the percentage of calories or proteins they contained . . . He sailed through the practical and theoretical exams with the same ease that he overcame any other obstacle. But if he gave his word, he had to keep it at any price, that is how I saw him go through the practical tests for nutrition after he had passed his final exam.

He cultivated friendship with dedication and care, nourishing it with his deep human sense. For him, friendship imposed on you sacred duties and granted equal rights. He practised both. He asked with the same ease with which he gave. And this was true of him for everything in life.

Distance did not imply absence for Ernesto. During each trip his letters, with more or less regularity depending on the vicissitudes of the road or on his finances, were a continuation of the friendly dialogue. Sometimes, because he loved photography, the letters were accompanied by his photos in the most diverse circumstances: ill in a southern hospital, almost unrecognisably thin; sitting on a wheel among the indigenous population of the Brazilian jungle, plump after a few weeks of rest; or in the publicity section of the magazine El Gráfico . . . he kept his friends' letters and he never left any without a reply.

When he returned from his last-but-one trip he recalled the days spent in Miami (I skip the details because they appear in all his biographies) as the most bitter and harsh days of his life. And this was not just because of the financial hardship he had to endure.

When he was preparing for his last trip out of Argentina

he arrived one day to tell me – laughing heartily, but also a little vexed – how the Venezuelan Consul was refusing to give him a visa (he had probably made a bad impression during his previous trip, in the eyes of those who govern the Americas) and how the man had mistaken his asthmatic fit for a fit of threatening temper.

Up to the day on which we said goodbye (he invited his closest friends to his home), I only knew Ernesto to be extremely sober: he didn't smoke, he didn't drink alcohol or coffee, and his diet was very strict. His asthma demanded that he comply with living conditions to which he adhered with total discipline.

Every letter from Ernesto was a page of literature, full of affection, of grace and irony. He would tell his adventures and misadventures with comic strokes, which took away the seriousness from even the most difficult situations. In each country he visited he blended in with the local people, and his interests would take him to visit Inca ruins as well as leper colonies and copper and tungsten mines. He understood the life of the people immediately and placed himself within their political and social context. His stories were entertaining, written with ease, but with purity and elegance. He depicted people and places with realism, without euphemisms and objectively. And when he mentioned his private life, be it with sadness or joy, he did so with sobriety and always demanded absolute discretion.

I believe that his love for life was so great that he managed an optimism that came from his personal brand of logic: 'When things are not going well I am consoled by the thought that they could be worse, but also that they could improve.'

In August 1958, when I was preparing to leave the country, I received a phone call from a young journalist. It was Masetti*. He had just spent two months in the Sierra

Maestra and he had brought two letters from Ernesto: one
for his mother and one for me, and in them he asked that we
should write to him as often as possible. I still remember his
pseudonym. It was Teté Calvache. And he gave various
addresses in Havana. His capacity for affection, far from
hardening him during the struggle, became richer, and he
thought with nostalgia of his country, his mother and his
friends. Masetti spoke at length about the Sierra Maestra,
about everything and everybody . . . But in his eyes nobody
had Ernesto's stature, because of his human features, his
bravery, for the variety of his talents. If the Civil Registry, or
a school, or the preparation of bread, or the repair and
manufacture of arms needed to be organised, there was
Ernesto to take charge and direct the work. And in combat,
he was always at the front.

There was already talk of his legendary courage, and the
anecdotes were many, such as the remarks from those
young men from Guatemala who met him in their country
and, after the fall of Arbenz, found a special brand of asylum
in Argentina.

On 2 January, while travelling, I learned of the triumph of
the revolution in Florence. From that 2 January 1959 his life
was no longer private and began to belong to history. There
is nothing more to say.

I had the extraordinary privilege of knowing him in depth,
of having enjoyed his trust, of having shared a great
friendship in which there was never neglect or deception. I
met him when he was very young, when he was plain
Ernesto. But the future Ernesto Che Guevara was already in
him. From those early years I saw him advancing along his
personal path, always going forward. He never stopped, and
those who knew him well knew that 'he would not stop
until he reached the Antipodes'; he was on his way to his
own destiny. And that would never be the destiny of

ordinary lives. I couldn't tell how or when it happened, but I had the certainty that he would reach his own destiny, no matter how arduous the road. There was always sudden news for me: a letter, a phone call, an item in the press. But nothing was ever surprising.

Today, more than a year after his death, I still find it difficult to put my memories and my spirit and the many souvenirs and images in order, because they are so drenched in affection, so intermingled with pain and admiration.

I feel so near and at the same time so far from his gigantic figure, from this demigod who reminds us of Hellenic legends and medieval heroes.

It is difficult to unite such greatness with his sensitivity and tenderness, his human richness.

He was too warm to carve him in stone. He was too large for us to imagine that he was ours only.

Ernesto Guevara, as Argentine as he was, was perhaps the most authentic citizen of the world.

Biographical notes

The following biographies are listed in page order and are indicated in the text by an asterisk after the first reference to the name.

Fidel Castro (1926–): lawyer and leader of the Cuban Revolution. Had previously led the failed attack on the Moncada Barracks in 1953. Founded the 26 July Movement, sailed from Mexico to Cuba with eighty men on board the *Granma*, commanded the Rebel Army during the revolution. Was Prime Minister (1959–76), President of the Council of State and the Council of Ministers (from 1976), Commander-in-Chief of the Armed Forces and First Secretary of the Communist Party.

Major General Fulgencio Batista (1901–73): Cuban military leader and dictator. Was de facto President of Cuba from 1940 to 1944 and then again from 1954 – when he won an election in which he was the sole candidate – until 1959 when he was overthrown by Fidel Castro and fled the country.

Raúl Castro (1931–): brother of Fidel Castro and *comandante* of the Rebel Army during the Cuban Revolution. Vice President of the Council of State and Council of Ministers, Second Secretary of the Communist Party of Cuba.

Juan Almeida (1927–): Cuban writer and guerrilla. A member of the 26 July Movement, he fought in the attack on the Moncada Barracks and was imprisoned with Castro in the Isla de Pinos. Went into exile and was one of the eighty-two men on board the *Granma* who left Mexico for the invasion of Cuba. Distinguished himself during the revolutionary war, held several posts in government and is to this day one of Castro's most loyal followers.

Ramiro Valdés (1932–): Cuban revolutionary and politician. Fought alongside Castro in the attack on the Moncada Barracks in 1953, being a founder member of the 26 July Movement. Member of the Politburo of the Communist Party since 1965, and Minister of the Interior (1955–8).

General Pedro Eugenio Aramburu (1903–70): de facto President of Argentina (1955–8), succeeding General Eduardo Lonardi, a member of the military junta that had ousted President Juan Perón. Met a violent death at the hands of Montoneros, a left-wing guerrilla organisation.

Hilda Gadea (1924–74): Peruvian economist of mixed Indian and Chinese ancestry. She was Che Guevara's first wife and introduced him to members of the 26 July Movement in 1953 in Guatemala, where she was a political exile, having been a member of the Partido Aprista Peruano. She had graduated in economic sciences at the University of San Marcos. After the triumph of the Cuban Revolution, she travelled to Havana with their daughter and held an official post as an economist. She and Guevara divorced amicably in 1959.

Hilda Beatriz Guevara (1956–95): Che Guevara's eldest daughter, known as Hildita.

José Martí (1853–95): Cuban poet, writer, political thinker and activist, hero of several of his country's attempts at independence from Spain and the USA. Died in battle in Dos Ríos, eastern Cuba.

Antonio 'Ñico' López: Cuban guerrilla who met Che Guevara in exile in Guatemala and Mexico and was one of the eighty-two on board the *Granma*. Was killed soon after landing for the invasion.

Julio Roberto Cáceres (nicknamed 'El Patojo'): Guatemalan guerrilla who followed Guevara to Cuba and was later killed in battle in Guatemala.

General Alberto Bayo: exiled Spanish Republican general who trained Fidel Castro's guerrillas in Mexico. Was unable to join the guerrillas in the invasion due to lack of space on board the *Granma*.

Generalísimo Francisco Franco (1892–1975): Spanish military dictator who ousted the Republican government with Nazi and Fascist help after a bloody civil war and ruled from 1945 until his death. Spain became a monarchy once again after his demise.

Jorge Beruff: represented Fidel Castro's 26 July Movement in Buenos Aires, Argentina.

Jules Dubois: American journalist, editor of the Miami-based *Diario de las Américas*. Turned out to be employed by the CIA.

Herbert Matthews: *The New York Times* war correspondent during the Spanish Civil War. Interviewed Fidel Castro in the Sierra Maestra during the Cuban revolutionary war.

Calixto García, Crescencio Pérez, Universo Sánchez and Gustavo Ameijeiras: Cuban guerrillas who were part of Castro's Rebel Army and took part in the skirmishes in the Sierra Maestra. With the exception of Ameijeiras, who was killed in 1958, all went on to be heroes of the Cuban Revolution.

Camilo Cienfuegos (1932–59): Cuban *comandante* who was Guevara's comrade and entered Havana in triumph at his side. Disappeared when his Cessna aircraft was lost at sea.

Ernest Hemingway (1899–1961): American novelist and journalist, who was part of the expatriate community in Paris in the 1920s. Was awarded the Nobel Prize for Literature in 1954. Author of *For Whom the Bell Tolls* and *The Old Man and the Sea*. Lived in Cojímar in Cuba for twenty years. Committed suicide in Ketchum, Idaho.

Eusebio Mujal (1915–85): Cuban trade unionist during the Batista regime. Leader of the Confederación de Trabajadores de Cuba (Confederation of Cuban Workers). Died leaving a fortune of eighteen million dollars, probably amassed from his illicit dealings during his tenure as head of the workers' guild of Cuba.

Juan Alberto Castellanos (1936–): Cuban guerrilla who fought with Che Guevara in the Sierra Maestra and was his personal escort. Was later a member of the group that attempted to create a guerrilla *foco* in Salta, northern Argentina, under Masetti. Was imprisoned in Argentina (1964–8) after the fiasco of Salta (Guevara was killed in Bolivia in 1967). Now lives in Managua.

Manuel Urrutia (1901–81): Cuban lawyer and first President of the revolutionary government of 1959. After six months in office he resigned following a series of disputes with Fidel Castro, and emigrated to the United States.

General Juan Manuel de Rosas (1793–1877): Argentine soldier and politician who ruled as dictator (1829–52). After his defeat at the battle of Caseros he went into exile in England and was buried at Southampton.

Cayetano Córdova Iturburu (1902–77): Argentine Communist poet. Covered the Spanish Civil War as war correspondent for a year. Was President of the Association of Intellectuals, Artists, Journalists and Writers (1965–7). Was awarded several important prizes for his poetry as well as his prose.

Germán Frers (1899–1986): Argentine all-round sportsman and founder of the Astillero Río de la Plata shipyard, whose designs revolutionised the way yachts were built. He won most of the continent's races, was a member of the Argentine team at the Olympics in Berlin in 1936, promoted the naval industry, and refused to sit the final exam to obtain his degree in engineering because, being an accomplished artist, painter and photographer, he did not want to be known as an engineer. He was Ernesto Guevara Lynch's cousin.

José María Guido (1910–75): when President Arturo Frondizi, who had arrived in power through the ballot box, and his Vice President were forced to resign by the military, Guido was the President of the Senate and therefore next in the line of succession, so he became provisional President of Argentina. In fact, it was a thinly disguised coup d'état.

Bernardino Rivadavia (1780–1845): statesman who was one of the leaders in repelling the English invasion of Buenos Aires. First President of Argentina (1826–7) when the colony gained independence from Spain. Was married to Juana del Pino, daughter of a former Viceroy.

Leandro Nicéforo Alem (1844–90): Argentine lawyer who fought in Paraguay as a volunteer against the forces of dictator Solano López. Founded the political party Unión Cívica Radical, was a provincial deputy and eventually national deputy and senator. Committed suicide in Buenos Aires after a failed insurrection that he led against institutional corruption.

Aimé Bonpland (1773–1859): French doctor and naturalist and friend and assistant of Alexander von Humboldt. Was fluent in Spanish and had a profound grasp of both botany and zoology.

Félix Manuel de Azara (1746–1821): Spanish military officer, naturalist and engineer. Was sent to South America in 1781 to settle a border dispute between the Spanish and Portuguese colonies.

Jean Antoine Victor Martin de Moussy (1810–69): French scientist and physician who explored the Uruguay and Paraná Rivers of Argentina, carrying out geographical and ethnological studies of the region for the Argentine authorities.

Baron Friedrich Henrich Alexander von Humboldt (1769–1859): German naturalist and traveller, who explored unknown territory in South America with Aimé Bonpland.

Moisés Bertoni (1857–1929): Swiss scientist who lived in the territory of Misiones and in Paraguay, carrying out studies and experiments in agriculture, botany, zoology, meteorology and ethnography.

Umberto Nobile (1885–1978): Italian aeronautical engineer and Arctic explorer, who piloted the first airship that both reached the North Pole and crossed the polar ice-cap between Europe and America.

Ricardo Güiraldes (1886–1927): Argentine novelist and poet and one of the most significant writers of his era. His most famous novel, *Don Segundo Sombra*, is set amongst the gauchos of his native country.

Jacques Antoine Marie de Liniers (1753–1810): French sailor and colonial administrator, on behalf of the Spanish Crown, of the Virreinato del Río de la Plata (1807–9). Was made provisional Viceroy in 1808, but was eventually shot by the new Argentine authorities for siding with the Spaniards in their war of independence. Is remembered with affection by Argentina for his part in repelling the English invasions.

Emilio Mola (1887–1937): Spanish general who commanded some of the Nationalist forces during the Spanish Civil War (1936–9). Coined the phrase 'fifth column' and died in a plane crash.

General Benito Mussolini (1883–1945): Italian Fascist dictator who ruled from 1922 until 1943. Formed the Axis with Hitler's Germany and entered the Second World War in 1940. In 1943 he resigned, was arrested, but was rescued by German parachutists. He was caught and shot in 1945.

Manuel Azaña (1880–1940): Spanish statesman, lawyer, author and lecturer at Madrid University. Was War Minister (1931), Prime Minister (1931–3) and President of the Spanish Republic (1936–9) before he resigned and went into exile. Died in Montauban, Switzerland.

Rafael Alberti (1902–99): Spanish writer and painter, regarded as one of the major Spanish poets of the twentieth century. Lived in exile in Argentina and Italy and returned to Spain in 1977, when he was elected Deputy for Cadiz in the First Legislature, on the Communist Party ticket.

Enrique Lister (1907–95): Spanish Communist politician and Republican Army General. Lived in Cuba in his early years, attended the Frunze Military Academy in the Soviet Union and joined the Republican Army at the outbreak of the Spanish Civil War. Was instrumental in the defence of Madrid, but when the Spanish Republic fell, he returned to the Soviet Union and fought in the Second World War as a Red Army general. Was also a general in the Yugoslav Army, thus becoming the only person ever to have been a general in three different armies.

Nino Nanetti (?–1937): Italian Communist member of the International Brigades, who fought in the battle of Guadalajara, where he commanded the 12th Division, as well as on the front of Biscay. Was the son of a proletarian family of Bologna and rose to the position of general of the Spanish Republic. Died during the withdrawal from Santander.

Cipriano Mera (1896–1975): Spanish military and political figure during the Spanish Republic. A bricklayer by profession, he joined the anarchist movement and presided over the construction union of Madrid of the National Confederation of Workers (CNT). Joined an uprising in the hope of accelerating the end of the war; when the Republic was defeated, he left for Casablanca, but was extradited back to Spain in 1942. Was condemned to death, but his sentence was commuted to thirty years in prison, although he was set free in 1945. Worked as a bricklayer in Paris until his death.

Alberto Granado (1922–): Argentine scientist and lifelong friend of Che Guevara, who travelled from Argentina to Venezuela with him. His travel diaries, *Travelling with Che Guevara*, were published in English in 2003. The film *The Motorcycle Diaries* was based on his own and Guevara's account of that journey. In 1961 he went to live in Cuba, where he became professor of medical biochemistry in the Faculty of Medicine at the University of Havana; later became director of the Department of Genetics until 1994, when he retired.

Joel Iglesias (1941–): Cuban guerrilla who joined the Revolutionary Army at the age of fifteen and was made a *comandante* at seventeen. Fought at the battle of El Uvero under Che Guevara, who taught him how to read and write. After the triumph of the revolution he graduated in social sciences, and in 1975 wrote *From the Sierra Maestra to El Escambray*, based on his experiences as a guerrilla.

Adolf Hitler (1889–1945): Chancellor of Germany from 1933, Führer from 1934 until his death. Was leader of the National Socialist German Workers' Party (the Nazi Party), and gained power in Germany as a result of the crisis after the First World War. The economy was restructured, the military rearmed, and an aggressive foreign policy was pursued with the intention of expanding Germany. His annexation of Austria and of Czech lands, as well as the invasion of Poland, triggered the Second World War. His racial policies cost the lives of eleven million people, mainly Jews, homosexuals, Communists and ethnic Roma. Committed suicide in his bunker when the Red Army of the Soviet Union overran Berlin.

Roberto Marcelino Ortiz (1886–1942): Argentine lawyer, who was President of Argentina (1938–40). As the election of 1937 was marked by fraud and violence, Ortiz returned to more proper electoral procedures, calling for federal intervention in the province of Buenos Aires, where a corrupt conservative machine had been in control. Suffered from diabetes that rendered him blind, so he was forced to resign in 1940.

Ramón Castillo (1873–1944): President of Argentina (1942–3), and previously Vice President (1940–2). Was overthrown by a military coup.

General Juan Domingo Perón (1895–1974): Argentine soldier and statesman, who took a leading role in the army revolt of 1943, achieved power and great popularity over the masses because of his social reforms and became President in 1946. Was ousted in 1955 and returned to power in 1973, and was President until his death.

Ernesto Sábato (1911–): Argentine novelist and literary critic. Attended the Sorbonne in Paris and worked at the Curie Institute. Began writing late in life and is the author of *The Outsider* and *About Tombs and Heroes*. His work was praised by Albert Camus and Graham Greene. Presided over the commission that investigated the fate of those who disappeared during Argentina's Dirty War of the 1970s, and in 1984 its report *Nunca Más* (*Never Again*) was published.

Miguel Najdorf (1910–97): Argentine chess player of Polish origin. Was born in Warsaw and was taught by Savielly Tartakower. At the age of twenty he was already an International Master. In 1939 the outbreak of the Second World War caught him in Buenos Aires, where he was a member of the Polish team at the 8th Chess Olympiad. He correctly perceived, being Jewish, that in Europe his life would be in danger and decided to stay on in Argentina, at considerable personal loss. Died in Malaga, Spain.

The Great Captain: General José Francisco de San Martín (1778–1850), a.k.a. the Saint with the Sword: Argentine soldier and patriot who liberated Argentina, Chile and Peru from Spanish domination. His crossing of the Andes from Argentina to Chile in 1817 with an army on horseback has been compared to Hannibal's crossing of the Alps. Although born in Argentina he had been sent to Spain to be educated at the military academy in Madrid and served with the Spanish army that fought against Napoleon. Died in self-imposed exile in France.

Jack London (1876–1916): American author who wrote more than fifty books of both fiction and non-fiction. He was enormously successful and one of the first Americans to make a living from writing.

General Juan Galo de Lavalle (1797–1841): Argentine soldier and First Sword of the Army of the Andes. Fought under San Martín in Argentina, Chile and Peru and under Bolívar in Ecuador. Was assassinated in northern Argentina by men from the forces of the dictator Juan Manuel de Rosas.

Víctor Paz Estenssoro (1907–2001): founded the Movimiento Nacionalista Revolucionario (MNR) in 1941 with Hernán Siles Suazo. Was three times President of Bolivia (1952–6, 1960–4, 1985–9).

Ricardo Rojo (1923–96): Argentine lawyer, author of *My Friend Che* (1968). Student leader with the Federación Universitaria de Buenos Aires, and later a politician and member of the Unión Cívica Radical del Pueblo (the largest opposition party when Perón was in office). Defended political prisoners in Latin America, made a spectacular escape from a police station in Buenos Aires and walked into the Guatemalan Embassy, where he was granted political asylum in 1953.

Tita Infante: Berta Hilda Infante (1924–76): Argentine doctor who befriended the younger Guevara in 1947 when they met at the Faculty of Medicine of the University of Buenos Aires when they were both students. She was a cultured and politically aware woman and a militant of the Communist Youth. They remained friends for life, although they did not meet again after Guevara left Argentina. She went on to study first in Marseilles and then at the Sorbonne in Paris, where she read psychiatry. Remained in Europe for ten years and only returned to Buenos Aires days after Guevara was killed in Bolivia. She regretted not heeding his call to move to Cuba to practise there, became very depressed because of the triumph of the military coup in Argentina and committed suicide in 1976.

Hernán Siles Suazo (1913–): President of Bolivia briefly in 1956 and then from 1956 to 1960. Returned from exile in Peru to serve again from 1982 to 1985.

Juan Lechín (1914–2001): Bolivian leader of the Central Obrera Boliviana (Trade Union Federation). Worked in the Cataví and Siglo XX tin mines as a machinist and became aware of the desperate conditions of the miners. In 1964 organised the Revolutionary Party of the National Left.

Manuel Arturo Odría (1897–1974): Peruvian dictator who was President from 1948 to 1950 and then again from 1950 to 1956.

Rómulo Betancourt (1908–81): President of Venezuela (1945–8 and 1959–64). His accomplishments included universal suffrage, instituting social reforms and securing half the profits generated by oil companies for Venezuela.

Juan Bosch (1909–2001): first democratically elected President of the Dominican Republic. Was ousted by a CIA coup in 1963 after only a few months in power.

Víctor Raúl Haya de la Torre (1895–1979): Peruvian thinker, lawyer and politician who spent a great part of his life in exile. Founded the American Popular Revolutionary Alliance (or APRA Party) while in exile in Mexico. In 1979 was briefly President of the Constitutional Assembly of Peru.

Colonel Carlos Castillo Armas (1914–57): de facto President of Guatemala from 1954 until 1957, when he was shot dead in the presidential palace by followers of Arbenz.

Colonel Jacobo Arbenz (1913–71): President of Guatemala (1951–4). Was ousted by a CIA coup that brought Castillo Armas to power.

Edelberto Torres: Nicaraguan professor, writer and politician. Was an indefatigable fighter against Central American dictatorships, in particular that of Anastasio Somoza of Nicaragua, his own country. This meant that he spent many years in exile as well as in jail. Wrote a detailed biography of the poet Rubén Darío, which took him twenty years to complete.

Augusto 'César' Sandino (1895–1934): charismatic Nicaraguan nationalist and anti-imperialist guerrilla leader. Was betrayed by the President after signing a ceasefire and assassinated by the National Guard.

Georg Wilhelm Friedrich Hegel (1770–1831): German philosopher, author of *The Phenomenology of Spirit*, *The Philosophy of Right* and *The Science of Logic*.

Marcos Pérez Jiménez (1914–2001): President of Venezuela (1952–8). After a general uprising, he left for the United States, but was returned to Caracas to face charges of embezzlement. Died in Spain.

Rafael Leonidas Trujillo (1891–1961): de facto dictator of the Dominican Republic from 1930 until his assassination in 1961. Was succeeded by Juan Bosch.

Luis Somoza (1922–67): President of Nicaragua from 1956 to 1963, when he relinquished power to his chosen successor. Eldest son of Anastasio Somoza (1896–1956), founder of the dynasty and officially twice President, although he effectively ruled as a dictator from 1936 until his assassination.

Juan José Arévalo (1904–90): President of Guatemala (1945–51).

Ike: Dwight D. Eisenhower (1890–1969): US soldier and politician, Supreme Commander of the Allied Forces in Europe during the Second World War and 34th President of the USA (1953–61).

Ulises Petit de Murat (1907–83): well-known Argentine screenwriter, who exiled himself in Mexico because he did not agree with the government of General Perón.

Nelson Rockefeller (1908–79): US politician and businessman, 41st Vice President of the USA (1974–7).

Pedro de Alvarado (1495–1540): Spanish soldier, a lieutenant of Hernán Cortés during the conquest of Mexico.

Hernán Cortés (1485–1547): Spanish conquistador of the Aztec empire, generally reviled in Mexico to this day.

John Foster Dulles (1888–1959): US Secretary of State (1953–9) under President Eisenhower. Was a significant figure in the early Cold War era and was awarded the Presidential Medal of Freedom in 1959. Famously refused to shake hands with Chinese Foreign Minister Chou En-lai at the Geneva conference in 1954.

Franklin Delano Roosevelt (1882–1945): politician who became the 32nd President of the United States of America (1933–45). Was elected to four terms in office and is the only American president to have served more than two terms. Creator of the New Deal to make the economy recover after the Great Depression. Provided support to Winston Churchill and his war effort until the Japanese attack on Pearl Harbor brought the USA into the war. In 1921 contracted polio, but refused to allow his infirmity to curtail his public life.

Professor Harold White: became great friends with Guevara when he was Minister for Industries in 1959 and Guevara invited him to visit him in Cuba. White stayed on and died in Havana in 1968.

Dr Alfonso Bauer Paiz (1918–): Guatemalan statesman and lawyer. Participated in the struggles to oust the military dictatorships of the 1940s. In 1948 was appointed Minister of Economy and Labour by President Arévalo and defended the country's interests against the United Fruit Company. Served in all the democratic governments before the 1954 coup against the government of Jacobo Arbenz, sponsored by the CIA. Went into exile in Mexico and returned in 1957 to continue the political struggle and his legal practice. In 1963 was forced to spend a year in hiding after the military coup led by Colonel Peralta, and in 1970 went into exile in Chile, where he worked with the democratically elected Marxist government of Salvador Allende. In 1993 returned to Guatemala and in 1999 was elected to Congress, where he served until 2003.

Karl Marx (1818–83): German philosopher, political economist and activist, often referred to as the Father of Communism. He believed that capitalism would be replaced by Communism and that the 'history of all hitherto existing society is the history of class struggle', as he stated in the introduction to the Communist Manifesto. He wrote *Das Kapital*. The demise of Communism has not diminished his influence in academic and political circles.

José Figueres (1906–90): served three terms as President of Costa Rica. Abolished the army and gave women the vote. Was a supporter of Fidel Castro.

Mao Tse Tung (1893–1976): Chinese Communist leader, who held office from 1945 until his death in 1976. Was one of the founders of the Chinese Communist Party. Set up a Chinese Soviet Republic in south-east China, defying the attacks of Chiang Kai-shek's forces until 1934, when he undertook the arduous Long March to north-west China with his followers. Resisted the Japanese from Yuanan and, when they collapsed, went on to shatter the regime of Chiang Kai-shek and proclaim the People's Republic of China.

Richard Nixon (1913–94): 37th President of the United States (1969–74), winning his second term in office by a landslide. A lawyer and Republican politician, he was Vice President in the administration of Dwight D. Eisenhower and the only person elected twice to both offices, as well as the only president ever to have resigned from office (as a result of the Watergate scandal and in order to avoid impeachment). Encouraged General Augusto Pinochet of Chile to overthrow the legitimate Socialist government of Salvador Allende. Waged war on North Vietnam and secretly bombed Cambodia.

Vladimir Ilych Lenin (1870–1924): Russian Communist politician who was the leader of the October Revolution and the first head of the Soviet Union, as well as the main theorist of Leninism, an interpretation of Marxism.

Aníbal Osvaldo Olivieri: Argentine admiral who had been a minister in Perón's government and rose against him twice. He opposed Perón in his break with the Roman Catholic Church.

Reynaldo Pastor: leader of one of Argentina's conservative

parties. Was involved in a failed coup against the government in 1951.

Monsignor Copello: Roman Catholic Archbishop of Buenos Aires, who did not conceal his right-wing ideology.

Arturo Frondizi (1908–95): President of Argentina (1958–62). He led the Unión Cívica Radical and was a brilliant lawyer who entered politics in 1930, being elected to the Chamber of Deputies in 1948. By 1962 he attempted to have the ban on the Peronist party lifted. Was deposed by a military coup while he was abroad attending a pan-American summit and sent to the island of Martín García as a political prisoner. The military could not tolerate that he had secretly invited Che Guevara to meet him in Buenos Aires while Guevara was visiting Uruguay at the head of a Cuban delegation.

Mauricio Yadarola: Argentine politician who opposed Perón from the 1940s. He was a member of the Unión Cívica Radical.

Silvano Santander: Argentine politician belonging to the right wing of the Unión Cívica Radical, and consequently in opposition to Perón. He accused Perón and his wife Eva of being Nazi agents.

John William Cooke (1920–68): Argentine politician and ideologist of the Peronist movement. When a coup by the military ousted Perón, Cooke was seized and imprisoned first in Buenos Aires and then in Patagonia. In 1957 he and other Peronist activists escaped from prison and settled in neighbouring Chile. In 1962 he backed the People's Guerrilla Army led by Jorge Ricardo Masetti, Guevara's lieutenant, which operated in Salta, northern Argentina, until it was wiped out in 1964. Wrote several books about Peronism and his relationship with Perón. Died of cancer in Buenos Aires.

Siddharta Gautama Buddha: Prince Siddharta was born around 538 BC, the son of the rajah of the Sakya tribe of India. When he was thirty he left the luxuries of the court, his beautiful wife and all earthly ambitions for the life of an ascetic. Was the founder of Buddhism, a faith that spread across India to Tibet, Nepal, Ceylon, Burma, Siam, China and Japan.

María Eva Duarte de Perón (1919–52): second wife of General Juan Domingo Perón, she died of leukaemia while Perón was still in office. Was a powerful political influence, campaigning for women's suffrage and social welfare for the masses.

Nazim Hikmet (1902–63): Turkish revolutionary poet and playwright, author of *A Sad State of Freedom*.

Freddie: Friedrich Engels (1820–95): German political philosopher who developed Communism with Karl Marx and co-wrote the Communist Manifesto with him. Edited the second and third volumes of *Das Kapital* after Marx's death.

Pablito: Pablo Neruda (1904–73): Chilean Communist poet and diplomat, author of 'A Song of Despair'. Was awarded the Nobel Prize for Literature in 1971.

Paul Muni (1895–1967): American actor in the 1932 film *I Am a Fugitive from a Chain Gang*, in which he portrayed a hunted convict.

Maxence Van der Meersch (1907–51): French author and lawyer, a humanist who wrote about the humble people of the northern region of his birth. Was awarded the Grand Prix de l'Académie Française in 1943 for *Corps et âmes* (*Bodies and Souls*), his novel about the world of medicine, which became an international success and was translated into thirteen languages.

Mario Dalmau and Darío López: Cuban guerrillas who participated in the attack on the Moncada Barracks and were exiled in Mexico.

Ricardo Gutiérrez (1936–96): Argentine poet and doctor. He wrote *The Book of Tears* and *The Book of Song*.

Sigmund Freud (1856–1939): Austrian neurologist and psychiatrist who co-founded the psychoanalytic school of psychology. He also made a long-lasting impact on many diverse fields, such as literature, film, Marxist and feminine theories, literary criticism, philosophy and psychology. Nonetheless, some of his theories remain widely disputed.

Panait Istrati (1884–1935): left-wing Romanian author who wrote both in Romanian and French. He was born in Brăila and died of tuberculosis at the Filaret Sanatorium in Bucharest.

Jorge Ricardo Masetti (1929–64): Argentine journalist who was the first Latin American to interview Fidel Castro in the Sierra Maestra. Founder and first director of the agency Prensa Latina. Close friend of Che Guevara. Led an insurrection in northern Argentina. Fell in combat on 21 April 1964 in the mountains of Salta, Argentina. His *nom de guerre* was Comandante Segundo.

Chronology

Entries in *italics* signify national and international events.

1928
14 June: Ernesto Guevara de la Serna is born in the port city
of Rosario, province of Santa Fe, Argentina, to an upper-
middle-class family of Spanish and Irish origin. He will be
the eldest of five children. Ernesto spends the first two years
of his life in Puerto Caraguatay, in the northern province of
Misiones, where his parents have a maté plantation. He
lives in contact with the wild tropical nature of the region.

1930
When he is two years old Ernesto is diagnosed as suffering
from asthma – a condition that will be with him all his life.

1933
The Guevaras move to Córdoba in search of a healthier
climate for their asthmatic son. Ernesto attends primary
school irregularly due to his asthma. His mother teaches
him the school syllabus at home, as well as French, in which
he will be fluent all his life.

1936
*The Spanish Civil War breaks out, a major conflict that
starts with a failed coup by a sector of the army against the
legitimate government of the Second Spanish Republic. It*

*rages from July 1936 until April 1939 and ends with the
victory of the rebels. This will lead to the dictatorship of the
Fascist General Francisco Franco, which lasts until his
death in 1975. The Republic has the support of the Soviet
Union, while Franco has the unconditional support of
Germany and Italy.*

1939
*The Second World War breaks out in Europe. Argentina
declares its neutrality. During the war Argentina sells iron
to the Axis and beef to Britain, thus emerging from the
conflict a rich and prosperous nation.*

1945
*General Juan Domingo Perón becomes President of
Argentina with a six-year mandate.*

*Argentina declares war on Germany and Japan one
month before the German capitulation. The USA drops
atomic bombs on Hiroshima and Nagasaki.*

1946
The Guevaras establish themselves in Buenos Aires.

1947
Ernesto enrols in the Medical Faculty of the University of
Buenos Aires.

1950
Ernesto fits his bicycle with a small motor and goes on a trip
to the provinces of north-west Argentina during the winter
holidays. He covers 4,700 kilometres.

1951
Ernesto travels twice on board Argentine merchant ships

from the southern port of Comodoro Rivadavia to Brazil, Venezuela and Trinidad as a male nurse.

In Bolivia, a right-wing military junta annuls the result of the elections and seizes power. Bolivian miners launch a strike as well as street protests.

1952

Ernesto goes on a trip through Latin America with his friend Alberto Granado and visits Chile, Peru, Colombia, Venezuela and Miami. They work in a leper colony in Peru.

General Juan Domingo Perón is re-elected in Argentina. Fulgencio Batista carries out a coup d'état in Cuba.

In Bolivia there is a revolutionary upsurge that arms the people's militias (mainly peasants and miners) and these replace the armed forces. Although the tin mines are nationalised, trade unions are legalised, land reform is initiated and the indigenous majority is enfranchised, the political system is not changed and continues to fail to represent vast sectors of the population, who suffer constant upheaval and coups throughout the years.

1953

Ernesto receives his medical degree from the University of Buenos Aires.

He is conscripted for National Military Service, but is declared physically unfit for active duty and released.

He leaves Buenos Aires by train and goes on his second trip through Latin America with Calica Ferrer.

Visits Bolivia, where he observes the impact of the 1952 revolution.

Travels to Guatemala, where Jacobo Arbenz is the constitutionally elected President.

26 July: Fidel Castro leads an attack on the Moncada

Barracks in Santiago de Cuba. The attack fails, Castro and other survivors are captured and imprisoned.

1954
January–June: in Guatemala, Guevara does odd jobs, studies Marx and meets several Cuban revolutionaries, who are veterans of the attack on the Moncada Barracks. He witnesses the invasion of Guatemala by CIA-backed forces and the downfall of President Arbenz, who refuses to arm the population. Takes refuge in the Argentine Embassy.

21 September: Ernesto leaves Guatemala and arrives in Mexico City, where he works as a doctor at the Central Hospital.

1955
In Mexico he meets Fidel Castro, who has been released from prison in Cuba.

Marries Peruvian economist Hilda Gadea.

He trains as a guerrilla with Castro and his men, who are preparing to return to Cuba to launch a guerrilla war.

He is nicknamed 'Che' by his Cuban friends, an expression then used throughout Latin America to refer to the people of Argentina.

In Argentina, General Juan Domingo Perón is ousted from power by a military coup.

1956
15 February: Guevara's first daughter, Hilda Beatriz Guevara, is born.

Gamal Abdel Nasser of the United Arab Republic (Egypt) nationalises the British- and French-owned Suez Canal, despite the opposition of combined Israeli, British and French forces.

24 June: Guevara and Castro are arrested by the Mexican

authorities, together with twenty-eight Cuban comrades who were training for the invasion. Guevara remains under arrest for fifty-seven days.

25 November: leaves from the Mexican port of Tuxpan for Cuba on board the *Granma* with Fidel Castro and eighty Cuban guerrillas, and arrives at Las Coloradas in Oriente province.

5 December: the rebels are surprised by government troops at Alegría del Pío and are dispersed. Guevara is wounded.

20 December: Guevara and his group manage to reunite with Fidel Castro and his men. Most of the invading force have been captured and killed. Castro's guerrillas number two dozen.

1957

January–May: first Rebel Army victories at La Plata, Arroyo del Infierno, Palma Mocha, El Uvero.

July: Guevara is promoted to *comandante* and is put in charge of the Columna Cuatro, so named to disguise the fact that there are only two. Later he will command Column 8.

Arturo Frondizi wins the presidential elections in Argentina and takes over from the military junta.

1958

24 May. In Cuba, Batista launches a military offensive against the Rebel Army in the Sierra Maestra.

July: Rebel Army victory at El Jigüe.

16 October: Guevara and his column arrive at the El Escambray mountains to consolidate the rebel forces.

December: Guevara captures strategic locations in the province of Las Villas in central Cuba.

28 December: the rebel forces commence the decisive battle for Santa Clara, the capital of Las Villas.

1959

1 January: Santa Clara falls to the Rebel Army column under Guevara. Fulgencio Batista flees to Miami.

2 January: Guevara enters Havana at the head of his troops and claims it for the revolution. He establishes himself at La Cabaña fortress and presides over the summary trials of the enemies of the revolution.

9 February: Guevara is made a Cuban citizen in recognition of his contribution to the revolution.

26 July: Fidel Castro becomes Prime Minister.

2 June: Guevara and Hilda Gadea have divorced amicably and Guevara marries Aleida March, his assistant during the military campaign. They will have two sons and two daughters.

Guevara goes on a fifteen-day visit to Nasser's United Arab Republic and the Suez Canal. The purpose of the trip is to study the UAR's methods of land reform.

Visits India and holds talks with Pandit Nehru.

Visits Burma, Thailand, Japan, Indonesia, Ceylon, Pakistan, Yugoslavia, Sudan, Egypt, Italy, Spain and Morocco, meeting heads of state while acting as roving ambassador for the Cuban Revolution. He signs several commercial, technical and cultural agreements.

Guevara is appointed Director of Industries for the National Institute of Agrarian Reform.

He is appointed Governor of the National Bank of Cuba and takes up the study of higher mathematics for the next three years.

1960

First declaration of Havana. Fidel Castro refers to 'Our America, the America that Bolívar, Hidalgo, Juárez, San Martín, O'Higgins, Tiradentes, Sucre and Martí wished to see free'.

Guevara publishes his book *Guerrilla Warfare – A Method*, which will become the handbook for guerrilla movements all over the world.

President Eisenhower orders the CIA to begin preparation of Cuban exiles to invade the island.

Cuba and the Soviet Union establish diplomatic relations. The Revolutionary Government nationalises the refineries of Texaco, Shell and Esso as a result of their refusal to refine oil from the USSR.

President Eisenhower reduces by 700,000 tons the amount of sugar the US will purchase from Cuba.

The USSR announces that it will purchase the Cuban sugar the USA refuses to buy.

Castro nationalises major US companies and foreign banks in Cuba as well as 382 large Cuban industries.

The USA declares a partial embargo against trading with Cuba.

In response to the US partial trade embargo, Guevara makes his first visit to the Socialist countries at the head of a Cuban delegation: he visits the USSR, the German Democratic Republic, Czechoslovakia, China and the People's Democratic Republic of Korea.

24 November: Guevara's daughter Aleida Guevara March is born.

1961

January: Patrice Lumumba, the first Prime Minister of the Republic of Congo, newly Independent from Belgium, is deposed in a US-backed coup and assassinated.

The USA breaks diplomatic relations with Cuba.

Guevara is appointed Minister for Industries.

President Kennedy abolishes Cuba's sugar quota.

1,500 exiled Cubans invade the Bay of Pigs and are routed by Cuban troops led by Fidel Castro. Guevara commands the troops at Pinar del Río. The invaders surrender at Playa Girón.

Guevara attends the Economic Summit of the Organisation of American States in Punta del Este, Uruguay, as head of the Cuban delegation and denounces the US Alliance for Progress. He then crosses over to Argentina secretly for a private visit to President Arturo Frondizi.

Guevara visits Brazil and is decorated by President Janio Quadros.

Cuba completes the first year of a nationwide literacy campaign.

1962

Algeria installs a revolutionary government, having won its independence from France after a long and bloody liberation struggle.

29 March: in Argentina the military oust President Arturo Frondizi and install his Vice President in his place when they discover that he has met Che Guevara in his presidential residence in the outskirts of Buenos Aires.

20 May: Guevara's son Camilo Guevara March is born.

The Organisation of American States votes to expel Cuba.

President Kennedy orders a total embargo on trade with Cuba.

27 August–7 September: Guevara visits the USSR for the second time at the head of an economic delegation.

President Kennedy imposes a naval blockade on Cuba and threatens the USSR with nuclear war as a result of Cuba's acquisition of missiles with nuclear warheads capable of attacking the USA. Soviet Premier Khrushchev agrees to remove the missiles from Cuba in exchange for Kennedy's pledge not to invade Cuba.

1963

The Chinese Communist Party splits Communist ideology, and gradually the world Communist parties divide between 'Muscovites' and 'Pekinistas'.

May: an attempt to establish a guerrilla movement in Peru to fight against the US-backed military dictatorship fails and its leader Javier Heraud is killed.

14 June: Guevara's daughter Celia Guevara March is born.

Guevara attends the ceremonies commemorating the first anniversary of Algerian independence and sets down the basis for good relations with President Ahmed Ben Bella. He also attends the International Seminar on Planning in Algiers.

In Cuba the Second Agrarian Reform law is drafted.

Guevara publishes his *Reminiscences of the Cuban Revolutionary War.*

In Argentina Dr Arturo Illia wins the elections.

1964

In Brazil a US-backed military coup overthrows the government of João Goulart and a period of bloodletting and struggle begins.

Colombia sees the formation of two subversive groups, the Revolutionary Armed Forces of Columbia (FARC) and the National Liberation Army (ELN). The armed struggle between FARC and the ELN against the government of Colombia and later the right-wing paramilitaries will last for more than forty years.

The insurrection started by Jorge Ricardo Masetti in Salta, northern Argentina – an initiative that had the blessing of Che Guevara and the support of both Cubans and Bolivians – is routed and Masetti is killed in combat.

Guevara travels to Geneva to speak before the United Nations Conference on Trade and Development.

Travels to Algeria via Prague to meet up with President Ben Bella and returns to Havana.

Visits the Soviet Union for the celebration of the forty-seventh anniversary of the October Revolution. Meets Ho Chi Minh.

Addresses the UN General Assembly in New York.

Travels to Algeria via Canada and Ireland, to meet President Ben Bella. During a three-month-long trip he visits President Modibo Keita of Mali and then travels to Dahomey.

1965

Guevara visits President Massemba-Debat in Congo-Brazzaville and President Sekou-Touré in Guinea. He has several meetings with President Nkrumah of Ghana in Accra.

Travels to Algeria. Makes a stopover in Paris and travels to Tanzania on an official visit.

Travels to Egypt to meet President Nasser and returns to Algiers for the Second Seminar of the Organisation of Afro-Asian Solidarity.

Returns to Egypt and spends time with President Nasser.

24 February: Guevara's son Ernesto Guevara March is born.

14 March: returns to Cuba and disappears from public life to train secretly for his Congo campaign.

April: departs from Cuba at the head of a group of Cuban guerrillas for an internationalist mission in Congo, which is to join forces with Laurent Kabila. Leaves his letter of resignation with Fidel Castro.

18 May: Guevara's mother, Celia de la Serna, dies.

June: the revolutionary government of Ben Bella of Algeria is overthrown in a military coup.

1 October: the Communist Party of Cuba is officially launched.

3 October: Fidel Castro reads Guevara's farewell letter.

December: after the failure of the Congo campaign, Guevara returns secretly to Cuba.

23,000 US troops invade Santo Domingo, in the Dominican Republic, in support of dictator Rafael Leonidas Trujillo.

Peru sees the formation of focos *(small bands of guerrillas) that sustain action for six months under saturation bombing with napalm and high explosives. The ELN of Peru, under Héctor Bejar, then begins action in La Convención, which ends in defeat in December.*

1966

Since 1961 in Venezuela groups of students and even dissident army officers have begun to form focos *to prepare for armed struggle, but by 1966 the armed offensive led by Douglas Bravo has failed, as the Communist Party abandoned the guerrillas operating in the mountains.*

3–14 January: the Tricontinental Conference of Solidarity of the Peoples of Asia, Africa and Latin America is held in Havana, and Cuba commits itself to support continental revolution.

July: in secret, Guevara selects and trains a guerrilla group for a mission in Bolivia in Pinar del Río province.

4 November: arrives in Bolivia in disguise and under a false Uruguayan passport to start the insurgency.

7 November: arrives at the site of his Bolivian camp at Ñacahuasu, where he is joined by seventeen Cubans and several Bolivian recruits.

In Argentina, General Juan Carlos Onganía puts an end to the democratic government of Dr Arturo Illia, in a bloodless coup.

1967

23 March: first successful guerrilla military action against a Bolivian army column.

16 April: Guevara's message to the Tricontinental, in which he calls for 'two, three, many Vietnams', is published.

31 July–10 August: the Organisation of Latin American Solidarity (OLAS) holds its conference in Havana. Guevara is made honorary chairman in his absence.

May–October: a massive force of Bolivian and US troops closes in on Guevara's guerrillas, who suffer heavy losses.

8 October: in Bolivia, Guevara is wounded, captured and then shot on 9 October.

18 October: Castro confirms that Guevara is dead and declares three days of official mourning. He delivers a memorial speech in the Plaza de la Revolución before a crowd of thousands.

1997

The remains of Ernesto Che Guevara are dug up in Bolivia and flown to Cuba.

Guevara is buried with full military honours in the city of Santa Clara, in the province of Las Villas, where he won the decisive battle of the Cuban Revolution.